SANDRA GUSTAFSON'S

CHEAP EATS IN ITALY

Florence • Rome • Venice

THIRD EDITION

A Traveler's Guide to the Best-Kept Secrets

CHRONICLE BOOKS
SAN FRANCISCO

Printed in the United States of America.

THIRD EDITION
ISBN 0-8118-1834-9
ISSN 1074-5084

Cover design: Yeong Sun Park
Cover photograph: StockFood America/Eising
Book design: Words & Deeds
Original maps: Françoise Humbert

Distributed in Canada by
Raincoast Books
8680 Cambie Street
Vancouver, BC V6P 6M9

10 9 8 7 6 5 4 3 2 1

Chronicle Books
85 Second Street
San Francisco, CA 94105

www.chroniclebooks.com

For Frank, Mary, Samantha, Gino, and Giovanni . . . all great Cheap Eaters in Italy

Contents

To the Reader

In Florence you think, in Rome you pray, and in Venice you love. In all three, you eat.

—*Italian proverb*

Italians are a people who think of themselves first as Romans, Venetians, Florentines, and Sicilians, and then as Italians. The link between them all is their love of and appreciation for food—whether the simple cooking of Tuscany, the seafood in Venice, the garlic, aromatic herbs, spices, and meats in Rome, or the Parma ham and robust pastas of Bologna. Italians have been trendsetters at the table ever since the Middle Ages. They were the first to use a fork, the first to wash their hands before a meal, and among the first to make a point of preparing their food using the freshest ingredients. When it comes to cuisine, few countries in the Western world have given so much to so many. Just think of all the foods you love, and no doubt a majority will be Italian: pasta, pizza, balsamic vinegar, Parmesan cheese, sundried tomatoes, porcini mushrooms, polenta, osso buco, prosciutto, minestrone—the list is endless. When we want satisfaction, comfort, or pure enjoyment, we eat Italian.

To Italians, life is meant to be lived fully. Food is not considered mere sustenance but rather a work of art to be enjoyed and relished at every meal. A great part of the Italian way of life revolves around eating. To an Italian, meals are to be shared and eaten in company. In fact, the word *company* is derived from two Italian words: *con,* meaning "with" and *pane* (bread), which means "breaking bread in friendship." But a meal only starts with the bread. From there you move on to the appetizer, a first and second course, vegetables, salad, cheese, fruit, dessert, coffee, and, finally, a digestive, which you will need after a lengthy meal. If you seriously overindulge, a shot of the strong herbal mix Fernet-Branca, available in most bars, will set you straight in no time.

In the last forty years, Italy has gone through a complete economic transformation. It is now the world's fifth-largest industrial power. As a result, prices have skyrocketed, the dollar goes up and down like a yo-yo, and inflation is rampant. *Nothing* is cheap in Italy, certainly not the food. Today it costs almost $2 to buy and send a postcard back to the States, most restaurants charge $30 to $35 for a meal, and you can easily spend $10 or more on a mediocre sandwich and a glass of rough house wine if you don't know where to eat. If you want a *cheap* Italian meal, you had better stay home and go to your local Italian restaurant. The pizza will not be as good as the wood-fired pie you will eat in Rome, nor the pasta as robust as the dish you will enjoy at Taverna San Trovaso in Venice, but I can assure you it will be cheaper.

Here is where *Cheap Eats in Italy* comes to your rescue. Before you read on, however, *please* be aware that this book is *not* a listing of the cheapest places to eat in Florence, Rome, and Venice. It is, instead, your reliable guide to quality food in each city with a realistic cost-to-value ratio. My commitment is to lead you to good meals in all price ranges, from Big Splurges to picnics on the piazza. *Cheap Eats in Italy* will help you plan your dining according to the constraints of your budget—you will know exactly where to get the maximum value for the minimum outlay. Just as important, you will dine where the natives dine, not where the tour buses stop.

When it comes to research, other guidebooks may send a questionnaire, or have someone stop by a random selection of restaurants. I do not do that. I am personally responsible for every entry in this book, and I have been to every address listed each time it appears. Updates are frequent. In doing the research for *Cheap Eats in Italy,* I spent months in Italy, plotting maps, walking hundreds of miles in every type of weather, checking on countless addresses, and eating meals that ranged from terrible and indifferent to delightful and gourmet. The result is this edition of *Cheap Eats in Italy,* which lists more than two hundred dining establishments. In the write-ups, I describe the atmosphere and decor, and tell you about the history of the restaurant and the family that runs it . . . even mentioning their children and pets you may see when you are there. I tell you about the other diners; how the food is prepared, presented, and tastes; and what it all costs. I recommend dishes to give you an idea of what the restaurant does best. I also tell you which ones to avoid. Because most menus in these three cities reflect the four seasons of the year, many of the foods I describe may not be served when you visit, but the quality and value will still be firmly in place. The subject of the many fine Italian wines is one I do not cover . . . that would necessitate another book. I do comment on some of the house wines and tell you if they are drinkable.

In the back of the book is a Readers' Comments page for your notes, suggestions, and comments. I hope you agree with me in my selections and pat me on the back when you do, but it is just as important to me to know about changes you may find, and any Cheap Eat discoveries you have made that you would like me to know about for the next edition. Please take a few minutes to drop me a note at the address listed, telling me about your experiences. As the countless readers who have written to me know, your letters are very important to me, and I read and answer every one I receive.

Whether you are traveling to Italy for business or pleasure, I urge you to go with an open mind. When you leave home, don't expect to encounter your way of life, or your favorite soul food. Enjoy the moment wherever you are, the people, the sights, the sounds, and even the smells. Sample a wide variety of foods, and roll with the punches, since travel is rarely trouble-free. If you can see the humor in a difficult situation, you will come home a more knowledgeable person, with a lifetime of happy memories.

By using this edition of *Cheap Eats in Italy,* I hope you will return with some of the best memories of all: those of sumptuous meals in wonderful settings, enjoyed all the more because they cost less. If I have been able to help you do this, I will consider my job well done. I want to hear from all of you. . . . Until then, *buona fortuna* and *buon appetito!*

How to Use Cheap Eats in Italy

Each listing in *Cheap Eats in Italy* includes the following information: the name and address of the establishment, the area of the city in which it is located, the telephone number, the days it is open and closed, annual closing dates, hours of service, whether reservations are necessary, whether credit cards are accepted, the average price of a three-course à la carte meal without beverages, the price of the *menù turistico* (set-price meal), the cover and service charges, and whether or not English is spoken.

The following abbreviations indicate which credit cards are accepted:

American Express	AE
Diners Club	DC
MasterCard	MC
Visa	V

At the end of the restaurant listings, you will find a glossary of menu and restaurant terms. Finally there is "Readers' Comments," which gives an address where you can send me suggestions or any comments you may have.

Tips for Enjoying Cheap Eats in Italy

The President could solve all the country's problems by having a big plate of spaghetti once a week. Congress can supply the meatballs.

—*Will Rogers*

1. When dining out, remember where you are when you are ordering and stay within the limits of the chef's abilities. Do not expect gourmet fare in a snack bar, and do not go to a fancy restaurant and order only a dish of pasta and a glass of wine.
2. If you see a headwaiter or chef standing in the doorway, tour buses parked outside, or an empty restaurant during prime time, keep going.
3. By law, all eating establishments must post a menu outside. *Always* read it before going in. This prevents you from being seated before finding out that you do not like what is being served, or worse, that the prices are too high.
4. Pay attention to the daily specials and the house specialties. You can be sure these will be the best the chef has to offer and will usually consist of seasonally fresh foods. If they are not on your menu, ask the waiter.
5. Drink tap water (*acqua naturale*) and stick to the house wine.
6. Don't sit down! Drink your morning cappuccino and eat your snack or sandwich for lunch while standing. If you sit down in a *caffè,* you will be charged up to twice as much for the privilege than if you consume your food on foot. If you sit at an outside table, the tab could be even more. The benefit of sitting is that you acquire something akin to "squatter's rights" and can linger at your table for the price of a coffee for hours without being bothered.
7. If you are eating in a self-service restaurant or *caffè,* or are doing the deli routine for lunch, arrive at the beginning of the service for the best selection and a chance to get a table.
8. For the Cheapest Eat, consider the *menù turistico* (set-price meal). Even though the choices may be boring and limited, it is usually a bargain buy because it includes at least two courses and the cover and service charges. Some also include dessert and/or beverage.

9. To keep the tab lower on an à la carte meal, skip the antipasto course and head straight for the pastas and entrées. Keep in mind that most main courses on an à la carte menu are not garnished, and orders of vegetables and salads will be extra. Also beware of dishes on the à la carte menu (such as fresh fish or Florentine beefsteak) marked "S.Q." or "L4,000 hg." *S.Q.* means you will be charged according to the total weight of the food ordered. For example, L4,000 hg means you will pay L4,000 *per* hectogram (3½ ounces). These hectograms can add up in a big hurry.
10. By law, restaurants must indicate when frozen food is used. Most often you will find that if anything is frozen, it will be the fish. If there is an asterisk (*) by any menu item, it is *congelato* (frozen). Most Italians would never order anything frozen, and neither should you. Make sure what you are ordering is *fresco* (fresh).
11. Your waiter will leave your plate in front of you as long as your cutlery is touching the plate and the table. Once you have placed your knife and fork on the plate, it will be taken away.
12. The *pane* (bread) and *coperto* (cover charge) is *per person* and the service charge is a percentage of the total bill. The good news is that *the service charge is the tip.* You do not have to pay one lira more unless you feel the service has been out of the ordinary. If you are having a coffee at the bar, leave the bartender L200. If the restaurant does not include or add the service charge themselves, leave 12 to 15 percent of the total bill as a tip. In Rome, the so-called cover charge has been banned and is now replaced by a "bread charge," which in theory is charged to the customer only if the bread in the basket is eaten. The service charge continues.
13. Every restaurant in Italy is required to give you a formal bill, which you are legally required to carry with you when you leave. Before leaving, compare the bill with the prices on the menu and add up the figures. Do not hesitate to question anything you do not understand. Mistakes are all too common.
14. If you are thirty years old or younger and plan to visit Venice, invest in a Rolling Venice Card (Carta Giovani). This bargain to end all bargains entitles the holder to discounts at participating restaurants, hotels, shops, and certain museums. For further details, see page 159 in the Venice section of this book.
15. If you have enjoyed a place recommended in *Cheap Eats in Italy,* tell the owner or manager where you found out about them. They are always very appreciative.

General Information

Everything you see I owe to spaghetti.

—*Sophia Loren*

When to Eat

Breakfast (*La Prima Colazione*): 7:30–10 A.M.

Hotels and pensiones usually serve a Continental breakfast that consists of coffee, tea, or hot chocolate, fresh rolls, butter, and preserves. Sometimes juice and cheese are included. Cheap Eaters should try to get their hotel to deduct this cost—which can be as much as $15 per person—from their bill and eat their breakfast at a bar or *caffè.* Doing so will cost half of what a hotel will charge, and the coffee will be better, the pastry fresher, and the local scene far more interesting. Remember: If you sit down, the price will increase by 50 to 250 percent *per person* than if you stand at the bar with all the other Italians.

Lunch (*Colazione*): noon or 12:30–2:30 P.M.

Lunch usually starts at 12:30 P.M. and lasts anywhere from thirty minutes (standing up) to three hours. Last order is supposed to be the time the restaurant lists as closing, but more often the last order will be taken about thirty minutes *before* closing. Lunch can be anything from a quick sandwich eaten standing at the corner bar to a full-blown four- or five-course meal ending with a strong coffee under the umbrellas on a busy piazza . . . which has to be one of the true pleasures of eating in Italy. Time, cost, calories, location, and hunger are the factors that will help you decide what to do for lunch. Sandwiches are available in a *paninoteca,* a bar selling sandwiches either made to order or ready-made and displayed under napkins in a case. If you are staying in one place for a few days, it is fun to become a "local" by eating your lunch each day in the same small restaurant or trattoria. The first day you will be treated with politeness. The second, your waiter will be pleased to see you back, and on the third, you will be treated as a "regular" and your waiter will already know what type of wine you like. Try it . . . you will be surprised. In most places, the menus for lunch and dinner are the same, and there is no price break offered at lunch.

Dinner (*La Cena*) 7:30–10:30 P.M.

If you want to eat with other foreigners, reserve a table for 7:30 P.M. If you want a more Italian experience, dine at 9 P.M. or later.

Where to Eat

At one time there was a distinct difference between a trattoria and a *ristorante,* based on the type of clientele and the prices charged. Now they are virtually interchangeable. A trattoria is generally a family affair, with Mama or Papà in the kitchen, and children helping out as needed. The decor and the menu are simple and the prices only *slightly* less than in a *ristorante.*

Fast-food *italiano* is a boon to all Cheap Eaters, and I am not talking McDonalds, where a burger, fries, and shake can cost upward of $12. Besides, who wants a Big Mac in Italy? Bars and *caffès* offer some of the Cheapest Eats, from an early morning *cornetto,* the Italian croissant, either plain or filled with custard or jam, to *tramezzini,* sandwiches made with sliced white bread. Inexpensive meals can also be found in stand-up snack bars that feature a *tavola calda,* which means "hot table." Usually frequented for lunch, these places feature a series of hot and cold dishes either to eat there or take out. *Rosticcerie* also offer hot and cold dishes to eat in or take out. At either the *tavola calda* or *rosticceria,* items are priced by the portion. You choose your food, pay the cashier, get a receipt, and give that to the person behind the counter, who will dish up your food. You will also encounter *pizzerias* (very often open only in the evening, especially in Rome and Florence) and places called *pizza a taglio* or *pizza rustica.* These hole-in-the-wall shops sell ready-made pizza by the slice. The pizza is cut to order and sold by weight. It is fun to try several small pieces. Alcoholic beverages are usually not served, but soft drinks and bottled mineral water will be. Seating is virtually nonexistent.

Other places for a quick bite or a simple meal include a *latteria,* which sells cheese, yogurt, and other dairy products; a *gelateria,* which serves ice cream; or a *pasticceria,* where you can go for a fresh pastry any time of the morning or afternoon. At an *il forno* you can buy bread, and at an *alimentari, salumeria,* or *gastronomia* you can buy cold cuts, cheese, wine, bread, mineral water, and other foods to put together a picnic in the piazza or back in your hotel room. For a glass or two of wine and a light meal or upmarket snack, go to an *enoteca,* or wine bar. *Osterias* were wine bars years ago, but now they are more restaurant than wine bar and feature old-fashioned homestyle cooking.

How to Eat Italian-Style

No man is lonely while eating spaghetti; it requires too much attention.
—*Christopher Morley*

Italians believe that God keeps an Italian kitchen, and so everyone should enjoy *la cucina italiana.* The following advice will help you do so in style.

Dealing with Italian waiters is similar to crossing Italian streets: you can do it if you are brazen enough, showing skill and courage and always looking like you own the place. A good waiter should explain the dishes on the menu and help you select a wine. But if you order coffee or tea during the meal, ask for the ketchup bottle, or request a doggie bag . . . watch out, you will be in big trouble.

Cocktails before dinner are associated negatively with Americans and the three-martini lunch. However, an aperitif, such as a flute of champagne or a *prosecco* (sparkling white or rose wine), to sip as you are deciding what to order is often served.

You do not have to order all of the courses in an Italian meal, but you will be expected to have more than a pasta and a salad in a nice place. When you add the cover and service charges, fine dining will not be a Cheap Eat. If you want a true Cheap Eat, go to a cafeteria or a snack bar, or dine alfresco with a picnic you have put together yourself.

A guiding principle in Italian dining is that you eat one food at a time, and that every food has its place. You will never see pasta, meat, and vegetables on the same plate. If you order a light supper of pasta and salad at an informal trattoria, you will be served the pasta first and the salad after. If you want to start your meal with a salad, the key word is *come,* as in *come antipasto, vorrei un insalata mista* (as an antipasto, I would like a mixed salad), or *comme secondo, vorrei un contorno* (as a second course, I would like a vegetable).

If the waiter does not bring the Parmesan cheese, it probably does not go with what you are eating. Parmesan is never used on pasta with fish or lots of garlic, but it is offered with many types of soup.

Bread is served with all Italian meals and is part of the *pane e coperto* charge. Butter is seldom served except with breakfast.

The container of olive oil on the table is for more than sprinkling on your salad. A plain broiled or grilled fish is enhanced with a few drops of *olio* and maybe some lemon.

Don't order fish on Sunday, when the markets are closed: the fish will be at least one day old. In Venice, extend this to Monday, since the Rialto fish market is closed then as well.

Coffee is served *after* a meal, never with it. For further coffee information and etiquette, see page 16.

Most places do not require men to wear a tie, but Italians always dress with casual elegance when they eat out, and they do not consider athletic shoes of any type to be acceptable with street clothes.

Taking children to restaurants in Italy is not the problem it can be in France. You can ask for a high chair (*seggiola* or *sediolina*) and for half portions (*mezze portione*).

Solo diners may be relegated to poor table locations. To avoid this as much as possible, reserve a table for two. Upon arrival, say your dining companion had to cancel at the last minute, and tell the waiter how sad this makes you. It usually works.

The Italian Menu

One cannot think well, love well, or sleep well, if one has not dined well.

—*Virginia Woolf*

The most important thing about eating in Italy is not to let the length of the menu frighten you, and to order according to the establishment. If you are in a simple trattoria, you probably will not be expected to order every course. But the better the restaurant, the more you will be expected to order.

Most Italian menus are laid out in the following order:

antipasti, or appetizer—which can be as simple as a few olives brought to your table or as lavish as a serve-yourself buffet, whereby you can almost make a meal from this course alone.

I primi, or *primo*—the first course, a choice of pasta, risotto, soup, or a light vegetable dish.

I secondi, or *secondo*—second or main course of meat, fish, or game.

contórnoi—vegetables and salads.

formaggi—cheese.

dolci—dessert.

caffè—espresso *only.*

digestivo—after-dinner liqueur (*grappa, amaro,* or *limoncello*).

Some restaurants and trattorias offer a *menù turistico* at an all-inclusive price. Do not let the name turn you off . . . it is only a fixed-price menu that at the very least includes pasta, a main course, and either a vegetable or a salad. It may also include dessert and beverage. *Pane e coperto* (bread and cover charge per person) and *servizio* (service charge) are almost always included, so there will be no additional expenses tacked onto your final bill. While this is the Cheap Eats way to go, the quality and quantity might not be up to the standard of an à la carte meal. You cannot expect the finest beef, soft-shell crabs, or the chef's best dishes. You *can* expect a filling if slightly boring meal.

Finally, it cannot be said enough: double-check your bill before you pay, and ask questions if you think something is incorrect. Mistakes, unfortunately, happen with great regularity.

IMPORTANT NOTE: If you are handed the English menu, it may not list the daily specials. Always ask to see the Italian menu along with the English one, otherwise you may miss out on the best dishes at the best prices. If you are a woman and are handed a menu without prices, insist on one with the prices clearly marked.

For a complete list of menu terms, and for phrases to help you while ordering, please see the Glossary on page 211.

How to Drink Italian-Style

A wine is like a man; it can have flaws and still be pleasing.

—*Italian village salami-maker*

An Italian *caffè,* or bar, is much more than a place to drink coffee or alcoholic beverages. Here you can eat breakfast, have a snack, buy a sandwich, eat an ice cream cone, make phone calls, use the toilet, read the newspaper, listen to or watch sporting events, meet your neighbor or lover, and argue over politics. If there is a black-and-white "T" (for tobacco) displayed outside, you can also buy cigarettes, matches, some toiletries, stamps, and bus tickets. No wonder there are more than five thousand such places in central Rome alone. In theory, and when the bar is busy, you pay for what you want at the *cassa* (cash desk) before you order it at the bar. Then take your receipt and put it on the bar for the barman to see. Remember, standing costs less. If you sit at a table, you will be charged more, but you can stay at your table as long as you like for the price of a cup of coffee.

What kind of coffee should you order in a *caffè*? The possibilities can be confusing to many Americans. This is a list of the most popular caffeine-laden drinks.

caffè	A small cup of very strong coffee, i.e., espresso
caffè Americano	American-style coffee, but stronger
caffè corretto	Coffee "corrected" with a shot of grappa, cognac, or other spirit
caffè freddo	Iced coffee
caffè Hag	Decaffeinated coffee
caffè latte	Hot milk mixed with espresso and served in a glass for breakfast
caffè macchiato	Espresso "stained" with a drop of steamed milk—a small version of a cappuccino
cappuccino	Espresso infused with steamed milk and consumed in the morning but never, never after lunch or dinner
corretto	Espresso with a drop of grappa or brandy
granitadi di caffè con panne	Iced coffee with whipped cream
latte macchiato	A glass of hot milk with a spot of espresso

Like the French, Italians never drink coffee or tea *with* any meal except breakfast, although coffee (*caffè*) is often ordered after a meal. Tea is considered a morning or between-meal beverage, or one to be used for medicinal purposes. It is the unknowing tourist who orders a cappuccino in a restaurant after lunch or dinner. When ordering your after-dinner coffee, do not ask for an espresso, ask for a *caffè, per favore.*

Even though coffee accounts for almost 80 percent of a bar's earnings, there are other things to drink, starting with *birra* (beer). Beer is either *alla spina* (on tap) or *alla bottiglia* (in the bottle). Wine is always available by the glass, but unless you are in an *enoteca* (wine bar), chances are it will be of low quality. The best bet is to order *prosecco* (dry sparkling white or rose wine). *Aperitivi* (aperitifs) are either alcoholic or nonalcoholic. The most popular are Campari soda, or Martini *rosso* or *bianco*. Finally, there is water, either from the tap, called *acqua naturale,* or bottled, which comes *non gassata* (still or plain) or *gassata* (with gas).

Chiuso (Closed)

All eating and drinking establishments have a regular *giorno de chiusura:* the one or two days a week they are closed. That doesn't mean much. Due to holidays, local customs, government red tape, the ever-present threat of *scioperi* (strikes), yearly vacations, restoration and remodeling, and much more than the non-Italian can ever fathom, the one place you really want to try may be closed. Though *Cheap Eats in Italy* listings include each establishment's days and hours of operations, be sure to call ahead to double-check, especially if you do not have a backup choice nearby or it is important that you eat at a particular place.

Bakeries, fruit and vegetable shops, and other food stores are closed all day Sunday and one afternoon per week. Their hours are generally 8:30 A.M. to 1 P.M. and 3:30 to 7:30 P.M. Open-air markets are open Monday through Saturday from 8 A.M. to 1 P.M.

Holidays

Very few restaurants in Italy are open 365 days a year. Most are closed at least one day a week and for an annual vacation of up to one month. Many close on some or all of the holidays listed below, and those closings depend on the economy at the moment as well as the whims of the owner. You can also count on most places being closed at least a few days between Christmas and the New Year. Because of these constantly changing policies, please call ahead to check if your visit falls during these holiday times or in the months of December, January, July, or August.

New Year's Day (*Capi d'Anno*)	January 1
Epiphany (*La Befana*)	varies; early in January
Good Friday	varies
Easter Sunday (*Pasqua*)	varies
Easter Monday (*Lunedi Pasqua*)	varies
Liberation Day (*Venticinque Aprile*)	April 25
Labor Day (*Primo Maggio*)	May 1
National Day	June 2
Assumption of the Virgin (Ferragósto)	August 15
All Saints' Day (*Tutti Santi*)	November 1
Feast of the Immaculate Conception (*Festa dell'Immacolata*)	December 8
Christmas Day (*Natale*)	December 25

Day after Christmas (*Santo Stefano*)	December 26
Patron Saints' Days:	
Florence: St. John the Baptist's Day	June 24
Rome: St. Peter's Day	June 29
Venice: St. Mark's Day	April 25

Smoking

Italian smokers outdo puffers in almost every other country in Europe. There is no Italian campaign saluting the health benefits of a smoke-free environment . . . or any hint of one in the future. During peak hours, especially in bars, *caffès,* and smaller restaurants and trattorias, the haze gets thick. If a restaurant listed in *Cheap Eats in Italy* is one of the few places where smoking is prohibited or that has a special nonsmoking section, it is noted. Otherwise . . . *buona fortuna!*

Reservations

Every *Cheap Eats in Italy* listing states the establishment's reservation policy. If reservations are advised, please make them. It is always better to arrive with reservations than to wish you had. If you feel uncomfortable calling yourself, ask your hotel to do it for you. They may even be able to get you a better table. Only a few places that are very busy do not honor their reservation times. However, you should arrive on time, call if you will be late, and definitely call to cancel if you will be unable to keep your reservation.

Italian telephone numbers are crazy. In Rome, some phone numbers have only five or six digits, although seven-figure numbers are the most common. Now the area codes for Florence, Rome, and Venice, including the beginning zero, are part of the number you dial. For example, in Florence you dial 055 plus the restaurant number; in Rome, dial 06 plus the number, and in Venice, 041 and the number. If you have difficulties, try calling the operator at 12. Operator assistance offers no guarantees, but it is worth a try.

Paying the Bill

Italian restaurant bills can be confusing. With the following information, you will be better able to avoid the pitfalls of being overcharged or confused when *il contro* (the bill) is presented.

In many small eating establishments, especially bars, *caffès,* bakeries, and snack bars, cash is king and plastic money (credit) is out. Every listing in *Cheap Eats in Italy* states the credit-card policy.

Italian law requires that all establishments give a bill to the customer and that the customer carry the bill out of the restaurant. Who knows if anyone ever checks, but it is a protection for the consumer—you must get a proper bill for your money spent.

Finally, always remember to add up the bill yourself and question any discrepancies. There are too many mistakes.

Prices

All *Cheap Eats in Italy* listings give the prices for à la carte meals and the *menù turistico* (fixed-price meal) if one is available. Almost every *menù turistico* includes at least two courses and the cover and the service charges. Sometimes a beverage is also included. À la carte prices never include any beverage, rarely include the cover, and only sometimes include the service. All printed menus are required to list whether or not there is a *pane/coperto* (bread or cover charge) and/or a *servicio* (service charge) and the amount. The à la carte prices quoted in this book represent the *average cost of a three-course meal only.* The prices quoted do not include the cover or service charge if there is one or (unless otherwise noted) any beverages. In determining the average price of a meal, the cheapest and the most expensive foods were avoided. Thus, you could spend more, or less, depending on what you decide to eat and drink. In using *Cheap Eats in Italy,* you should expect a margin of labor costs and the owner's view of the economy.

Bread and Cover Charge (*Pane e Coperto*)

Pane e coperto (literally, "bread and cover") is one charge levied per person and is not to be confused with the service charge. In Rome, the cover charge has been banned, but Roman restaurateurs don't give up easily, so there is now a bread charge to take its place. In theory it is not applicable if you do not touch the basket of bread, but theory and fact do not always agree. In Florence and Venice the cover charge is intact and includes the table settings, flowers, and everything else the owner wants to toss into this catch-all charge, *plus* the bread, whether or not you want it or eat it. All menus *must* clearly state the cost of the bread/cover charge, which is listed separately in the bill, and added to the total on which you will pay service. If you order the *menù turistico,* or eat standing at a bar counter, you will avoid the bread/cover charge, and in most cases the service charge as well.

Service Charge (*Servizio*)

Servizio incluso and *servizio compreso* mean the service charge is included in the price of the meal, and no further tip is necessary (nor will there be another charge added to your bill). *Servizio non-incluso* or *servizio non-compreso* means that the service charge has not been added, and you will be expected to pay an additional 10 to 15 percent of the total bill, including the cover. Sometimes the service is not included, but the restaurant will automatically add the service to your bill, and this will appear as a separate charge. All of the listings in *Cheap Eats in Italy* describe how the service charge is handled: they say either "service included," "service not included," "no service charged," or "12% service added" (though this percentage will vary).

Please remember that *the service charge is the tip,* and you are not required to leave anything more unless the service has been especially good and you are feeling generous, in which case you can round off the total. For service above and beyond, consider the ultimate tip: informing the person's employer by writing a letter of praise.

Big Splurges

Restaurants in the Big Splurge category are included for those who have more flexible budgets, or for special-occasion dining to celebrate a birthday, anniversary, or any other memorable day. These restaurants are marked by a ($) in the list of restaurants for Florence, Rome, and Venice, and again by the restaurant heading in the text for each city. Please refer to the Index for a separate listing of each city's Big Splurges.

FLORENCE

Their smiles and laughter are due to their habit of thinking pleasurably about the pleasures of life.

—*Peter Nichols,* Italia, Italia, *1973*

Whichever way you turn, you are struck with picturesque beauty and faded splendors.

—*William Hazlitt,* Notes of a Journey through France and Italy, *1826*

For nearly three centuries, from Giotto's time to Michelangelo's, Florence was the cultural center of Europe, producing countless art treasures and generating ideas that formed the cornerstone of twentieth-century thought. Five centuries after the Renaissance was born here, Florence has become a victim of her own beauty and is in danger of being consumed by traffic, pollution, and crowds from the four corners of the planet. Streets designed to accommodate horse-drawn carriages and pedestrians now cope with cars, trucks, and hundreds of smog-inducing tour buses. Despite this, visitors continue to flock to this beautiful city to immerse themselves in the art, the literature, and the soft Tuscan light. The home of Dante and *David,* Machiavelli, the Medicis, and the Guccis, Florence is still the perfect place to fall in love all over again.

The food in Florence is simple and hearty, without rich sauces or elaborate spices. The cuisine reflects the Tuscan emphasis on bread, beans, deep-green extra-virgin olive oil, wild game, free-range poultry, and grilled and roasted meats. Most of Florence's restaurants are not gourmet, but many regional dishes are prepared so well that the food is considered to be some of the best in Italy. Because of the influx of more than one million visitors a year, the good-value restaurants are known to visitors and natives alike. To avoid eating with your fellow compatriots, plan to eat dinner when the Italians do, after 8:30 or 9 P.M.

In Florence you will probably consume more bread than you will pasta. Most of the bread is baked without salt, which seems odd at first, but once you develop a taste for it, the plain unsalted bread is almost addictive. Stale bread goes into some of the best dishes. *Crostini* (toasted bread spread with pâté) is a delicious antipasto or light snack. *Ribollita,* a hearty vegetable soup with beans and black cabbage, reheated and poured over a thick slice of bread, is a favorite first course. In summer, *panzanella,* a salad of torn bread tossed with tomatoes and onion in red wine and virgin olive oil, is a light and refreshing lunch. The meat courses are a delight to all carnivores, especially the *bistecca alla fiorentina,* a two- to three-inch slab of Chianti beef, salted and coated with olive oil and served juicy rare. Chianti wine is always a fit accompaniment for any meal. For

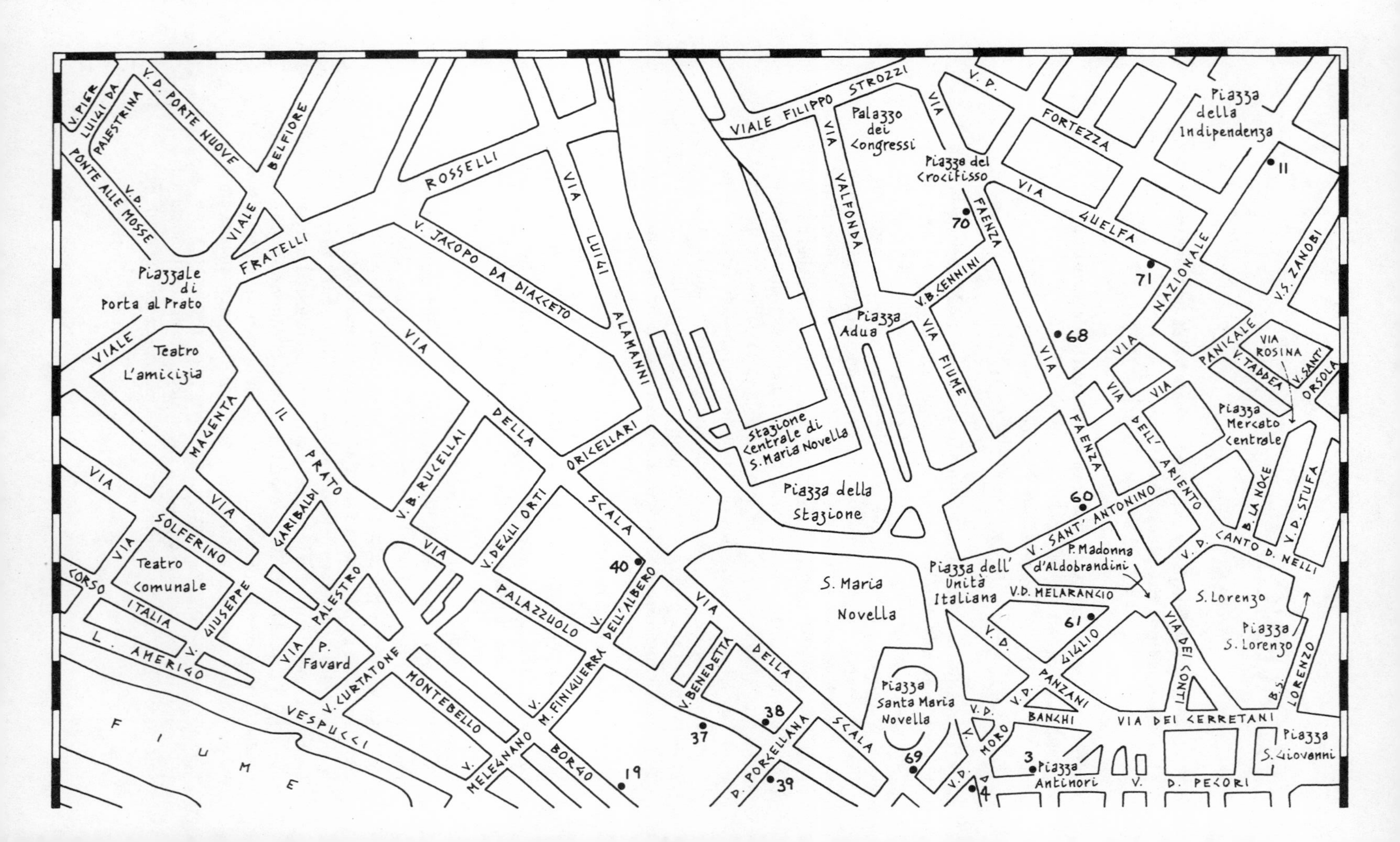
V. PIER LUIGI DA PALESTRINA
V. D. PORTE NUOVE
V. D. PONTE ALLE MOSSE
BELFIORE
VIALE FRATELLI ROSSELLI
Piazzale di Porta al Prato
VIALE
Teatro L'amicizia
V. JACOPO DA DIACCETO
VIA LUIGI ALAMANNI
VIA DELLA SCALA
VIA IL PRATO
MAGENTA
VIA
VIA SOLFERINO
VIA
Teatro Comunale
CORSO ITALIA
L. AMERIGO VESPUCCI
GIUSEPPE GARIBALDI
VIA PALESTRO
P. Favard
V. CURTATONE
MONTEBELLO
V. MELEGNANO
BORGO
V. M. FINIGUERRA
V. PALAZZUOLO
V. B. RUCELLAI
ORICELLARI
V. DEGLI ORTI
VIA
V. DELL'ALBERO
V. BENEDETTA
D. PORCELLANA
F I U M E
19
37
38
39
40
Stazione centrale di S. Maria Novella
Piazza della Stazione
VIALE FILIPPO STROZZI
VIA VALFONDA
Palazzo dei Congressi
Piazza del Crocifisso
70
VIA FAENZA
V. B. CENNINI
Piazza Adua
VIA FIUME
V. D.
VIA FORTEZZA
Piazza della Indipendenza
11
VIA GUELFA
71
NAZIONALE
V. S. ZANOBI
68
VIA PANICALE
VIA ROSINA
V. TADDEA
V. SANT' ORSOLA
Piazza Mercato Centrale
VIA
VIA DELL' ARIENTO
B. LA NOCE
V. D. STUFA
60
V. SANT' ANTONINO
V. D. CANTO D. NELLI
P. Madonna d'Aldobrandini
Piazza dell' Unità Italiana
V. D. MELARANCIO
61
S. Lorenzo
Piazza S. Lorenzo
B. S. LORENZO
S. Maria Novella
V. D. GIGLIO
V. D. PANZANI
VIA DEI CONTI
Piazza Santa Maria Novella
69
V. D. MORO
BANCHI
VIA DEI CERRETANI
Piazza S. Giovanni
3
Piazza Antinori
V. D. PECORI
V. D.
4

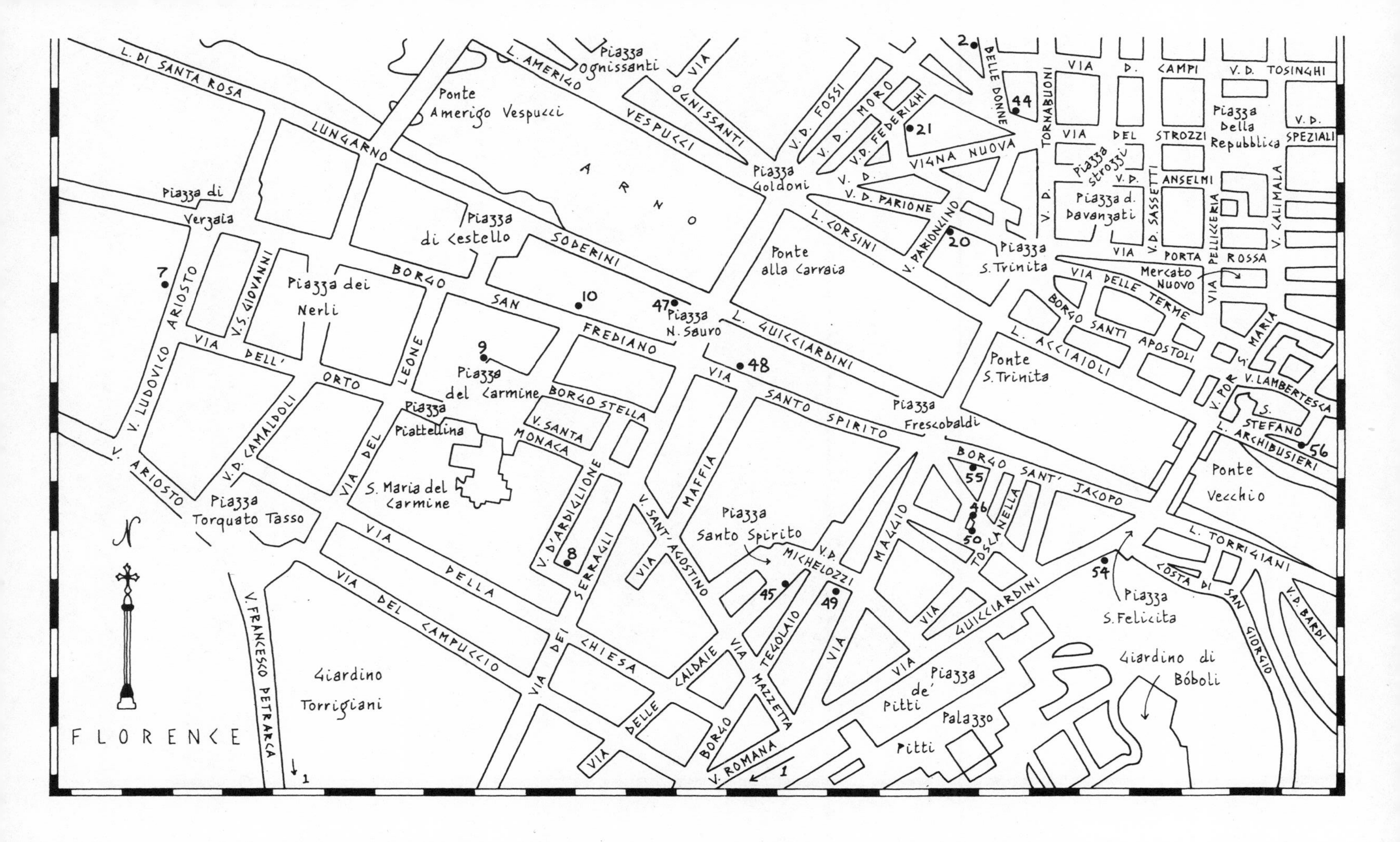
FLORENCE
N
ARNO
L. DI SANTA ROSA
LUNGARNO
L. AMERIGO
Piazza Ognissanti
VIA OGNISSANTI
VESPUCCI
Ponte Amerigo Vespucci
Piazza di Verzaia
V. LUDOVICO ARIOSTO
V. ARIOSTO
V. S. GIOVANNI
Piazza dei Nerli
VIA DELL' ORTO
VIA DEL LEONE
V. D. CAMALDOLI
Piazza Torquato Tasso
Piazza di Cestello
SODERINI
BORGO SAN FREDIANO
Piazza del Carmine
Piazza Piattellina
S. Maria del Carmine
BORGO STELLA
V. SANTA MONACA
V. D'ARDIGLIONE
SERRAGLI
VIA DELLA
VIA DEL CAMPUCCIO
VIA DEI CHIESA
VIA DELLE CALDAIE
V. FRANCESCO PETRARCA
Giardino Torrigiani
Piazza N. Sauro
L. GUICCIARDINI
VIA SANTO SPIRITO
VIA MAFFIA
V. SANT' AGOSTINO
VIA
Piazza Santo Spirito
V. D. MICHELOZZI
VIA TEGOLAIO
VIA MAZZETTA
BORGO
V. ROMANA
VIA MAGGIO
VIA GUICCIARDINI
VIA
Piazza de' Pitti
Palazzo Pitti
Giardino di Bóboli
Piazza S. Felicita
COSTA DI SAN GIORGIO
L. TORRIGIANI
V. D. BARDI
Ponte Vecchio
BORGO SANT' JACOPO
TOSCANELLA
Piazza Frescobaldi
Ponte S. Trinita
L. ACCIAIOLI
BORGO SANTI APOSTOLI
VIA DELLE TERME
Mercato Nuovo
VIA PORTA ROSSA
VIA PELLICCERIA
V. CALIMALA
V. D. SPEZIALI
Piazza Della Repubblica
V. D. TOSINGHI
VIA D. CAMPI
VIA DEL STROZZI
V. D. ANSELMI
V. D. SASSETTI
Piazza Strozzi
Piazza d. Davanzati
V. D. TORNABUONI
BELLE DONNE
VIGNA NUOVA
V. D. FEDERIGHI
V. D. MORO
V. D. FOSSI
V. D.
V. D. PARIONE
V. PARIONCINO
L. CORSINI
Piazza Goldoni
Ponte alla Carraia
Piazza S. Trinita
V. POR S. MARIA
V. LAMBERTESCA
S. STEFANO
L. ARCHIBUSIERI
Ponte Vecchio
1
2
7
8
9
10
20
21
44
45
46
47
48
49
50
54
55
56

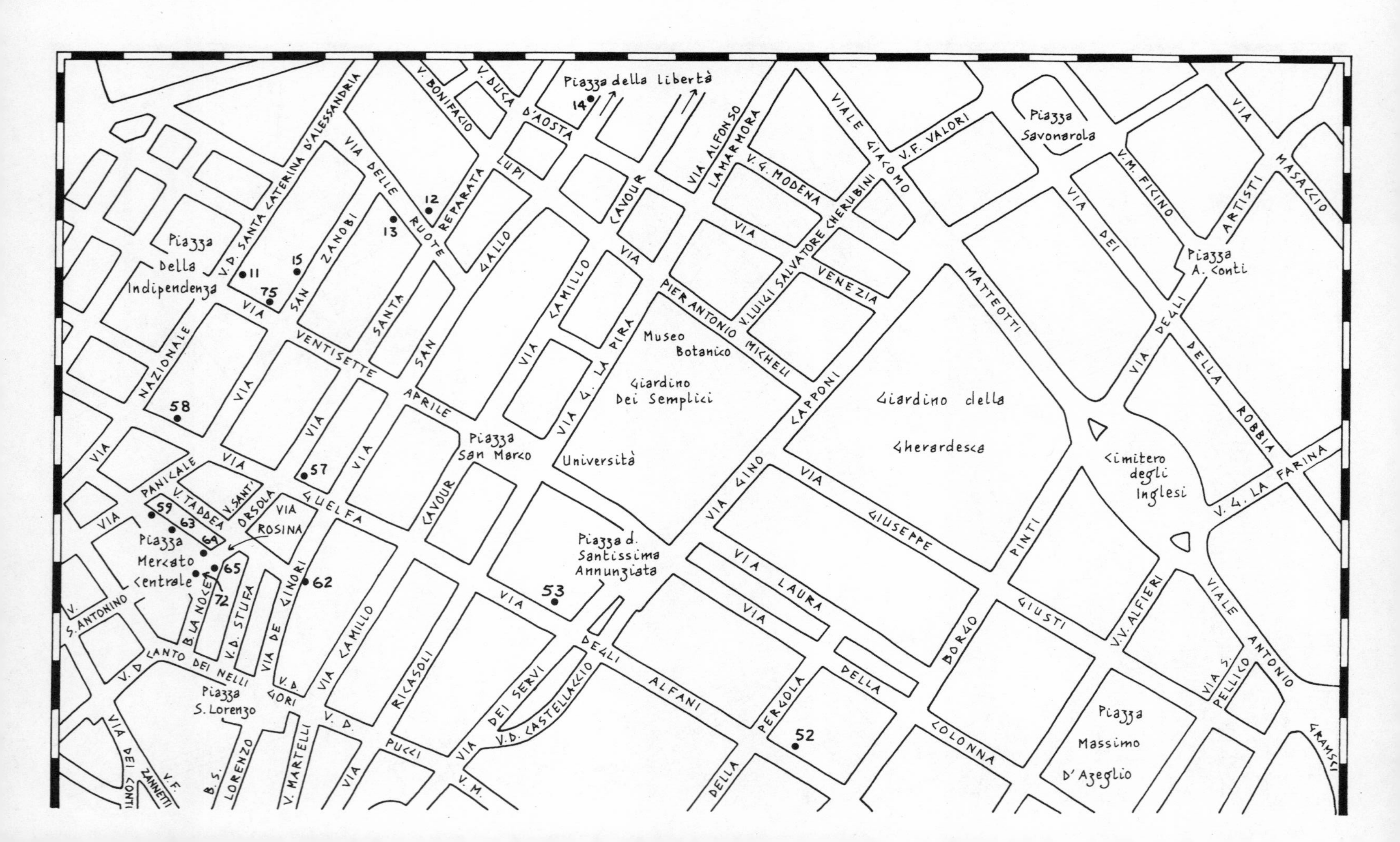

Piazza della Libertà
Piazza Savonarola
Piazza A. Conti
Piazza Della Indipendenza
Museo Botanico
Giardino Dei Semplici
Università
Piazza San Marco
Giardino della Gherardesca
Cimitero degli Inglesi
Piazza d. Santissima Annunziata
Piazza Mercato Centrale
Piazza S. Lorenzo
Piazza Massimo D'Azeglio
V. Bonifacio
V. Duca d'Aosta
Via Alfonso Lamarmora
Viale Giacomo
V.F. Valori
V.M. Ficino
Via dei
Via Masaccio
Artisti
Via degli
Della Robbia
V. G. La Farina
Viale Antonio
Gramsci
Via S. Pellico
V.V. Alfieri
Giusti
Pinti
Borgo
Colonna
Della
V.D. Santa Caterina d'Alessandria
Via delle Ruote
Reparata
Lupi
Gallo
Via Camillo Cavour
V.G. Modena
V. Luigi Salvatore Cherubini
Via Venezia
Pier Antonio Micheli
Via G. La Pira
Capponi
Matteotti
Via Gino
Via Giuseppe
Via Laura
Via della Pergola
Via degli Alfani
Via dei Servi
V.D. Castellaccio
Via San Zanobi
Santa
San
Via Ventisette Aprile
Via Nazionale
Via Panicale
V. Taddea
V. Sant' Orsola
Via Rosina
Guelfa
Cavour
Via de Ginori
V.D. Stufa
B. La Noce
V.D. Canto dei Nelli
V.D. Gori
Via Camillo Ricasoli
V.D. Pucci
V. Martelli
B.S. Lorenzo
V.M.
V. S. Antonino
Via dei Conti
V.F. Zannetti
Via
11
12
13
14
15
52
53
57
58
59
62
63
65
69
72
75

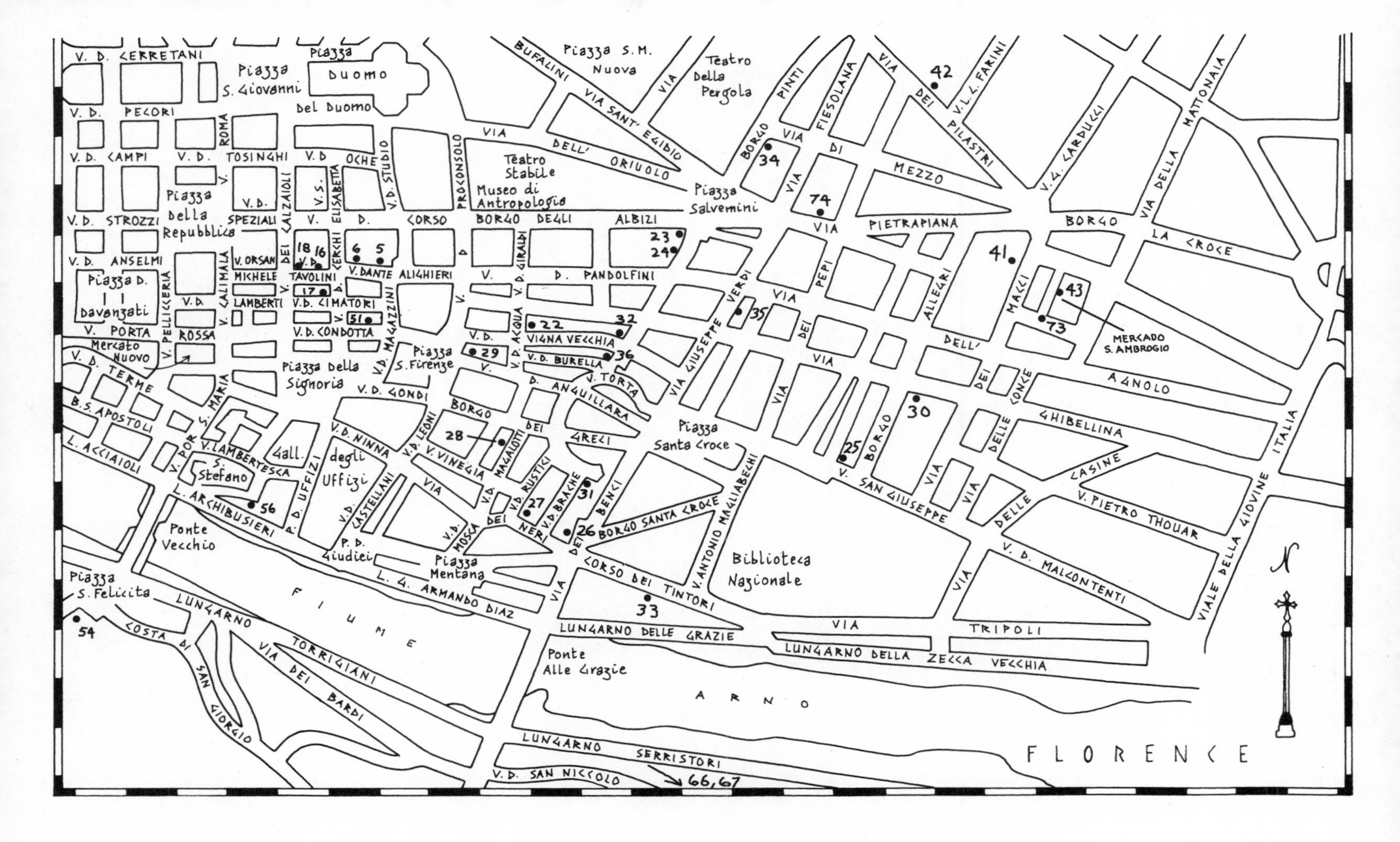
FLORENCE
N
V. D. CERRETANI
Piazza Duomo
Piazza S. Giovanni
Del Duomo
V. D. PECORI
ROMA
V. D. CAMPI
V. D. TOSINGHI
V. D OCHE
V. D. STUDIO
Piazza della Repubblica
V. D. STROZZI
V. D. SPEZIALI
DEI CALZAIOLI
V. S. ELISABETTA
V. D. CORSO
CERCHI
V. D. ANSELMI
V. ORSAN MICHELE
TAVOLINI
V. DANTE ALIGHIERI
Piazza D. Davanzati
V. PELLICCERIA
V. CALIMALA
LAMBERTI
V. D. CIMATORI
V. D. CONDOTTA
V. D. MAGAZZINI
V. PORTA ROSSA
Mercato Nuovo
Piazza Della Signoria
Piazza S. Firenze
V. D. TERME
B. S. APOSTOLI
L. ACCIAIOLI
V. POR S. MARIA
V. LAMBERTESCA
S. Stefano
Gall. degli Uffizi
P. D. UFFIZI
L. ARCHIBUSIERI
Ponte Vecchio
Piazza S. Felicita
COSTA DI SAN GIORGIO
LUNGARNO TORRIGIANI
VIA DEI BARDI
FIUME
ARNO
V. D. GONDI
V. D. NINNA
V. D. LEONI
V. VINEGIA
V. D. CASTELLANI
P. D. Giudici
V. D. MOSCA
Piazza Mentana
L. G. ARMANDO DIAZ
BORGO DEI GRECI
V. D. MAGALOTTI
V. D. RUSTICI
V. D. NERI
V. D. BRACHE
VIA DEI BENCI
BORGO SANTA CROCE
CORSO DEI TINTORI
LUNGARNO DELLE GRAZIE
Ponte Alle Grazie
LUNGARNO SERRISTORI
V. D. SAN NICCOLO
66, 67
PROCONSOLO
VIA BUFALINI
Piazza S. M. Nuova
VIA SANT' EGIDIO
VIA DELL' ORIUOLO
Teatro Stabile
Museo di Antropologia
BORGO DEGLI ALBIZI
V. D. GIRALDI
V. D. PANDOLFINI
V. D. ACQUA
VIGNA VECCHIA
V. D. BURELLA
D. ANGUILLARA
V. TORTA
Piazza Santa Croce
VIA GIUSEPPE VERDI
Teatro Della Pergola
VIA
BORGO PINTI
VIA FIESOLANA
VIA DI MEZZO
Piazza Salvemini
VIA PIETRAPIANA
VIA PEPI
VIA DEI PILASTRI
V. L. C. FARINI
V. G. CARDUCCI
VIA DELLA MATTONAIA
BORGO LA CROCE
MACCI
MERCADO S. AMBROGIO
VIA DELL' AGNOLO
ALLEGRI
DEI CONCE
BORGO
V. SAN GIUSEPPE
V. ANTONIO MAGLIABECHI
Biblioteca Nazionale
VIA DELLE CASINE
GHIBELLINA
V. PIETRO THOUAR
V. D. MALCONTENTI
VIALE DELLA GIOVINE ITALIA
VIA TRIPOLI
LUNGARNO DELLA ZECCA VECCHIA
42
34
74
23
24
41
43
73
18
16
6
5
17
51
22
32
35
29
36
30
25
28
31
27
26
56
33
54

an even better wine, look for Chianti Classico, with the *gallo nero,* or black rooster, label on the neck.

Dessert is not the main focus of the meal. It is usually a piece of fresh fruit or a glass of *vin santo,* a sweet wine made from dried grapes. *Cantuccini di Prato* (also called *biscotti di Prato*) are hard "almost" cookies usually dipped in the wine, a nice finish to any Tuscan meal.

NOTE: In Florence, the street numbers of commercial establishments (stores, restaurants, and businesses) are indicated by a red "r" following the number of the address (i.e., 34r). A blue or black "b" means the address is a private residence. To add to the fun, addresses are seldom in sequence as we think they should be. Instead, they are in sequence according to the "r" or the "b" numbers, but they are not necessarily next to one another, which can create confusion for the unknowing visitor.

Also, *oltrarno* refers to "the other side of the Arno," often considered the Left Bank of Florence. Crossing the Ponte Vecchio from the central part of the city, visitors usually walk and shop along Via Guicciardini until they reach the enormous Pitti Palace, now an art gallery with works by Titian, Tintoretto, Rubens, and Raphael. Hidden along the side streets are antique stores to behold, artisan workshops, and galleries. The hilly Boboli Gardens make up the only park in the center of Florence, and are a wonderful place to spend a nice, quiet afternoon admiring the long expanse of cypress trees, a miniature island, the statuary, and lovely plantings.

Restaurants in Florence

The number in parentheses before each restaurant corresponds to a number that marks the restaurant's location on the Florence map (an entry with no number before it is located outside the parameters of the map); a dollar sign ($) indicates restaurants in the Big Splurge category.

RESTAURANTS

FOOD SHOPPING IN FLORENCE

Boboli Gardens

Behind the Pitti Palace are eleven rolling acres of gardens known as the Giardinia di Boboli, which was the playground of the Medicis when they lived in the Pitti. Laid out by the great landscape architect Triboli, the gardens are popular today for quiet walks amid the statuary and fountains. A climb to the top of Fort Belvedere rewards visitors with a sweeping view of Florence.

(1) TRATTORIA BOBOLI
Via Romana, 45r

TELEPHONE AND FAX
055-23-36-401
OPEN
Thur–Tues
CLOSED
Wed, Aug
HOURS
Noon–3 P.M., 7:30–10 P.M.
RESERVATIONS
Suggested
CREDIT CARDS
AE, DC, MC, V
À LA CARTE
L34,000–40,000

Remember your mother, or others interested in your well-being, telling you, "Keep your eyes and ears open, never give up, and you never know what good thing is awaiting you around the next corner?" Well, I can tell you it is a saying that works, especially in my job of scouting out the best Cheap Eats and Sleeps in the cities this series covers. Such was the case one rainy day in Florence near the Boboli Gardens. I had just reinspected a hotel nearby that unfortunately had to be dropped from *Cheap Sleeps in Italy* because management had become complacent, favoring deferred maintenance to conscientious upkeep. I was tired and hungry when I noticed this friendly looking trattoria across the street.

MENÙ TURISTICO
L25,000, two courses, beverage, cover, and service included

MENU DEGUSTAZIONE
L40,000, three courses, bottle of excellent Chianti wine, coffee, cover, and service included

STUDENT MENU (OCT–MARCH)
L10,000, one main course plus potatoes; L18,000, two courses and potatoes; beverage extra; cover and service included in both

COVER AND SERVICE CHARGES
Cover L3,000, no service charge

ENGLISH
Yes

Any port in a storm, I thought, as I hung up my dripping raincoat and settled into a cozy corner table in a typical room crowded with wine racks and plates on the walls, plants here and there, and a ceiling fan.

Since I did not qualify for the bargain student Cheap Eats, the *menù turistico* looked worthy of consideration. It offered plenty of food and value, with either a soup or choice of three pastas to start, followed by fried chicken, veal scaloppine with tomatoes and peas, pork with potatoes, or liver, and accompanied by wine or water. I decided to splurge a little and ordered the Menu Degustazione, which included a bottle of excellent Chianti wine. I started with *crepes à la Florentine,* a duet of crepes filled with spinach and ricotta and covered with a cream sauce and cheese gratinée. Next I had a grilled steak topped with arugula and a side of potatoes. My dessert was a plate of *biscotti* for dipping into a glass of *vin santo,* followed by coffee. I was graciously served by Gilberto and his wife, who have been taking care of their loyal patrons for over two decades. No, it is not destination dining, but it is much more than a mere port in a storm if you are near the Boboli Gardens and want a nice, simple meal.

Il Duomo

Florence is a city-museum, whose art treasures are unparalleled anywhere in the world. This city of refinement and elegance gave Italy its national language and was the birthplace of the Renaissance. The city symbol is Il Duomo, the thirteenth-century cathedral crowned by a dome by Brunelleschi with a distinctive pink, white, and green marble exterior that dominates the Piazza del Duomo and all around it.

(2) BELLE DONNE
Via delle Belle Donne, 16r

TELEPHONE
055-23-82-609

OPEN
Mon–Fri

CLOSED
Sat, Sun, Aug

HOURS
Noon–2:30 P.M., 7–10 P.M.

RESERVATIONS
Advised

There is no sign or menu outside Belle Donne, only a cluster of Florentines waiting for a vacant seat. The inside is overpowered by massive fruit and vegetable displays and a forest of green plants. The closely spaced tables, set for two or four, are always filled to capacity. The menu, written on a blackboard, is seldom the same two days in a row. You can eat lightly and order only one course, or go full tilt and have several courses if you are starved. If available, do not pass up the cream of chestnut soup or the avocado and zucchini salad. For a main course, look for the chicken in lemon, carpaccio with *rucola* (thinly sliced raw beef fillet served with a salad of bitter greens), or, if you are up to it, the tripe. If you are having a vegetable, watch for anything au gratin, and for dessert, do yourself a favor in the early spring and summer and order the strawberry tart. The service can be rushed and borders on the rude, especially during the peak lunch hour. Don't let this deter you . . . it doesn't the locals.

CREDIT CARDS
None

À LA CARTE
L30,000–35,000, beverage extra

MENÙ TURISTICO
None

COVER AND SERVICE CHARGES
Cover L1,500, service included

ENGLISH
Limited

(3) CANTINETTA ANTINORI ($)
Piazza Antinori, 3r

Many years ago, owners of large estates around Florence kept small cellars in their palaces, and sold products from little windows on the street. Following this long-standing tradition, the Antinori family has established the Cantinetta in their fifteenth-century Renaissance Palazzo Antinori in the heart of Florence. Without question, this is a magnificent showplace for the vintages of the oldest and most distinguished wine producer in Tuscany. The dark-paneled bar and restaurant are filled with the beautifully clad Florentines who have made this the most popular wine bar in their city. All of the food comes from the family estates, which are known especially for their rich extra-virgin olive oil, outstanding cheeses, and fine wines. Full meals can run into the Big Splurge category, but are worth every delicious bite. If you want to spend less and still enjoy this memorable experience, order an appetizer, a salad, or a plate of assorted cheeses along with a glass or two of their excellent wines. If you sit at the bar, you will save both the cover and service charges.

TELEPHONE
055-29-22-34

FAX
055-23-59-87

OPEN
Mon–Fri

CLOSED
Sat, Sun, Aug, Dec 24–Jan 8

HOURS
12:30–2:30 P.M., 7–10:30 P.M.

RESERVATIONS
Essential

CREDIT CARDS
AE, DC, V

À LA CARTE
L75,000 (three courses); individual courses from L18,000, beverage extra

MENÙ TURISTICO
None

COVER AND SERVICE CHARGES
Cover L4,500, 10% service added

ENGLISH
Yes, and menu in English

(4) CROCE AL TREBBIO
Via delle Belle Donne, 49r

A meal at Croce al Trebbio is pleasant and unhurried, with good service and food to match. The interior is upmarket rustic, with beams, bountiful food displays, and two walls papered with foreign money. The basement features a hundred-year-old arched brick ceiling and rough stone walls. If romance is on your agenda, this is a more intimate place to dine, especially in the evening when the lights are low.

Newcomers and old-timers alike go for either the *menù turistico* or the daily specials, which vary according

TELEPHONE
055-28-70-89

OPEN
Daily

CLOSED
Nov–Feb, Mon

HOURS
Noon–2:30 P.M., 7–10:30 P.M.

RESERVATIONS
Advised for dinner

CREDIT CARDS
AE, DC, MC, V

À LA CARTE
L35,000–40,000, beverage extra

MENÙ TURISTICO
L22,000, three courses, cover, and service included, beverage extra

COVER AND SERVICE CHARGES
Cover L2,000, 10% service added for à la carte

ENGLISH
Yes, and menu in English

to the season. The à la carte choices are broader, but they are only borderline bargains. The meal gets off to a stunning start if you order a simple *insalata caprese* (salad with tomatoes and buffalo mozzarella cheese) or the *risotto alla creme d'asparagi* (asparagus risotto). Other first-course standouts include a *tortellini panna e prosciutto* (tortellini with cream and ham), *pasta ai quatro formaggi* (pasta with four cheeses), and an especially worthy *ribollita* (the famed Florentine reboiled soup). Osso buco with peas, roast beef with potatoes, and the ever-present tripe are three *piatti pronti*—ready-to-serve main courses. Taking a little more time but definitely worth the wait are any of the veal or lamb dishes, especially scaloppine with lemon or mushrooms or the sliced lamb with fresh artichokes. The desserts are rather limited, but if it's on, the *tiramisù* is worth the calorie splurge.

(5) DA PENNELLO
Via Dante Alighieri, 4r

TELEPHONE
055-29-48-48

OPEN
Tues–Sat; Sun, lunch only

CLOSED
Mon, Aug, Dec 25–Jan 2

HOURS
Noon–2:30 P.M., 7–10 P.M.

RESERVATIONS
Definitely

CREDIT CARDS
AE, DC, V

À LA CARTE
L40,000, beverage extra

MENÙ TURISTICO
L30,000, three courses, beverage extra

COVER AND SERVICE CHARGES
None

ENGLISH
Yes

Da Pennello has been discovered, but never mind. The brightly lit restaurant is deservedly popular with everyone who visits or lives in Florence, and is always packed to the walls, so if you arrive without a reservation, especially during prime lunchtime, be prepared to wait up to an hour. It is located on a narrow street near Dante's house, about a five-minute stroll from Il Duomo in the direction of the Uffizi Gallery and the Arno River. The kitchen is known for producing an impressive variety of outstanding antipasti, and if you wish, you can make an entire meal out of these wonderful appetizers.

The *menù turistico* offers good Cheap Eating. There is a choice of *primi piatti* (first courses) of several pastas or the soup of the day. The *secondi piatti* usually lists a roast, veal scaloppine, and an omelette of some sort, along with vegetables or a salad and dessert. The value here is that you can exchange either the first or second courses with a trip to the antipasti table. Wine is extra. If you want *only* to take advantage of the groaning antipasti table, that is a nice option for Cheap Eaters who want a light meal. If you are going to do this, I suggest going for lunch when it is all fresh. At dinnertime, most antipasti tables are recycled from lunch.

(6) TRIPE STAND
Via Dante Alighieri, 22r

Almost all American visitors to Florence eventually find themselves in the American Express office on Via Dante Alighieri. If you are here between 9 A.M. and 2 P.M., or later from 5–7:30 P.M., a portable food cart with a blue-and-white awning will be sitting out front. There will be a line, and the busy man behind the cart won't miss a beat as he serves his hungry customers. What is he selling at this popular pit stop? Tripe. Thirty kilograms per day—which means sixty-six pounds. That is a lot of tripe!

Wait a minute . . . tripe isn't *that* bad, and here it is really quite good. Obviously it is a big success among local tripe fanciers, who have been stopping by Miro's cart for two decades. Big pieces of tripe are pulled from two steaming pots, sliced thinly onto fresh rolls, dipped into the juice (optional), served with salt, pepper, and green salsa, and rolled in wax paper. Afraid to go whole hog on a sandwich? Then order a small helping of just the tripe, served again on waxed paper and accompanied by toothpicks. If you are cooking in, you can buy fresh tripe from this stand at L1,100 for 100 grams. What to drink with your repast? Remember, this *is* Italy, so you can purchase a chilled minibottle of wine, a more pedestrian soda, or a beer to complement your meal.

TELEPHONE
None

OPEN
Mon–Fri; Sat, breakfast and lunch only

CLOSED
Sat afternoon, Sun, Aug

HOURS
9 A.M–2:30 P.M., 5–7:30 P.M.

RESERVATIONS
Not accepted

CREDIT CARDS
None

À LA CARTE
L3,500 for a sandwich

MENÙ TURISTICO
None

COVER AND SERVICE CHARGES
None

ENGLISH
No

Piazza del Carmine

Santa Maria del Carmine is a Baroque building with restored frescoes by Masaccio and Masolino and viewing times limited to a mere quarter of an hour.

(7) ALLA VECCHIA BETTOLA
Viale Ludovico Ariosto, 32–34r

Tuscany's simplest foods tend to be its most successful, and nowhere is this more evident than at Alla Vecchia Bettola, a picturesque trattoria specializing in the region's native cuisine. Under the same ownership is Nerbone (see page 66).

The handwritten but legible menu changes almost daily. A bottle of house wine is on the table for you to pour into green glasses, paying only for as much as you drink. Seating is at marble-topped row tables on benches along the wall or on four-legged, backless stools. Despite the rather rustic decor, the atmosphere is upscale and so

TELEPHONE
055-22-41-58

OPEN
Tues–Sat

CLOSED
Sun, Mon, Aug, Dec 23–Jan 2

HOURS
Noon–2:30 P.M., 7:30–10 P.M.

RESERVATIONS
Essential

CREDIT CARDS
None

À LA CARTE
L40,000, beverage extra

MENÙ TURISTICO
None

COVER AND SERVICE CHARGES
Cover L2,000, service included

ENGLISH
Yes

are the diners, arriving when the doors open and standing in line as the night goes on. As you can see, management does not stress creature comforts. It does, however, definitely stress good food offered at fair prices.

If it is available, start with the *pecorino con baccellie,* a basket of raw, unshelled fava beans (similar to limas) and two slabs of smoky pecorino cheese. You shell the beans and pop them into your mouth with a piece of the cheese and a chunk of country bread. It is different and good, not heavy as one might expect. Move on to *topini al pomodoro,* a light gnocchi bathed in tomato sauce, or *risotto alle zucchine,* followed by a second course of roast veal or rabbit served with crisply fried artichokes. The salads are disappointing, especially the tired spinach version, drenched in too much oil. The desserts, on the other hand, won't let you down. Try the house apple cake or the plate of assorted *biscotti,* consisting of macaroons and almond cookies for you to dip into a glass of sweet *vin santo.*

(8) I RADDI
Via d'Ardiglione, 47r

TELEPHONE
055-21-10-72

OPEN
Mon–Sat

CLOSED
Sun, 10 days in Feb and 10 days in Aug (dates vary)

HOURS
12:30–2:30 P.M., 7:30–10:30 P.M.

RESERVATIONS
Advised for dinner

CREDIT CARDS
AE, MC, V

À LA CARTE
L30,000–40,000, beverage extra

MENÙ TURISTICO
None

COVER AND SERVICE CHARGES
Cover L2,000, 10% service added

ENGLISH
Yes, and it is excellent

When things change at a restaurant, I worry. When I find that the restaurant is even better, I am pleased. Such is the case at I Raddi.

Luciano Raddi was a European and Italian boxing champ of the '50s who switched careers and became a restaurant owner. Along with his wife and daughter, he cooked and served homestyle Florentine dishes in a trattoria somewhat off the usual tourist track, but close enough for a nice walk after lunch to the Piazza Santo Spirito, with its interesting church, or to the Pitti Palace museum, a few blocks farther. On my last trip to Florence, I learned that Luciano had died and the restaurant had been sold. The new owners are Duccio Lapini and Toshi Mitsubiki, a chef who despite his name is one good Italian cook. Duccio spent two years studying in San Francisco and worked in New York for two more. I don't need to tell you that his English is excellent. The two worked with Luciano's wife and daughter for six months before taking it over themselves, and in the process changed nothing inside . . . only improved the menu and the cooking.

The well-spaced tables are double-covered with red and white cloths and set in a rough-hewn room dominated by a heavy-beamed ceiling. The lunch crowd is sparse, making it easy to get a good table without advance reservations. Things pick up at night, however, when the neighborhood pours in for an evening of conversation, fine Chianti, and generous helpings of delicious food. The menu does not go on forever, a sure sign that everything is fresh. The daily specials are usually the best bets, especially the tagliatelle with eggplant, butter, and fresh herbs. If you are like me and can barely think of dinner without a dessert of some sort, you will like the *dolce della casa,* either cheesecake or lemon or chocolate mousse. The wines are very good, especially the Capezzana-DOCG, a full-bodied Chianti Montalbano.

(9) TRATTORIA DEL CARMINE
Piazza del Carmine, 18r

Tucked away from the tourist glare is the appealing Trattoria del Carmine, a simple choice where everything seems to turn out. I like to go in the summertime and sit under an umbrella on the sidewalk terrace. During the cooler months, seating is on ladderback chairs in two whitewashed rooms filled with attractive watercolors and leafy green plants.

The *menù turistico* is definitely the best Cheap Eat going in the neighborhood. It gives you a selection of several first and second courses, along with dessert, which could be the Florentine favorite of *vin santo con biscotti,* hard almond cookies to dip in sweet wine, or *crostata de frutta,* a fruit tart. On the à la carte side, look for the chef's daily recommendations. Perhaps you might start with risotto with artichokes and follow this with roast pork garnished with rape, a bitter green that complements this meat, and a side order of potato puree.

TELEPHONE
055-21-86-01

OPEN
Mon–Sat

CLOSED
Sun

HOURS
Noon–2:30 P.M., 7:15–10:30 P.M.

RESERVATIONS
Advised

CREDIT CARDS
AE, DC, MC, V

À LA CARTE
L30,000–35,000, beverage extra

MENÙ TURISTICO
L20,000, three courses, cover and service included, beverage extra

COVER AND SERVICE CHARGES
Cover L2,000, service included

ENGLISH
Yes

(10) TRATTORIA SABATINO
Borgo San Frediano, 39r

Almost fifty years ago you would have noticed that the trim on the outside walls is the same as the paint on the inside, that a large icebox (not a refrigerator) occupies a center stage location, that the tile floors are faded but clean, and that sheets of plastic cover the green tablecloths. That half-century-old scene remains intact . . . absolutely nothing has changed, nor will it anytime in the foreseeable future. And therein lies the charm and appeal of Trattoria Sabatino, a favorite for

TELEPHONE
055-28-46-25

OPEN
Mon–Fri

CLOSED
Sat, Sun, Aug

HOURS
Noon–2:30 P.M., 7:30–10 P.M.

RESERVATIONS
Not necessary

CREDIT CARDS
None

À LA CARTE
L22,000–28,000, beverage extra
MENÙ TURISTICO
None
COVER AND SERVICE CHARGES
Cover L2,000, no service charge
ENGLISH
Yes

generations of families who come for their daily rations of *pappa al pomodoro* in winter and *panzanella* or rice salad in summer, the Tuesday tripe, the Friday *baccalà,* or the daily portions of Florentine beefsteak and roast lamb. It is all graciously presided over by members of the Sabatino family, who treat everyone with a courtesy that dates back to the day they opened. For a touch of real Florence, it is hard to top.

Piazza della Indipendenza

Piazza della Indipendenza is a large green space near the train station.

(11) IL GIARDINO DI BARBANO
Piazza della Indipendenza, 3/4r

TELEPHONE
055-48-67-52
OPEN
Mon–Tues, Thur–Sun, dinner only
CLOSED
Wed, 3 weeks Feb (dates vary)
HOURS
6 P.M.–1 A.M.
RESERVATIONS
Not necessary
CREDIT CARDS
AE, DC, V
À LA CARTE
L22,000, beverage extra; pizzas from L6,000, pastas from L9,000
MENÙ TURISTICO
None
COVER AND SERVICE CHARGES
Cover L1,000, service included
ENGLISH
Yes, and menu in English

Handsome Gian Carlo, who with his pretty wife, Tosca, has been running this successful restaurant for over fifteen years, told me, "I was born in Florence, my entire family lives here, and I will die here." He has definitely captured the essence of being Florentine. From 5 P.M. until 1 A.M. every night but Wednesday, most of the restaurant's 120 seats are filled with a happy crowd that ranges from tourists and tradesmen to fashionable men and women. In summer, the table to request is one in either the glassed-in or outdoor garden; in winter, ask for a booth in front. The specialty is *pappardelle al cinghiale,* wide, flat noodles sauced with wild boar meat. If that doesn't speak to you, perhaps one of the fifty pastas or risottos will. Still not enticed? Then order one of the thirty-four pizzas. There are also salads, appetizers, and a host of desserts, including the house version of profiteroles, all guaranteed to keep you fully contented for some time.

(12) IL VEGETARIANO
Via delle Ruote, 30r

TELEPHONE
055-47-50–30
OPEN
Tues–Fri; Sat–Sun, dinner only
CLOSED
Mon, holidays, Aug
HOURS
12:30–2:30 P.M., 7:30–10:30 P.M.
RESERVATIONS
Not accepted

Exceptional vegetarian food, served in a warm, friendly atmosphere, is dished out cafeteria style to faithful diners, many of whom eat here with great regularity. Murals of Tuscany, fresh flowers on the tables, and a summer garden create an appealing natural setting.

The menu changes daily and varies with the seasons. Once you enter the restaurant, check the printed blackboard, decide what you want, write it down on the form provided, and take it to the cashier to pay. The dishes for each course are priced the same, allowing you to add up your total easily. After paying, take your menu form to the cafeteria counter to be served. You can eat at communal tables either in the smoking or nonsmoking section. The varied selection of food usually includes rice and pastas, casseroles made from beans and legumes, quiches, soufflés, vegan and macrobiotic choices, lots of salads, and, for dessert, anything from pumpkin pie to vegan cake.

NOTE: There is no sign outside the restaurant. Look for the round sign with a red telephone receiver hanging above the entrance at Via della Ruote, 30r. This is it.

CREDIT CARDS
None

À LA CARTE
L20,000–23,000, beverage extra

MENÙ TURISTICO
None

COVER AND SERVICE CHARGES
Cover L2,000, service included

ENGLISH
Yes

(13) TAVERNA DEL BRONZINO ($)

Via delle Ruote, 25r

Eating at the Taverna del Bronzino is always a great pleasure. It is the perfect place for Big Splurge occasion dining, be it a birthday, an anniversary, or a romantic evening with the love of your life.

The understated and elegant interior is done in muted colors with flattering lighting. You will sit comfortably at nicely appointed tables with crisp linens, heavy silver, and fresh flowers. Formal waiters offer gracious and unobtrusive service that is always one step ahead of what you need.

You are bound to be as impressed with the food as with the surroundings. It all starts with a glass of the house aperitif and a plate of tiny appetizers to enjoy while you decide what to order. If you ask, your waiter will make knowledgeable suggestions to help you plan your meal. The imaginative dishes are inspired by the seasonal best of the Italian harvest. The appetizers lean toward fresh prawns, shrimp, and smoked fish, or a seasonally wonderful artichoke strudel. The fresh pastas are blanketed under robust sauces of fresh seafood, *funghi porcini,* or black truffles. The meat, poultry, and fresh fish are perfectly cooked, gently perfumed with wines and herbs, and attractively served.

Sublime desserts and a distinguished wine list round out a meal you will favorably recall long after you have forgotten many others.

TELEPHONE
055-49-52-20

OPEN
Mon–Sat

CLOSED
Sun, Aug

HOURS
12:30–2 P.M., 7:30–10 P.M.

RESERVATIONS
Essential

CREDIT CARDS
AE, DC, MC, V

À LA CARTE
L55,000–60,000, beverage extra

MENÙ TURISTICO
None

COVER AND SERVICE CHARGES
Cover L5,000, service included

ENGLISH
Yes

MISCELLANEOUS
Coat and tie recommended

(14) TRATTORIA DA TITO
Via San Gallo, 112r

TELEPHONE
055-47-24-75
OPEN
Mon–Sat
CLOSED
Sun, Aug
HOURS
Noon–3 P.M., 7–10:30 P.M.
RESERVATIONS
Advised
CREDIT CARDS
MC, V
À LA CARTE
L35,000–40,000, beverage extra
MENÙ TURISTICO
L25,000, three courses, plus vegetables; beverage, cover, and service included
COVER AND SERVICE CHARGES
Cover L1,500, L1,000 service added
ENGLISH
Yes, and menu in English

Tito remains one of my Florentine favorites because it is so typically Tuscan, complete with yellowing walls lined with photos of dubious value, quick and friendly service, and reasonable prices for food of uncompromising quality. It is also out of the tourist mainstream, thus attracting a very local crowd.

At lunchtime you will need a shoehorn to get in because it is packed with regulars, who consider this their neighborhood command post. Cheap Eaters will like the all-inclusive *menù turistico,* which is a virtual steal considering the choices for three courses that include a vegetable and a choice of wine, water, or soft drink. Otherwise, you could loosen the money belt a notch or two and order from the *piatti del giorno* (daily specials). Carbohydrate fans will have a field day with the long list of authentic pastas and rice dishes. The *ribollita* (reboiled vegetable and bean soup), tortelloni with spinach, ricotta cheese, and asparagus, or any of the pastas dressed with seasonal items such as fresh *funghi porcini* or artichokes, are especially good. Carnivores can choose from a range of top-quality meats, and fish eaters will like the grilled salmon or baked sole. In the event that there is room for dessert, indulge in the *dolce della casa* (special house dessert of the day) or an assortment of Tuscan cheeses and another glass of wine.

(15) TRATTORIA SAN ZANOBI
Via San Zanobi, 33A/r

TELEPHONE
055-47-52-86
OPEN
Mon–Sat
CLOSED
Sun, Aug (1 week)
HOURS
Noon–2:30 P.M., 7–10:30 P.M.
RESERVATIONS
Advised for dinner
CREDIT CARDS
AE, MC, V
À LA CARTE
L30,000–35,000, beverage extra
MENÙ TURISTICO
L20,000, three courses; beverages, cover, and service included

It's a simple trattoria . . . red-tile floors, original brick archways, and wood-framed windows. Each room takes its design cue from a famous Florentine landmark: Il Duomo, the Palazzo Vecchio, and the Palazzo da Vanzati. The *menù turistico* should appeal to every committed Cheap Eater, not only for the price-to-quality ratio but for the portions, which more than satisfy. The printed à la carte menu covers the bases, but, as usual, prime plates are those the chef recommends that day. You will see this neatly written on a small sheet of paper fastened to the inside of the menu.

The kitchen produces uncomplicated interpretations of *ribollita, pasta e fagioli, tagliatelle* with duck, roast lamb with potatoes, and breaded lamb chops garnished with fried artichokes. Homemade *tiramisù* and *panna cotta* add just the right sweet finishing notes to the kind of meal typical Florentines survive on.

COVER AND SERVICE CHARGES
Cover L3,000, 12% service added
ENGLISH
Yes

Piazza della Repubblica

Ringed by *caffès* and countless shops lining the streets leading into the large square, this is the commercial heart of Florence. In ancient times it was a huge marketplace filled with merchants, farmers, and beggars, all doing business successfully.

(16) CANTINETTA DEI VERRAZZANO
Via dei Tavolini, 18–20r

On one of my early morning walks, I found this elegant *caffè* that is also a bakery, wine shop, wonderful lunch stop, and elegant teatime rendezvous. Starting at 8 A.M., the bakers send out heaping trays of breakfast goodies along with loaves of brown, white, olive, or wine-flavored breads. I would stop in after walking, order a glass of freshly squeezed orange juice, a *cornetto,* and a double cappuccino to enjoy while glancing through the morning paper. The gleaming glass display cases are filled with a colorful assortment of individual tarts, marvelous cakes sold whole or by the slice, beautiful piles of *biscotti,* and sandwiches made with salmon, cucumber, thinly sliced beef, or ham. By noon, the wood-burning oven along the back is in full force, turning out individual pizzas or focaccia bread split in half while still hot and layered with your choice of fillings. I also loved the assorted open-faced sandwiches garnished with a slice of hard-boiled egg, a sprinkle of chives, and a splash of olive oil. Later in the day, it is a good choice for a glorious Italian pastry treat to eat here or have packaged to go; and anytime between noon until 8 P.M., it is a nice place to sip a glass of wine while contemplating your next shopping, sightseeing, or walking destination.

TELEPHONE
055-26-85-90
OPEN
Mon–Sat
CLOSED
Bakery is closed Wed afternoon; Sun
HOURS
8 A.M.–9 P.M., continuous service
RESERVATIONS
Not accepted
CREDIT CARDS
AE, DC, MC, V
À LA CARTE
From L5,500, beverage extra
MENÙ TURISTICO
None
COVER AND SERVICE CHARGES
Included
ENGLISH
Yes

(17) I FRATELLINI
Via dei Cimatori, 38r

One of the best ways to cut food costs and have a Cheap Eat in the bargain is to have lunch at a snack bar. Here you will be joined by savvy Italians who know they can order the blue-plate special or a meaty sandwich and a glass of wine for a mere fraction of a restaurant meal. Further savings are possible if the meal is eaten while

TELEPHONE
055-23-96-096
OPEN
Mon–Sat
CLOSED
Sun, Aug (2 weeks)
HOURS
8 A.M.–8 P.M.

RESERVATIONS
Not accepted
CREDIT CARDS
None
À LA CARTE
Sandwiches from L4,500
MENÙ TURISTICO
None
COVER AND SERVICE CHARGES
None
ENGLISH
Very limited

standing rather than seated at a table. Only you can decide how far you want to pinch your lire on that score.

This brings me to I Fratellini, a stand-up wine bar and sandwich counter that has been going strong since 1875, and is now run by two friendly, hardworking brothers. You can order your freshly made sandwiches to eat here or to go. They serve twenty to twenty-seven sandwiches, including wild boar with goat cheese and Spam and artichokes (!), and they specialize in those made with *prosciutto crudo* (air-dried, salt-cured ham) and homemade chicken liver pâté spread on thinly sliced bread. To round out the repast, order a glass of their Chianti Classico . . . but be careful. If you ask for the large, it will be served in a tall water tumbler. There are no tables, you are expected to stand. If you can't manage holding both your big sandwich and glass of wine at the same time, look for a spot along the little shelves on each side of the stand. That's where you can put your wineglass between sips.

(18) PERCHÈ NÒ!
Via dei Tavolini, 19r

TELEPHONE
055-23-98-969
OPEN
Daily
CLOSED
Tues in winter; Nov 5–25
HOURS
Summer 8 A.M.–midnight; winter 8 A.M.–8:30 P.M.
RESERVATIONS
Not accepted
CREDIT CARDS
None
À LA CARTE
From L2,500
MENÙ TURISTICO
None
COVER AND SERVICE CHARGES
None
ENGLISH
Limited

Perchè Nò! (at Via dei Tavolini and Via dei Calzaioli) opened its doors in 1939 and is recognized today as the oldest *gelateria* in Florence. In addition to its longevity, it has an impressive history. During World War II, it supplied the American troops stationed in Florence with ice cream. When the city's electrical supply was shut off, officers ordered soldiers to reconnect the electrical supply that serviced Perchè Nò! and the surrounding area. After the war, the owners installed the first counter showcase for ice cream, which became a model for all others.

From the beginning, they have been known for their varieties of *semifreddo,* that illegally rich and creamy ice cream that has untold fat grams and tastes like a gift from heaven. Be sure you sample their white chocolate, rum crunch, hazelnut mousse, or coffee mousse. In summer, the green apple *sorbetto* is a refreshing change of pace. The yogurt ice cream is a big seller, as is the brioche filled with whipped cream. You can have your gelato in a cone or a cup and dipped in a flurry of chocolate pieces and nuts—or just plain if you are dieting.

Piazza Goldoni

The Piazza Goldoni serves as a crossroads joining the Ponte alle Carraia with Via del Fossi leading to the Piazza Santa Maria Novella, the train station, and Lungaro Amerigo Vespucci and Lungaro Corsini following along the Arno.

(19) ARMANDO
Borgo Ognissanti, 140r

Armando, on my short list of best-value restaurants in Florence, offers cooking that will not only please but nourish very well. Handed down from father to son, this typically Tuscan trattoria is as authentic as the cuisine, with friendly service provided by family and long-term staff in an ever-crowded and cheerful atmosphere. As the evening wears on, it can get loud, but that is part of the fun of eating here. Keep in mind that Italians dine late; in fact, at 9:30 P.M. they are still milling about waiting for a table to clear.

The Oscar for the best pasta dish goes to their *ravioli al burro e salvia,* homemade ravioli stuffed with ricotta cheese and sage and lightly covered in a buttery sauce. Throw cholesterol and fat counting to the wind just once and treat yourself to this. Another hands-down favorite in the pasta category goes to the *spaghetti alla carriettiera,* pasta topped with a spicy sauce made from garlic, fresh basil, tomato, and red pepper. This dish will wake up your taste buds in a hurry. Even if you have spent a lifetime turning up your nose at liver, please consider it here and try the *fegato alla salvia,* calves' liver broiled just to the tender pink stage. In the dessert department, nothing is a spectacular standout, so opt for an assortment of local cheeses, a scoop of cool gelato, or save these calories for a better opportunity.

TELEPHONE
055-21-62-19

OPEN
Tues–Sat; Mon, dinner only

CLOSED
Sun, major holidays, Aug (dates vary)

HOURS
12:30–3 P.M., 7:30–10:30 P.M.

RESERVATIONS
Advised, especially for dinner

CREDIT CARDS
MC, V

À LA CARTE
L40,000–45,000, beverage extra

MENÙ TURISTICO
None

COVER AND SERVICE CHARGES
Cover L2,500, 10% service added

ENGLISH
Yes

(20) COCO LEZZONE ($)
Via Parioncino, 26r

There is no sign outside, but that does not mean that this beloved spot has not been found by everyone from Florentine workers and blue bloods to Prince Charles and Luciano Pavarotti. The inside has barely changed since it opened a century ago. It still has plain white-tile walls and elbow-to-elbow seating along narrow tables. The hearty, traditional cooking is prepared with high-quality, fresh ingredients. The only nod to modern times

TELEPHONE
055-28-71-78

OPEN
Mon–Sat

CLOSED
Sun, all holidays, July–Aug (5 weeks), Dec 22–Jan 7

HOURS
Noon–2:30 P.M., 7–10:30 P.M.

RESERVATIONS
Not accepted

CREDIT CARDS
None

À LA CARTE
L45,000–50,000, beverage extra

MENÙ TURISTICO
None

COVER AND SERVICE CHARGES
Cover L4,000, 10% service added

ENGLISH
Yes

is the note printed on the menu, *il trillo dei telefoni cellulari disturba la cottura della ribollita* (the ringing of your cellular telephone disturbs the cooking of the *ribollita*).

There is a weekly menu, but not all of the dishes are available every day. Listen to what the waiter says about the daily specials, and remember that you can always depend on osso buco on Monday, beef stew on Tuesday, *involtini* (stewed rolls of meat) on Wednesday, tripe for your Thursday main course, and *baccalà* on Friday. Diners are expected to order full meals, to eat them with zeal, and to drink plenty of wine in the process. That is very easy to do, especially if you start out with a light *primo piatto* (first plate) of *pappa al pomodoro,* their famous *ribollita,* or the seasonally available *farfalle con piselli* or *tartufo* (pasta with peas or truffles). For the *secondo piatto,* go with the daily special, or if you are a beef eater, dig into one of the Florentine steaks, cooked rare and literally overflowing the plate. If you have been working up the courage to try tripe, here is your chance. Served in a tomato sauce with freshly ground Parmesan cheese, it is perfectly tender and delicious. The desserts are all made here and reflect on the season and the mood of the chef.

(21) IL LATINI ($)
Via dei Palchetti, 6r

TELEPHONE
055-21-09-16

OPEN
Tues–Sun

CLOSED
Sun, Aug (dates vary)

HOURS
12:30–2:30 P.M., 7:30–10:30 P.M.

RESERVATIONS
Advised for large parties

CREDIT CARDS
AE, DC, MC, V

À LA CARTE
L45,000, beverage extra

MENÙ TURISTICO
None

COVER AND SERVICE CHARGES
Cover L3,000, service included

ENGLISH
Yes, and menu in English

Narciso Latini opened Il Latini around the turn of the century as a *fiachetteria,* or wine shop. In the fifties, his nephew took over, expanded, and began to serve sandwiches and hot food prepared by his wife, first in her own kitchen at home and later on in the restaurant. For most of us, the popular trattoria is synonymous with good food, good wine, and good cheer. It is everything one expects and hopes for, from the interior festooned with hanging hams and trestle tables to the big servings of typical Tuscan dishes served with plenty of their own bottles of wine and extra-virgin olive oil. Others find it impossibly crowded and somehow lacking. Frankly, I am in the first camp . . . I like it and continue to recommend it because I have always had fine food and service, but I must tell you that some readers have not been as satisfied.

A recommended opening course is their signature soup, *zuppa di fagioli con farro,* made with wild grain and puréed kidney beans and seasoned with garlic and rosemary. For the meat dish, you have a wide choice, ranging from saddle of pork, leg of lamb, herb-scented squab, and roasted veal to the red-meat blowout to end them all—the *piatto misto,* a mixed plate made up of a piece of all of their meats. To end, you must have either their silky rendition of *tiramisù,* a slice of their own plum cake topped with ice cream, or *contuccini con vin santo* (home-made almond cookies dipped in sweet white wine).

Piazza Santa Croce

Santa Croce is considered the pantheon of Italy's great men: Michelangelo, Machiavelli, Galileo, Rossini, and Foscolo are buried here. Inside are frescoes by Giotto. To the right of the church stands Brunelleschi's beautiful Pazzi Chapel. The Piazza Santa Croce is anchored by the church and ringed with lovely medieval *palazzos.* In back of the piazza is one of the most interesting working areas of Florence and the bustling Sant' Ambrogio Market.

(22) ACQUA AL 2
Via della Vigna Vecchia, 40r

Everyone loves Acqua al 2, one of the most firmly established and well-known restaurants in Florence. Located at Via della Vigna Vecchia and Via dell'Acqua, it consists of three rooms with stone walls, arched brick ceilings, wooden banquettes, hard wooden chairs and benches, and tables set with fresh flowers, candles, and paper place mats. The animated diners come from all walks of life and every corner of the globe to enjoy Chef Stefano's hearty food. His menu doesn't leave much to chance, with twenty-six pastas (seven of which are vegetarian), hamburger prepared five ways, several omelettes, at least ten variations of veal, and a dozen salads. The house specialties offer some particular treats, especially the *assaggio di primi,* your choice of any five pastas, or a gooey, rich serving of focaccia, split, stuffed, then baked. The desserts don't sparkle. Go down the street and around the corner and treat yourself to the heavenly ice cream at Vivoli (see page 52).

TELEPHONE
055-28-41-70

OPEN
Tues–Sun, dinner only

CLOSED
Mon

HOURS
7:30 P.M.–1 A.M.

RESERVATIONS
Advised

CREDIT CARDS
AE, DC, MC, V

À LA CARTE
L40,000, beverage extra

MENÙ TURISTICO
None

COVER AND SERVICE CHARGES
Cover L2,000, 10% service added

ENGLISH
Yes

(23) ANTICO NOÈ
Volta di San Piero, 6r

Ask any student in Florence where to go for the best sandwiches and the answer will be Antico Noè, a real hole-in-the-wall where good food and good cheer have been served since 1561. To say it is hidden is an

TELEPHONE
055-23-40-838

OPEN
Mon–Sat

CLOSED
Sun, Aug (2 weeks)

understatement, even though it is not too far from the Santa Croce Church. The best directions if you are coming from the church are to walk north along Via Giuseppe Verdi to Piazza Salvermini; on your left you will see a covered passageway (Volta di San Piero) that usually has a man selling flowers right in front. Antico Noè is in the passageway. Look for a crowd of students standing in front eating and drinking.

HOURS
10:30 A.M.–8:30 P.M.

RESERVATIONS
Not accepted

CREDIT CARDS
None

À LA CARTE
Sandwiches from L3,500

MENÙ TURISTICO
None

COVER AND SERVICE CHARGES
None

ENGLISH
Yes, Linda is Canadian and also speaks French

Except for a few bar stools, there is no seating, but no one minds standing up to eat their overstuffed made-to-order sandwiches. Prices start at around L3,500 for a plain meat sandwich; each addition (e.g., tomato, lettuce, cheese) costs an additional L500. The best sandwiches are the spiced rolled roast beef or the turkey washed down with a beer or a glass of wine. The house wine is cheap, but spend a few hundred lire more and enjoy a glass of their Chianti Classico. For dessert, stroll over to Vivoli (see page 52) and enjoy a cone or a cup of their famous gelato.

(24) ANTICO NOÈ #2

Volta di San Piero, 6r (two doors from the sandwich shop by the same name)

TELEPHONE
055-23-40–838

OPEN
Mon–Sat

CLOSED
Sun, Aug (2 weeks)

HOURS
Noon–3:30 P.M., 7 P.M.–midnight

RESERVATIONS
Recommended for Fri and Sat dinner

CREDIT CARDS
MC, V

À LA CARTE
L30,000–35,000, beverage extra

MENÙ TURISTICO
L17,000 lunch and dinner, two courses, vegetable, half-liter water; cover and service included

COVER AND SERVICE CHARGES
L2,000 cover, no service charged or accepted

ENGLISH
Yes, Linda is Canadian and also speaks French

For more comfortable, serious dining on a Cheap Eating budget, walk two doors down to Linda and Daniele's new sit-down restaurant. Here they have thirty-five backless rush-seated stools arranged around plain wooden tables. The 400-year-old space was in another life a butcher shop and still has the same old beams, marble walls, meat hooks, and slanted floor—easier to hose down at the end of a messy day—it had before modern times and high rent took over. Dining here puts you dead center in the midst of "junior-year-abroad American students studying in Florence." There are six cooperating universities in the area and it seems all of the American students and their parents and friends *live* at Antico Noè. No wonder. You can order either the *menù a prezzo fisso,* a two-course meal that includes a vegetable garnish and a half-liter of water, or have whatever you want à la carte. The grub is simple and filling, with no whistles or bells to attract a serious gourmet, but it is decent fare and there is plenty of it. An added attraction is the wine list, with two hundred varieties offered. That should certainly keep Mom and Dad happy during their visit to Florence.

(25) BALDOVINO
Via San Giuseppe, 22r

Follow the *bel mondo* to Baldovino, one of the best, and definitely most popular, trattorias in the neighborhood. Opened a few years ago on a shoestring by a delightful Scottish duo, David and Catherine Gardner, it hit the ground running and became a favorite among Florentines and visitors alike. Success allowed them to expand across the street, and there you will find their wine bar and terrace, which open in the morning for coffee served with Catherine's homemade muffins and other pastries, and continuing throughout the day and evening dispensing creative snacks and sandwiches, all tossed down with a glass or two of fine wine. In addition to the selection of wines, they sell a wide variety of balsamic vinegars, some of the best dried pasta on the market, honey, extra-virgin Tuscan olive oil, and three type of coffees, all packaged and ready to send home to lucky friends.

The restaurant has three rooms, each painted in wild color combinations of orange and purple, or just plain green. Once you are inside the front door, wend your way through the first room and the exhibition kitchen to the more desirable back rooms, which have less waiter and patron traffic running back and forth. The inventive menu puts an imaginative twist on the bounty of the Tuscan region. Appetizers to whet your appetite include grilled vegetables marinated in olive oil and served with a hunk of fresh mozzarella. A plate of smoked fish gets star billing, as do four types of focaccia bread seasoned with olive oil and rosemary and topped with chopped tomatoes, garlic, basil, and olive oil or piled with smoked salmon, arugula, and slivers of fresh Parmesan. Six meal-in-one salads start with the Baldovino, featuring chicken breast, grapes, walnuts, and celery, and finish with a raw vegetable combination dusted with shavings of pecorino cheese. Pastas and wood-fired pizzas, main courses of roasted seabass, the traditional Florentine T-bone steak, veal pan-seared with *vin santo,* or grilled chicken all prove winners in the eyes of the trendsetters who fill the restaurant on a daily basis. The homemade desserts, guaranteed to keep you on the treadmill an extra twenty minutes per day for the next week, tempt with a honey-nut, banana, or chocolate torte served with vanilla ice cream, a whiskey-infused bread pudding, and cheese-cake with strawberry salsa.

TELEPHONE
055-24-17-73

OPEN
Tues–Sun

CLOSED
Mon, last week of Nov and first week of Dec

HOURS
Restaurant: noon–2:30 P.M., 7–11 P.M. Wine bar: 10 A.M.–11 P.M.

RESERVATIONS
In the restaurant, recommended for lunch, essential for dinner; not necessary for the wine bar unless you want to sit on the terrace

CREDIT CARDS
AE, DC, MC, V

À LA CARTE
Restaurant: Pizza from L9,000–13,000; three-course meal L35,000–45,000, beverage extra. Wine bar: L7,000–15,000, beverage extra

MENÙ TURISTICO
None

COVER AND SERVICE CHARGES
Cover L3,000, service included

ENGLISH
Yes

MISCELLANEOUS
There is a no-smoking dining room

(26) FIASCHETTERIA AL PANINO
Via dei Neri, 2r

TELEPHONE
055-21-68-87

OPEN
Mon–Sat, bar and lunch only

CLOSED
Sun, Aug (dates vary)

HOURS
Bar 9 A.M.–9 P.M., lunch 12:30–3 P.M.

RESERVATIONS
Not accepted

CREDIT CARDS
None

À LA CARTE
Sandwiches from L4,000, two courses for L10,000–15,000, beverage extra

MENÙ TURISTICO
None

COVER AND SERVICE CHARGES
No cover, service included

ENGLISH
No

Smart Italian Cheap Eaters eat their lunches in snack bars that serve a hot noon meal. One of the best of these around the Santa Croce Church is the Fiaschetteria al Panino. You won't be able to miss its corner location . . . just look for the hungry crowd standing outside patiently waiting for the food rewards inside. This is a fast-paced place where dallying over long conversations is not part of the acceptable game plan during lunch, when everyone eats quickly at the bar or sits on a stool at the marble counters circling the windows. At other times during the day you can walk by and see the same cast of neighbors sitting at the same tables playing cards, nursing a glass of wine, or just looking at you looking at them.

The food is guaranteed to do wonders for your well-being. Following the Italian tradition of preparing a special dish each day, the chef has *pappa al pomodoro* on Monday and *zuppa di faro* on Tuesday. Wednesday he makes *tagliatelle,* and on Thursday, cannelloni stuffed with spinach and ricotta cheese. Friday is fish day, and the pasta has a clam sauce. Every day you can count on lasagna, an assortment of *frittatas,* and warm foccacia, split and filled with meat or cheese. For dessert, abandon all diet worries and try the chocolate mousse torte, a rich pie that chocoholics will dream of for years to come. The other desserts are a lemon and honey torte that is good but not fabulous and fried doughnut holes that are absolutely forgettable, heavy lumps that sit like wet laundry in the pit of your stomach for days. Espresso is served, but no other coffee drinks.

(27) GELATERIA DEI NERI
Via dei Neri, 20–22r

TELEPHONE
055-21-00–34

OPEN
Mon–Tues, Thur–Sun

CLOSED
Wed

HOURS
1 P.M.–midnight

RESERVATIONS
Not accepted

CREDIT CARDS
None

À LA CARTE
Cups or cones L2,500–8,000; cakes L15,000–20,000

How do you know the gelato here is made from fresh ingredients? One look through the streetside window into the kitchen presided over by Mauricio, the hardworking owner, tells it all. This ice cream maestro works six days a week from 1 P.M. until midnight churning out some of the best gelato I have ever tasted. If you are lactose intolerant, not to worry; he has developed a sugarless, vegetarian soya ice cream that belies any notions that anything healthy can't possibly taste good. His chocolate mousse *semifreddo* is worth a trip to his shop, as is the lemon cream yogurt ice cream. Not content to rest his laurels on dipping ice cream, Mauricio also makes ice cream cakes to order. Clearly he has orders, and lots of them, because I have never passed his shop without admiring his masterpieces displayed in the front window, waiting to be picked up.

MENÙ TURISTICO
None

COVER AND SERVICE CHARGES
None

ENGLISH
Limited

(28) I' CCHÈ C'È C'È
Via d. Magalotti, 11r

In Italian the name means "what you find, you find," which in this case always means excellent Tuscan fare and service.

Owner and chef Gino Noci is a native Florentine with lots of experience in the restaurant business, including time spent in a French restaurant in London. He emphasizes that his establishment is a casual, family run place where everyone is welcomed in the same friendly way. For lunch, the long wooden tables are set with paper place mats and napkins. At night, linen replaces the paper. Ringing the room are shelves of wine bottles and paintings of varying quality.

Cheap Eaters will want to pay close attention to the *menù turistico,* which includes a first and second course and either a salad or frozen fried potatoes. When deciding what to order, always ask your waiter what Gino is cooking that day, and also take a long look at the grilled fresh fish. Everything is kept simple, using only the best olive oils and fresh ingredients. The house wine, poured from large barrels, is drinkable and recommended.

NOTE: If you are going to Siena, ask Gino for directions to Trattoria Mama Rosa, which he owns. It is at Via Cassia, 32.

TELEPHONE
055-21-65-89

OPEN
Tues–Sun

CLOSED
Mon, Aug 17–Sept 10

HOURS
12:30–2:30 P.M., 7:30–10:30 P.M.

RESERVATIONS
Essential; not accepted for *menù turistico* for lunch

CREDIT CARDS
AE, MC, V

À LA CARTE
L40,000–45,000, beverage extra

MENÙ TURISTICO
L20,000, two courses; cover and service included, beverage extra

COVER AND SERVICE CHARGES
Cover L2,000, service not included

ENGLISH
Yes

(29) IL BARROCCIO
Via della Vigna Vecchia, 31r

For Sunday lunch, Il Barroccio is a full house with a mix of Italian families, area regulars, and tourists visiting the Santa Croce Church. The closely spaced tables are set with white and red linen cloths, polished silver, china, and fresh flowers. Tuscan watercolors crowd almost every inch of space on the smoke-yellowed walls.

The menu has all the Tuscan standbys, plus a selection of seasonal and daily specials. All the pastas, sauces, and desserts are made here and are free of preservatives and additives. You can actually taste the potatoes in the gnocchi, with its fresh basil and tomato sauce. The *ravioli alle noci,* ravioli with nuts in a cream sauce, is a

TELEPHONE
055-21-15-03

OPEN
Mon–Tues, Thur–Sun

CLOSED
Wed

HOURS
Noon–2:30 P.M., 7:15–10:30 P.M.

RESERVATIONS
Advised for Sun lunch

CREDIT CARDS
AE, DC, MC, V

À LA CARTE
L30,000–35,000, beverage extra

MENÙ TURISTICO
None

COVER AND SERVICE CHARGES
Cover L3,000, 10% service added

ENGLISH
Yes

very interesting first course. Main courses to rely on include the *carpaccio Parmigiano e rucola*—thin slices of raw beef served with fresh Parmesan and bitter greens. Veal is fixed several ways, and there are always grilled meats. The desserts consist of *panna cotta,* a pudding, *tiramisù, biscotti con vin santo,* sorbet, and fresh fruit. A nice alternative is the plate of assorted Italian cheeses paired with a glass of wine.

NOTE: If you are the host for a small group, the restaurant can provide a set menu with wines if notified in advance.

(30) LA BARAONDA ($)
Via Ghibellina, 67r

TELEPHONE AND FAX
055-23-41-171

OPEN
Tues–Sat; Mon, dinner only

CLOSED
Sun, Aug

HOURS
1–2:30 P.M., 7:30–10:30 P.M.

RESERVATIONS
Strongly advised

CREDIT CARDS
AE, DC, MC, V

À LA CARTE
Lunch: L35,000–40,000, includes water, wine, and coffee; dinner: L65,000, includes house wine, other beverages extra

MENÙ TURISTICO
None

COVER AND SERVICE CHARGES
Lunch: cover L3,000; dinner: cover L5,000; 10% service added for both lunch and dinner

ENGLISH
Yes

La baraonda means "hubbub," an apt description of this trattoria at noon, when the prices are lower than at night and every seat is occupied. It is owned by Duccio Magni and his wife, Elena, who is responsible for the kitchen. Florentine regulars flock here for the wholesome yet imaginative food prepared with only seasonally grown produce. The three-room interior consists of pure white tiles halfway up the walls, beamed ceilings, a bar with a few antique prints of boxing matches, and Villeroy and Bosch china placed on white linen–clad tables.

Lighter, Cheap Eater–friendly lunches keep everyone coming back for more, especially between October and May, when favorite dishes are featured each day on the menu. Tuesday you will find kidneys, tripe, or other organ meats; Wednesday, pigeon; Thursday, rabbit; Friday, codfish; and Saturday, a delicious roast leg of pork. During the hot months, the menu offers lighter fare, including meat salads and fresh goat cheese. And every day for the past twelve years they have served veal meatloaf covered in fresh tomato sauce, which always sells out, and vegetable soufflés, which are actually more like a quiche than an airy soufflé.

At dinnertime, there is no printed menu, and each course has only one price. The meal begins with complimentary appetizers served with a basket of homemade bread and a crock of black olive pâté. I like the risotto baked with greens and the penne tossed with lots of garlic and broccoli as sturdy first courses. If I don't have one of the daily specials or the veal meatloaf, then I might order the braised beef in a lemon sauce or the leg of pork. All main courses are garnished, saving the extra expense of a side order of vegetables or a salad. An apple torte, similar to a thin pancake piled high with lightly cooked apples, is billed as the house dessert. A glass of Italian grappa, *vin santo,* or Nocino (a walnut liqueur), along with a piece of candy, finalizes the excellent meal.

(31) OSTERIA DA QUINTO ($)
Piazza Peruzzi, 5r

A jungle of plants lines the stairs leading to this basement restaurant owned by a man who sang for twenty-five years in the theater in Naples. As the evening wears on, and he has had enough wine and encouragement, Quinto usually bursts into song, accompanied either by a tape or the pianist who plays when he isn't belting out a familiar opera aria or popular tune. The interior reflects years of collecting bits of everything, from a scale and utensils to De Cerrico dishes, gourds, and hanging hams and sausages you can almost smell. My dinner companion captured the essence of the interior with this observation: "good grief, this place is tastefully hideous!" I don't know if you will agree with him or not, but whatever your mood for dining—festive, romantic, solitary, or starved—you will leave satisfied and agree that the food is honest and well presented.

When you are first seated, you are brought the usual basket of bread and asked what you want to drink. When that is taken care of, they ask you what you want to eat. Did someone mention a menu? There is one, and you are welcome to look at it, but it shouldn't seriously interest you, because I don't think the chef has paid attention to it for some time. Here you depend on your waiter to tell you what is fresh in the kitchen and what the chef is doing with it. The regular customers walk back to the kitchen to see for themselves, but you can trust your waiter to take good care of you. If the ravioli with ruccola (bitter red lettuce) or the risotto with fresh mushrooms is available, I can strongly vouch for them both. Florentine beefsteak is another winner. Salads and vegetables should also play leading roles in your choices. The wine, food, music, and atmosphere, however "tastefully hideous" you may think it is, add up to a memorable not-so-Cheap Eats experience.

TELEPHONE
055-21-33-23

OPEN
Tues–Sun

CLOSED
Mon

HOURS
12:30–2:30 P.M., 7:30–10:30 P.M.

RESERVATIONS
Recommended for dinner

CREDIT CARDS
AE, MC, V

À LA CARTE
L45,000–50,000, beverage extra

MENÙ TURISTICO
None

COVER AND SERVICE CHARGES
Cover L3,000, service not included

ENGLISH
Enough

MISCELLANEOUS
Piano player begins around 8 P.M.

(32) PALLOTTINO
Via Isola delle Stinche, 1r

TELEPHONE
055-28-95-73
OPEN
Tues–Sun
CLOSED
Mon, 15 days in Aug (dates vary)
HOURS
12:30–2:30 P.M., 7:30–10:15 P.M.
RESERVATIONS
Accepted for dinner only
CREDIT CARDS
AE, DC, MC, V
À LA CARTE
Dinner only, L35,000, beverage extra
MENÙ TURISTICO
Lunch only, L14,000, two courses, dessert or coffee; cover and service included, beverage extra
COVER AND SERVICE CHARGES
Dinner only, cover L3,000, 10% service added
ENGLISH
Enough, à la carte menu in English

Ask the natives living around Santa Croce Church where they eat and the unanimous reply is: Pallottino! Where else? Because it was located very close to my flat, I had the opportunity of trying it several times, and I certainly share the enthusiasm, especially for the *menù turistico,* served *only* at lunch. This is a Cheap Eat to behold. To keep the regulars interested and coming back in droves, the menu, two courses plus dessert or coffee, changes daily and offers several choices for each course. Whole-wheat bread comes with the meal, but veggies and wine do not. The house wine is cheap and drinkable.

What about dinner? The *menù turistico* is replaced by à la carte choices, which provide enough variety of the usual Tuscan favorites to keep everyone well-fed and happy. Naturally, the offerings are a little more sophisticated, but the prices are still reasonable enough not to crash the budget.

(33) RISTORANTE DEL FAGIOLI
Corso dei Tintori, 47r

TELEPHONE
055-24-42-85
FAX
055-24-18-83
OPEN
Mon–Fri
CLOSED
Sat, Sun, one week at Christmas and Easter, Aug
HOURS
12:30–2:30 P.M., 7:30–10:30 P.M.
RESERVATIONS
Recommended
CREDIT CARDS
None
À LA CARTE
L35,000–40,000, beverage extra
MENÙ TURISTICO
None
COVER AND SERVICE CHARGES
Cover L3,000, no service charge
ENGLISH
Yes

During my last research trip to Florence, I stayed in a beautiful penthouse apartment on the piazza facing Santa Croce Church. My neighbors were a delightful couple who were celebrating retirement by spending six months in Florence and another six months in a villa in Tuscany. What a way to start retirement! As part of their immersion into Italian life in Florence, they ate out at least once a day and would often report their findings to me. One of their *hottest* tips was this family owned and run trattoria right around the corner from our flats. Indeed, it is a great Cheap Eat find and one I could happily go to night after night.

There are two rooms, but you definitely want to sit in the first room. The menu delivers first-rate Tuscan specialties prepared by Luigi, the father, and served graciously by his two sons, Antonio and Simone. While contemplating what to have, ask for the *pinzimonio misto di stagione,* a plate or bowl of raw seasonal vegetables to dip into olive oil, a light and refreshing way to start your meal. The portions are more than generous, especially the *ribollita,* brought to you in a big bowl so you can help yourself to as much as you want. It would be easy to make a meal on this rich, twice-cooked bean and bread soup highlighted with vegetables, garlic, oil, and herbs, but please save room for the comforting dishes that follow, such as osso buco, *baccalà* with tomato, Chianti beefsteaks, and spicy sausages. They make all of their own desserts, but frankly, I never had room for more than a few *biscotti* dipped into *vin santo*. When it came time to pay the bill, I always appreciated having it explained to me item by item so there would be no misunderstandings. More restaurants in Florence should follow suit.

(34) RISTORANTE LA GIOSTRA ($)
Borgo Pinti, 10r

TELEPHONE
055-24-13-41

OPEN
Daily

CLOSED
Never

HOURS
12:30–2:30 P.M., 7 P.M.–midnight

RESERVATIONS
Essential

CREDIT CARDS
AE

À LA CARTE
L50,000, beverage extra

MENÙ TURISTICO
None

COVER AND SERVICE CHARGES
Cover L3,000, service included

ENGLISH
Yes

The motto on the business card says "In Food We Trust." Judging from its popularity, it is obvious the Florentines have come to trust the food as well.

You will recognize Dimitri, the Russian owner of this very "in" place, when he comes out of the kitchen in full chef's garb and goes from table to table greeting his guests. He is a dignified and well-educated man, with doctorates in both chemistry and biology. Always a lover of fine food and cooking, he was told for years by his friends, "You are such a good cook, why don't you open your own restaurant?" Several years ago he came out of retirement and opened La Giostra Club with the help of his twin sons and his daughter. The restaurant was an instant hit, and it remains fully booked for both lunch and dinner seven days a week. The name means "carousel," and you can see a picture of one to the right of the entry.

Lunchtime does not seem to be a drawn-out affair, though dinner can be. If you go when the restaurant opens, chances are the service will be more attentive. As the evening progresses, the waiters are stretched beyond their limits, resulting in long delays between courses. Almost the minute you are seated, you are served a flute of champagne and a plate of assorted *crostini,* toast with various toppings. This helps with the long lag until the waiter comes back to take your order and again until the appearance of the first course. Be patient—the menu is small but choice. All of the *primi piatti* (first courses) are good, especially the ricotta-filled crepe, the *pappardelle* with artichokes and ham, and the *tagliatelle* with a flavorful sauce of *funghi porcini.* One of the most popular main courses is the *filetto di bue Lorenzo il Magnifico,* finely sliced beef topped with fresh spinach and brought to your table on a sizzling hot plate that sits on a breadboard. Another favorite is the *scamorza,* slices of ham covered with cheese that has been browned and bubbled under the broiler just before it arrives at your table. For dessert, forget the *torta di mele,* a dreary apple tart, and opt instead for a cool lemon sorbet or the wickedly fattening *tiramisù.* The wine list is not cheap, but vintages are happily served by the glass, thus enabling you to sample more than one without ruining the budget completely.

(35) SALUMERIA/GASTRONOMIA VERDI
Via Guiseppe Verdi, 36r

TELEPHONE
055-24-45-17

OPEN
Daily

CLOSED
Sometimes on Sun

HOURS
8 A.M.–3 P.M., 5–8 P.M.

RESERVATIONS
Not accepted

CREDIT CARDS
None

À LA CARTE
Sandwiches start at L3,500, all other food sold by weight

MENÙ TURISTICO
Lunch: L12,000, two courses plus vegetable and half-liter of mineral water

COVER AND SERVICE CHARGES
None

ENGLISH
Yes

Glorious picnics, terrific takeout, and Cheap Eater–friendly lunches all begin at Pino's Salumeria/Gastronomia Verdi, a few short blocks from Piazza Santa Croce. Walking by, you can smell the good things awaiting you inside, where the artistically presented food is not only lovely to look at but delightful to taste. Pino gets up with the chickens to be at the market when it opens to find the best ingredients for the many dishes skillfully prepared by Antonella, a sweet French cook who grew up in Monte Carlo. With these two virtuosos in my neighborhood, I would never have to go near the kitchen to cook again! They work long hours every day, including Sunday, dishing out a fabulous selection of pastas, sweet and savory crepes, tortes, salads galore, and a host of sandwiches made with the best cold meats and cheeses—or any other ingredient you can think of to put between two slices of freshly baked bread. Tuscan and Venetian wines are available to complement your repast.

Everything can be packaged to go, or consumed in the small side room dedicated to what Pino calls "speed lunches." These meals consist of a first and second course with vegetable garnish and a half bottle of mineral water for less than a hamburger, shake, and fries would cost you in a fast-food joint at home. These are Cheap Eat deals to be sure.

(36) VIVOLI
Via Isola delle Stinche, 7r

TELEPHONE
055-29-23-34

FAX
055-23-02-621

Since 1930, the largest and creamiest selections of ice cream have been scooped out at Vivoli, located across the street from Florence's only English-language movie house. It is most active in the evening, when young Florentines strut their stuff, and on Sundays, when it becomes a family affair. These are the times you will be able to witness the Italian phenomenon of the *passeggiata,* the see-and-be-seen stroll all Italians love.

Baskets of fresh berries, cases of bananas, and crates of oranges go into the thousand-plus quarts of ice cream made and consumed here *each day.* For my gelato lire, the absolute best flavor, and one of their specialties, is the orange-chocolate cream, a cloudlike mixture of chocolate, cream orange liqueur, and pieces of fresh orange. Any of the *semifreddo* choices are fabulous, provided you can stand the fat-gram blowout from the whipped cream–based ice cream. Dieters need not feel left out: the fruit flavors are fat free, with the exception of banana. The gelato is served only in cups, and you pay for the size of the cup, not the number of flavors you want in it. Avoid the strange rice cream flavor, a bland-tasting vanilla with hard pieces of almost raw rice sprinkled throughout. Also available are drinks at the full bar and homemade morning pastries and sandwiches.

OPEN
Tues–Sun

CLOSED
Mon, Jan, Aug (last 2 weeks)

HOURS
7 A.M.–1 A.M.

RESERVATIONS
Not accepted

CREDIT CARDS
None

À LA CARTE
Gelato from L2,500–16,000

MENÙ TURISTICO
None

COVER AND SERVICE CHARGES
None

ENGLISH
Depends on server

Piazza Santa Maria Novella

The Gothic-Renaissance church of Santa Maria Novella was the Florentine seat of the Dominicans. The piazza outside, one of the largest in the city, is frequented by backpackers coming and going from the train station.

(37) DA GIORGIO
Via Palazzuolo, 100r

If the line is too long down the street at Il Contadino (see below), walk up to Da Giorgio, another Cheap Eat with a set-price-only menu. If I had to choose between the two, I would give the edge to Da Giorgio. In spite of the shared tables with plastic-covered linen, there are cloth napkins, green plants, a few pictures scattered on the walls, and a larger selection of dishes.

Of course, there is no printed menu; you must depend on the waiter to tell you what is available that day. For starters, there might be macaroni with a spicy sauce, *pasta al pesto,* risotto with peas, tomatoes, and meat, or *fettuccine al freddo.* On Thursday, there is always gnocchi. Your second course of meat, chicken, or fish is garnished with vegetables, salad, or potatoes. Wine or mineral

TELEPHONE
055-28-43-02

OPEN
Mon–Sat

CLOSED
Sun, Aug (2 weeks, dates vary)

HOURS
Noon–3 P.M., 6–10 P.M.

RESERVATIONS
Not accepted

CREDIT CARDS
AE, DC, MC, V

À LA CARTE
None

MENÙ TURISTICO
L16,000, two courses; beverage, cover, and service included

COVER AND SERVICE CHARGES
Both included
ENGLISH
Yes

water is included, but coffee is extra. The only dessert option is a piece of fresh fruit, which costs extra and is not worth it.

(38) IL CONTADINO
Via Palazzuolo, 71r

TELEPHONE
055-23-82-673
OPEN
Mon–Sat
CLOSED
Sun, Aug (2 weeks, dates vary)
HOURS
Noon–2:30 P.M., 6:30–9:30 P.M.
RESERVATIONS
Not accepted
CREDIT CARDS
None
À LA CARTE
None
MENÙ TURISTICO
Lunch L16,000; dinner L17,000; two courses; beverage, cover, and service included
COVER AND SERVICE CHARGES
Both included
ENGLISH
Yes

You will probably have to wait in line with the Italians at lunch and the tourists at dinner if you want one of the Cheapest Eats in Florence. Il Contadino is across the street from the area's other bargain Cheap Eat, Da Giorgia (see above), and they both serve just about the same food and appeal to the same type of thrifty eater.

At Il Contadino, interior decor is nonexistent: not a picture, plant, or flower of any sort graces the two white-tiled rooms, which are filled instead with eager eaters, sleeves rolled up and ties loosened. The food is unimaginative but filling, and there is plenty of it. House wine or mineral water are included. For both courses, there are usually at least five selections, such as ravioli, minestrone, *pasta e fagioli,* pork, and beef, with fish on Wednesday and Friday. The main courses are garnished with either a salad, vegetable, fries, or beans. Coffee and fresh fruit cost extra.

(39) SOSTANZA ($)
Via del Porcellana, 25r

TELEPHONE
055-21-26-91
OPEN
Mon–Fri
CLOSED
Sat, Sun, Aug
HOURS
Noon–2:10 P.M., dinner seatings 7:30 P.M. and 9 P.M.
RESERVATIONS
Essential
CREDIT CARDS
None
À LA CARTE
L45,000–50,000, beverage extra
MENÙ TURISTICO
None
COVER AND SERVICE CHARGES
Cover L4,000, 10% service added
ENGLISH
Enough

Sostanza is one of the city's oldest and best-loved trattorias, frequented by the great, the near-great, and the just-plain folks. Forty places are crammed into a long room that despite its pristine plainness becomes hectic as the meal progresses and the diners crowd in together. The waiters wear jackets, but formality ends here. The wine is served in tumblers, bread is handed to you, and plates are passed. Lots of hugging, kissing, and waving goes on among the regulars. Reservations are essential for the two nightly dinner seatings.

The handwritten menu is easy to read, and states at the top, *si serve solo pranzo completo.* That generally means, "don't come here if you are only going to order a pasta and a salad." Dishes to remember are the *tortino di carciofi* (artichoke omelette) and the *bistecca alla Fiorentino,* a six-hundred-gram T-bone steak geared for lumberjacks but ordered, and finished, by wafer-thin models. The only dessert made here, an orange meringue cake, is a must—

you will think you don't have room, but will end up not sharing one bite.

(40) TRATTORIA GIARDINO
Via della Scala, 61r

Trattoria Giardino fits the bill for a hearty Cheap Eat in the area around the train station and Piazza Santa Maria Novella. Bruno, the present owner, a former waiter here, bought it thirty-four years ago and is still on hand daily, along with his attractive English-speaking daughter, who takes care of the dinner rush hour. It is a comfortable, friendly place where everyone is welcome and treated with the same degree of kindness and respect. The main room is paneled in knotty pine, and in summer, a garden terrace in back is open for dining. The *menù turistico* is positively philanthropic when you consider that the price includes three courses, a beverage, and the cover and service charges. À la carte diners will fare well with any of the *piatti del giorno* selections neatly printed on a piece of paper and stuck to the regular menu. For dessert, either the chocolate cake or the *torta della nonna,* a cream-filled yellow cake, should set you on your merry way.

TELEPHONE
055-21-31-41

OPEN
Mon, Wed–Sun

CLOSED
Tues, July 15–Aug 15

HOURS
Noon–3 P.M., 7–10 P.M.

RESERVATIONS
Not necessary

CREDIT CARDS
AE, DC, MC, V

À LA CARTE
L30,000, beverage extra

MENÙ TURISTICO
L20,000, three courses; beverage, cover, and service included

COVER AND SERVICE CHARGES
Cover L2,000, 10% service added

ENGLISH
Sometimes at lunch, always at dinner

Piazza Sant' Ambrogio

This is an interesting working-class neighborhood and the most local of markets in Florence. The best time to experience all the fauna and flora is on a Saturday morning.

(41) IL PIZZAIUOLO
Via dei Macci, 113r

Pizza pundits debate who has the best pizza in town, but all of them would agree on one thing: if you like Neapolitan pizza, this place has the best in Florence. It is a casual spot, across the square from the busy market at Piazza Sant' Ambrogio. You can arrive for lunch without a reservation, but forget it if you arrive without one at dinner. In the evening, reservations are taken for 8, 9, 10, or 11 P.M., and without your name on the book for one of these times, you will not get in. The twenty-five or so pizzas range from a simple *Napoli*—with tomatoes, mozzarella, anchovies, capers, and oregano—to the *pizza bomba ripena,* which has the usual tomato and mozzarella,

TELEPHONE
055-24-11-71

OPEN
Mon–Sat

CLOSED
Sun, 1 week at Easter and Christmas, Aug

HOURS
12:30–3:30 P.M., 7:30 P.M.–midnight

RESERVATIONS
Required for dinner

CREDIT CARDS
None

À LA CARTE
L8,000–15,000
MENÙ TURISTICO
None
COVER AND SERVICE CHARGES
None
ENGLISH
Sometimes

plus *prosciutto cotto* (cooked prosciutto), ricotta, mushrooms, and salami. If you don't see the combination you want, they will create it for you. Also on board are a half dozen pastas, but if you are eating here, you eat pizza, perhaps share a salad, and bypass the pasta for another meal.

(42) I PILASTRI
Via dei Pilastri, 16r

TELEPHONE
055-24-52-00
OPEN
Mon–Sat; Wed, half-day only
CLOSED
Sun, Aug
HOURS
Bar: Mon–Fri 7:30 A.M.–7:30 P.M., Wed 7:30 A.M.–2 P.M., Sat 8 A.M.–3 P.M.; hot food daily 8 A.M.–3 P.M., 5:30–7:30 P.M.
RESERVATIONS
Not accepted
CREDIT CARDS
None
À LA CARTE
From L5,500
MENÙ TURISTICO
None
COVER AND SERVICE CHARGES
None
ENGLISH
Sometimes

Takeout doesn't have to be tacky, and it is certainly anything but at this bustling bar, *enoteca,* gourmet deli, lunch counter, and grocery store. Whatever you need in the way of packaged food or drink, chances are I Pilastri has it. The hot food is ready before noon, and by 1 P.M., the place is teaming, the selection dwindling, and the tables all occupied. If you arrive early, and I recommend you do, you are bound to be lost in the endless choices before you: lasagna with mushrooms or asparagus, zucchini torte, fat sausages with braised fennel, roast chicken, curried rice, fish fixed numerous ways, salads and veggies galore, and myriad meats and cheeses waiting to be stacked on fresh rolls. It will be impossible to leave hungry. Depending on the mood of the owner, however, you could leave ticked off . . . sometimes he is beyond rude, but the regulars ignore this and you should also try to.

(43) TAVOLA CALDA DA ROCCO
Mercato di Sant' Ambrogio

You know everything is fresh . . . the Rocco family shops at the market daily for the food they prepare in their open kitchen in the center hall of this wonderful Florentine food landmark. The hot dishes are ready around 11:30 A.M. or noon, and are served to seriously hungry market workers and regulars who lap it up while perched on stools closely placed at blue formica tables. The menu, which changes daily and is written on a board, always includes robust soups and stews, hearty pastas, and, in winter, baked pears in red wine for dessert. Even if you ordered every course, you would have trouble spending ten or twelve dollars, and that would include a generous plastic cup filled with the rough-and-ready house *vino.* After your meal, saunter across the aisle to the Bar-Jolly Caffè-La Caffetteria del Vecchio Mercato and have one of the cheapest espressos in town.

Piazza Santa Trinità

The Piazza S. Trinità joins with the Ponte S. Trinità, the second most important bridge (after the Ponte Vecchio) crossing the Arno. From this piazza, visitors can continue walking to Via dei Tornabuoni, Florence's most elegant and expensive shopping street.

(44) TRATTORIA MARIONE
Via della Spada, 27r

Mario and Sergio prove their Italian pedigree with their *cucina casalinga* (homestyle cooking) and a decor scheme composed of typical rows of wine and assorted paintings lining the walls, and rush-seated chairs positioned around tables topped with white linens over blue liners. Dining here will be a good experience from beginning to end. Especially appealing is their *menù turistico,* which includes two courses, fruit for dessert, wine or water, and the cover and service charges. While this *prezzo fisso* (fixed-price menu) has seven choices for first and second courses, it offers few surprises. Upping the ante a bit and going à la carte is not fraught with budget peril, and allows for a slightly more interesting dining experience, with orders of gnocchi with salmon, fresh *pappardelle* with wild boar sauce, fresh grilled fish, roast lamb or veal served with creamy potatoes, and the red-meat-eater fix of *bistecca alla Fiorentina.* Dessert? Not here, thank you, unless you want fruit or *biscottini.*

TELEPHONE
055-23-47-56

OPEN
Mon–Sat

CLOSED
Sun, holidays, Aug

HOURS
Noon–3 P.M., 7–10 P.M.

RESERVATIONS
Not necessary

CREDIT CARDS
AE, DC, MC, V

À LA CARTE
L25,000–30,000

MENÙ TURISTICO
L23,000, two courses plus fruit and wine or water; cover and service included

COVER AND SERVICE CHARGES
Cover L1,500, 10% service added

ENGLISH
Yes, and menu in English

Piazza Santo Spirito

The Augustinian church of Santo Spirito was designed by Brunelleschi in 1444. Its austere exterior houses numerous works of art, including a *Madonna and Child* by Filippo Lippi. The piazza is lively during the week with a morning farmer's market and two Sundays a month with a flea market.

(45) BAR RICCHI
Piazza Santo Spirito, 9r

What a pleasant Cheap Eat the Bar Ricchi continues to be. I dashed in one day several years ago to avoid being drenched by a sudden rainstorm. I had planned to have a quick sandwich and regroup for the rest of the afternoon, but when I saw the lunch plates being served to eager patrons who have been dining here for years, I quickly changed my order.

TELEPHONE
055-21-58-64

OPEN
Mon–Sat, bar and lunch only

CLOSED
Sun (see "Note"), Aug (last 2 weeks)

HOURS
Bar 7 A.M.–8 P.M. (summer bar hours, 6 A.M.–6 P.M.); lunch noon–3 P.M.

RESERVATIONS
Not accepted

CREDIT CARDS
AE, MC, V

À LA CARTE
L9,000–18,000, beverage extra

MENÙ TURISTICO
None

COVER AND SERVICE CHARGES
Cover L2,000, service included

ENGLISH
Yes

Every time I have visited the Bar Ricchi, I have found the food to be simple yet delicious. When you go in winter, sit in the room next to the stand-up bar and settle into a soft, tufted banquette seat before a tiny marble-topped café table. Covering the walls here and in the bar is a fascinating display of framed photographs of the Santo Spirito Church. On warm days, enjoy your lunch outside on the terrace with its commanding view of the church.

The power behind the success of the kitchen is Alfonsina, the wife of the owner of the Bar Ricchi. Her menu selections are limited, but they change every day with the exception of the roast beef and creamy mashed potatoes and the big one-plate salads. On my last visit, in addition to these two staples, she had salmon quiche, moussaka, and veal with fresh peas in an herb, onion, and wine sauce. This is *not* the place to skip dessert. Treat yourself and indulge in one of Alfonsina's almost illegally rich pastries, a piece of fruit-topped cheesecake, or a serving of their homemade ice cream. As with most "insider" Cheap Eats, the best dishes go quickly, so plan to arrive early for your lunch.

NOTE: Bar Ricchi is open for lunch on the second Sunday of every month (except August), when there is an open-air market on Piazza Santo Spirito.

(46) CAFFÈ DEGLI ARTIGIANI
Via dello Sprone, 16r

TELEPHONE
055-28-71-41

OPEN
Mon–Sat

CLOSED
Sun

HOURS
12:30–10:30 P.M., continuous service

RESERVATIONS
Not necessary

CREDIT CARDS
AE, MC, V

À LA CARTE
L8,000–22,000, beverage extra

MENÙ TURISTICO
None

COVER AND SERVICE CHARGES
None

ENGLISH
Yes

Both the furniture and the staff are laid-back at this *caffè* annex of Trattoria Quatro Leoni across the square. There, the atmosphere is smart and sophisticated; here it is chilled out and relaxed in rustic surroundings. Downstairs is the prep center for the food, which is cooked in the kitchen at Trattoria Quattro Leoni, and a stand-up bar where you can grab a noontime sandwich on the run, get a quick coffee and pastry, or enjoy an afternoon beer. The more serious dining takes place upstairs on assorted old tables, some refinished, others with green paint waiting to be removed. Seating is on odd chairs, benches, and an old settee lounge. A mirror along one wall adds some dimension to the white-walled room, which often has loud music wafting over it. The interior may be a bit rough around the edges, but the food is clearly well-prepared. The good thing about the *caffè* is that you can come in for a bowl of soup, plate of pasta, a salad, or one of the daily specials, or go the three-course route and still leave satisfied and happy that your Cheap Eating budget has suffered no serious dents.

(47) PASTICCERIA MARINO
Piazza N. Sauro, 19r

For some of the best croissants (called *cornetti* or brioche) in Florence, the name to remember is Pasticceria Marino, a bar and pastry shop on the Piazza N. Sauro at the end of the Ponte alla Carraia (from Piazza Goldoni, cross the Arno River and you will be on the Piazza N. Sauro). Dozens of other pastries are also made here, but the best are these buttery croissants that come out of the oven all morning long.

The croissants are available plain or filled with chocolate or vanilla custard (called *crema*) or with marmalade. If they are temporarily out when you arrive, be patient—another batch is undoubtedly baking in the back. Order a cappuccino to consume with your treat, and stand with the crowd around the bar, or sit at one of the stools placed at the counter along one wall.

TELEPHONE
055-21-26-57
OPEN
Tues–Sun
CLOSED
Mon, Aug (dates vary)
HOURS
6:30 A.M.–8 P.M
RESERVATIONS
Not accepted
CREDIT CARDS
None
À LA CARTE
Cornetti are L1,500
MENÙ TURISTICO
None
COVER AND SERVICE CHARGES
None
ENGLISH
Depends on server

(48) TRATTORIA ANGIOLINO
Via Santo Spirito, 36r

Angiolino certainly gets an A for authenticity, with an interior filled with hanging braids of garlic and bunches of dried herbs, a big marble bar along the first room, and white linen–clad tables lining each wall. The food matches the setting: strictly Tuscan in scope and presentation. The menu is a textbook for the region's favorites of *ribollita, pappa al pomodoro,* tripe, grilled steaks, and a handful of chef's specialties that reflect the seasons. It is a good place to remember for a leisurely lunch or dinner anytime you are on this side of the Arno prowling around Piazza Santo Spirito, checking out the outrageously priced antiques along Via Maggio, or walking in the Boboli Gardens.

TELEPHONE
055-23-98-976
OPEN
Tues–Sun
CLOSED
Mon
HOURS
12:30–2:30 P.M., 7:30–10:30 P.M.
RESERVATIONS
Preferred
CREDIT CARDS
AE, DC, MC, V
À LA CARTE
L35,000–45,000, beverage extra
MENÙ TURISTICO
None
COVER AND SERVICE CHARGES
L3,000 cover, 10% service added
ENGLISH
Yes

(49) TRATTORIA LA CASALINGA
Via dei Michelozzi, 9r

If you are a collector, or just an admirer of fine furniture and antiques, be sure to walk down Via Maggio and browse the many beautiful shops and boutiques selling one-of-a-kind items with prices to match. Try to time your visit to include a meal at this typical Florentine trattoria, which is extremely popular with everyone from

TELEPHONE
055-21-86-24
OPEN
Mon–Sat
CLOSED
Sun, 15 days in Aug (dates vary)
HOURS
Noon–2:30 P.M., 7–9:30 P.M.

RESERVATIONS
Advised for four or more
CREDIT CARDS
AE, MC, V
À LA CARTE
L20,000–30,000, beverage extra
MENÙ TURISTICO
None
COVER AND SERVICE CHARGES
Cover L2,500, no service charge
ENGLISH
Yes

students, families, and toothless pensioners to Japanese tourists and ladies-who-lunch.

The two rooms with knotty pine wainscoting and high ceilings have closely spaced white linen–covered tables. It is run by the Bartarelli family: the father is the cook and mother gives him a hand, while out in front an uncle and a sister named Andrea handle the service, which is bright and friendly. The basic menu of pastas, grills, roasts, and vegetables remains the same. The daily specials are handwritten, and, as usual, these are the dishes to pay attention to. Because the tables are turned at least twice during each meal, service is quick, so you can count on being in and out in an hour or so—a real accomplishment in Italy.

(50) TRATTORIA QUATTRO LEONI
Via dei Vellutini, 1r

TELEPHONE
055-21-85-62
OPEN
Mon–Tues, Thur–Fri
CLOSED
Wed
HOURS
12:20–2:30 P.M., 7:30–10:30 P.M.
RESERVATIONS
Absolutely
CREDIT CARDS
AE, MC, V
À LA CARTE
L40,000–45,000, beverage extra
MENÙ TURISTICO
None
COVER AND SERVICE CHARGES
Cover L2,000, 10% service added
ENGLISH
Yes

Cheap Eating Florentines hope you won't discover one of their favorite places between the Pitti Palace and Santo Spirito Church. Arriving without a reservation is a big mistake: the place is filled from the minute it opens with dining hopefuls standing in the bar waiting for a miracle. Despite the crunch, the chef and staff pay attention to details that matter when eating out, and no one ever makes you feel rushed.

A wider selection of antipasti than usual adds variety to the proceedings. On cold days, you could start with the *crostini misti*—mixed toasts, grilled vegetables, or *mozzarella di bufala* with either tiny tomatoes or prosciutto. In summer, try the *tegamino di zucchine,* with smoked, dried beef, creamy white cheese, zucchini, and tartufo oil, or *cuore di carciofo, a* tempting dish made with smoked meat, small artichokes, gorgonzola cheese, tartufo oil, and pine nuts sprinkled on top. The pasta list is short, offering *ribollita,* gnocchi, risotto, *taglierini* with porcini mushrooms, and the usual penne with assorted sauces. The grilled chicken is a good main-course bet, as is the liver with fresh sage or the tender veal cutlets. For garnishes, you could order deep-fried vegetables, sautéed greens, fat white beans topped with extra-virgin olive oil, or a pedestrian *insalata mista* (mixed salad). Desserts allow you three choices: *biscotti* with *vin santo,* the house sweet of the day, or fresh pineapple.

For lighter, more casual Cheaper Eats, try their Caffè degli Artigiani across the square. Please see page 58 for details.

Piazza Signoria

Although never completed, the Piazza della Signoria is considered one of the most beautiful in Italy, and is certainly Florence's civic showplace. The square, once the forum of the Republic and the center of secular life during the rule of the Medici family, is dominated by a series of magnificent statues, including a copy of Michelangelo's *David* (the original is housed in the Galleria dell'Accademia on Via Ricasoli), an equestrian bronze of Cosimo I by Giambologna, and the *Fountain of Neptune,* by Ammannati.

(51) OSTERIA VINI E VECCHI SAPORI
Via del Magazzini, 3r

Look for the Chianti bottle sitting on a wine barrel and the green plants hanging in front of Emore Cozzani's great little Florentine wine bar, around the corner from Piazza Signoria. *Little* is the operative word here: there are only five tables inside, which means you could do your drinking and eating milling with the other patrons on the sidewalk. This is a hands-on operation for Emore, who works both the bar and the crowd, proving that the best things do come in small packages. The food and wines celebrate the goodness of Tuscany with *pasta e fagioli* (pasta and white beans), *salsicce e fagioli* (sausage and white beans), penne with mushrooms and peas, tripe, *crostini*, and *biscotti* to dip in *vin santo* for a semisweet ending.

TELEPHONE
055-293-045
OPEN
Tues–Sun
CLOSED
Mon
HOURS
10 A.M.–1 A.M., continuous service
RESERVATIONS
Not necessary
CREDIT CARDS
None
À LA CARTE
L7,000–15,000
MENÙ TURISTICO
None
COVER AND SERVICE CHARGES
None
ENGLISH
Yes

Piazza SS. Anunziata

This piazza is one of the loveliest in Florence, surrounded on three sides by arches and on its easternmost corner by the Foundling's Hospital, built by Brunelleschi and decorated by Della Robbia. The hospital, the first of its kind in Europe, cared for many of the domestic slaves' babies who were left in a small revolving door set into a wall. Today the square is a favorite gathering place for students from the nearby university.

(52) BUFFET FREDDO
Via degli Alfani, 70r

When I see an eating place that is SRO every time I pass by, no matter what time of the day or evening, I know they are dishing out delicious food at prices the

TELEPHONE
055-239-6400
OPEN
Mon–Sat
CLOSED
Sun, 15 days in Aug (dates vary)

HOURS
8:30 A.M.–8:30 P.M., continuous service; hot lunch noon–2:30 P.M.
RESERVATIONS
Not accepted
CREDIT CARDS
None
À LA CARTE
L8,000 for one-dish meal, L15,000–17,000 for three courses, beverage extra
MENÙ TURISTICO
None
COVER AND SERVICE CHARGES
None
ENGLISH
Limited

locals appreciate. The lively clientele, drawn from both the university and blue-collar ranks, gathers to meet, greet, and eat at the five shared marble-topped tables. And eat well they do. A daily blue-plate special, two to three pastas, a soup, and enormous custom-made sandwiches filled with every combination of meat, cheese, and vegetable known to the civilized world are consumed in great quantities until 8:30 P.M. every day but Sunday.

(53) MAXIMILIAN
Via degli Alfani, 10r

TELEPHONE
055-24-78-080
OPEN
Tues–Sun
CLOSED
Mon, Aug (last 2 weeks usually)
HOURS
1–3 P.M., 7:30–11:30 P.M.
RESERVATIONS
Advised
CREDIT CARDS
AE, DC, MC, V
À LA CARTE
Minimum order is L25,000, average is L35,000, beverage extra
MENÙ TURISTICO
None
COVER AND SERVICE CHARGES
Cover L4,000, service not included
ENGLISH
Enough

"How do you do it?" I asked Adelina Vicini, the energetic owner and one-woman virtuoso of Maximilian. She not only plans the menu, shops for the food, and prepares and serves both lunch and dinner but does the cleanup six days a week with only occasional help from a friend when things really get busy. She told me she sleeps only four or five hours a night. That must be on a good night. I am exhausted just *thinking* about it all.

She has been in her little trattoria on this street away from the tourist masses long enough for the natives to have discovered her, and to hope you won't. Because she must depend on repeat local business, she has found what works and cooks accordingly. Her food is not exotic or gourmet but the simple home cooking we all know and love . . . and wish we had more of. It is nice to start with an *insalata mista,* filled with assorted greens, carrots, and tomatoes and brought to the table with a cruet of olive oil and vinegar. Vegetarians will lap up her garlic-filled pastas and grilled seasonal vegetables. Meat eaters are treated to fried brains, calves' liver with mashed potatoes, or succulent roast rabbit. If you don't see what you want on the menu, and she has the ingredients in the kitchen, she will be happy to fix it for you. For dessert, even if you think you are full, you will find yourself scraping the bottom of the generous dish of profiteroles smothered in thick chocolate.

As you can imagine, when the tables are full, service may be a little slow because everything is prepared to order. Don't worry, order a bottle of Chianti Classico, sit back, enjoy the experience, and give Adelina credit for a job very well done.

Pitti Palace

The Palazzo Pitti, a fifteenth-century palace designed by Brunelleschi as a residence for the powerful Medicis, is across the Arno on Florence's "Left Bank." Only a ten-minute stroll from the Ponte Veccio, the fortress palace holds one of Europe's greatest art collections, scattered through several museums. The most famous is the Galleria del Palatina, with paintings hung four or five feet high on damask-covered walls.

(54) IL FORNAIO
Via Guicciardini, 3r

For a sandwich on the run or a pastry to go, you cannot beat Il Fornaio, a chain of bakeries with several locations in Florence. They open early in the morning, selling trays of hot *cornetti* (croissants), brioche, and other treats and temptations. The lunch lines for sandwiches and slices of pizza are legion, proving that when you offer good food at decent prices the world will beat a path to your door. All of the food is to go, and the service is frenetic during the crazy lunch scene. If, however, you go about noon, or wait until after 1:30 P.M., when admittedly the selection will be diminished, you will at least be able to place your order without a long wait.

Another popular location is at Via Sant'Antonino and Via Faenza in the Mercato Centrale.

TELEPHONE
None
OPEN
Mon–Tues, Thur–Sat; Wed, morning only
CLOSED
Sun
HOURS
7:30 A.M.–7:30 P.M., continuous service
RESERVATIONS
Not accepted
CREDIT CARDS
None
À LA CARTE
From L1,500, beverage not available
MENÙ TURISTICO
None
COVER AND SERVICE CHARGES
None
ENGLISH
Depends on server

(55) OSTERIA DEL CINGHIALE BIANCO
Borgo Sant' Jacopo, 43r

Massimo Masselli, along with his wife and son, represents the third generation of well-known restaurateurs in Florence. Their popular establishment, set in a fourteenth-century tower, specializes in wild boar, a delicacy best made into sausage, salami, or ham and served as an antipasto or stewed with red wine and vegetables and served with polenta as a main course.

There is an absolute bargain Cheap Eat *menù turistico* for lunch, but often it is not offered; you must ask for it. The choices for this two-course meal are good, and include two large salads. Headlining the Tuscan dishes on both the à la carte and *menù turistico* menus are *pappa al pomodoro* (a filling bread soup made with tomatoes,

TELEPHONE
055-21-57-06
OPEN
Mon, Thur–Sun
CLOSED
Tues, Wed, July (3 weeks)
HOURS
Noon–2:30 P.M., 7–10:30 P.M.
RESERVATIONS
Essential
CREDIT CARDS
None
À LA CARTE
L40,000–45,000, beverage extra

MENÙ TURISTICO
Lunch only: L16,000, two courses plus a glass of wine or 1/4 liter of mineral water; cover and service included

COVER AND SERVICE CHARGES
Cover L2,000, service included

ENGLISH
Yes

garlic, and olive oil) and *ribollita* (a hearty, long-simmered soup made with beans, vegetables, and bread). These age-old recipes date back to the times when peasants did not have much to eat and had to make do with what few ingredients they could find. Another wonderful dish is the *strozzapreti al burro,* boiled spinach pasta dumplings filled with cheese and drizzled with butter. Delicately crafted desserts include a *crema di Mascarpone* served with cookies and a *tiramisù* made with ricotta cheese that turns out to be light and less sweet than the regular, heavier versions.

Please keep in mind that reservations are essential for lunch and dinner, and that the romantic mezzanine table must be booked several days in advance.

Ponte Vecchio

The famous Ponte Vecchio, the narrowest bridge in Florence, dates from 1345. It is lined with wooden shops displaying an awe-inspiring collection of gold and magnificent jewels, and is thronged with tourists on their way to and from the Pitti Palace.

(56) BUCA DELL' ORAFO
Volta dei Girolami, 28r

TELEPHONE
055-21-36-19

OPEN
Tues–Sat

CLOSED
Sun, Mon, Aug

HOURS
12:30–2:30 P.M., 7:30–10:30 P.M.

RESERVATIONS
Essential as far in advance as possible

CREDIT CARDS
None

À LA CARTE
L35,000–45,000, beverage extra

MENÙ TURISTICO
None

COVER AND SERVICE CHARGES
Cover L3,000, service included

ENGLISH
Yes

Hidden under an archway near the Ponte Vecchio is the Buca dell' Orafo, a favorite for years with Florentines and visitors for its good value and authentic cuisine. The two owners are on tap every day to run the kitchen and serve their guests. Everyone seems to know one another, particularly at lunch, when lots of laughing and talking goes on between the tables. If you go for lunch or after 9 P.M., you will likely share your dining experience with Italians. If you go for an early dinner, you will hear mostly English spoken and probably run into your cousin's neighbor from Detroit.

The regulars know to come on the specific days their favorite dishes are served. Friday it is always fresh codfish. Thursday, Friday, and Saturday *ribollita* headlines the openers. And every day you can count on finding a special, such as *stracotto e fagioli,* braised beef with beans in a sauce with garlic, onions, and sage. A spring favorite is the *tortino di carciofi,* an artichoke omelette that will change your mind about what can be done with an artichoke. The dessert to melt your heart and your willpower is the house special *dolce,* a sponge cake with cream layers and meringue and almonds on top. It will be one of the best desserts you have on your entire trip.

San Lorenzo Central Market

The Piazza Mercato Centrale houses two floors of the glories of Tuscan food. If you love food, this is a must-see in Florence. Along the surrounding streets are countless stalls, all selling basically the same things: polyester scarf copies of the real Guccis or Fendis, leather bags, belts, jackets, and boxes, T-shirts, Florentine paper goods, souvenirs, and accessories. Bargains are rare because the competition is so intense that the prices are almost fixed, so look around and buy from the vendor who treats you the best.

(57) CAFAGGI
Via Guelfa, 35r

One of the best ways to find out about places to eat is to ask the natives where they go. The top contender on Via Guelfa, between Piazza della Indipendenza and Piazza San Marco off Via Cavour, is Cafaggi. This plain-Jane restaurant has been in the Cafaggi family for decades, and consists of two rather large cream-colored rooms. The second room off the kitchen is slightly more appealing due to a few plants scattered about and some flowers on the tables. Smart Cheap Eaters will join the well-dressed businesspeople at lunch and the attractive neighborhood evening crowd who come prepared to dine well, not to lounge in magnificent surroundings. After you have had your first glass of wine and have tasted the fine food, you will quickly forget about the dull atmosphere. Some Cheap Eaters will want to stay with the set-priced menu, which includes a first and second course. However, with a bit of careful ordering, à la carte will not be prohibitive.

The real boss of the kitchen is Sra. Cafaggi, who oversees a chef who prides himself on turning out carefully prepared dishes using the freshest seasonal ingredients, reflecting the best the market has to offer. In fact, the front window has a vivid display of the types of fresh fish, meat, and produce you can expect to see on your plate. The chef is a wizard with fresh fish and veal, especially the veal served in a buttery asparagus sauce.

TELEPHONE
055-29-49-89

OPEN
Mon–Sat

CLOSED
Sun, mid-July–Aug (dates vary)

HOURS
Noon–2:30 P.M., 7–10:30 P.M.

RESERVATIONS
Advised, especially weekends and holidays

CREDIT CARDS
AE, MC, V

À LA CARTE
L40,000–50,000, beverage extra

MENÙ TURISTICO
L24,000, two courses; cover and service included, beverage extra

COVER AND SERVICE CHARGES
Cover L3,500, service included

ENGLISH
Yes, and menu in English

The desserts are all made here and are beautiful. Try the *millefoglie alla crema,* layers of flaky pastry filled with whipped cream. The house wine is adequate, so there is no need to splurge on anything else. The service is friendly, yet professional and to the point.

(58) I' TOSCANO
Via Guelfa, 70r

TELEPHONE
055-21-54-75

OPEN
Mon, Wed–Sun

CLOSED
Tues, Aug

HOURS
Noon–2:30 P.M., 7:30–10:30 P.M.

RESERVATIONS
Advised for dinner

CREDIT CARDS
AE, DC, MC, V

À LA CARTE
L40,000, beverage extra

MENÙ TURISTICO
L28,000, three courses plus mineral water or wine; cover and service included

COVER AND SERVICE CHARGES
Cover L3,000, service included

ENGLISH
Yes, and menu in English

The chef at i' Toscano displays his varied skills with dishes of fresh, flavorful food attractively presented in two rather formal rooms—formal by Florence standards, that is. A bouquet of flowers adds one of the only spots of color in the brightly lit, stark white surroundings. The properly set tables are spaced wide enough to prevent being a part of your neighbor's conversation, and the friendly waiters make an effort to explain any dish you are not sure about.

The food has just enough creativity and imagination to lift it out of the ordinary and place it into the near-gourmet category. The three-course *menù turistico,* an excellent value, changes every two weeks and offers three or four dishes for each course, plus mineral water or wine. For not too much more, you can order à la carte and have a more interesting meal, starting with a plate of cold slices of wild boar, deer, and other game meats, or something typically Florentine, toasted bread topped with black cabbage, garlic, and olive oil. The spinach ravioli with herbs and fresh tomato is a satisfying first course, as is the gnocchi in a vegetable sauce. For the main dish, if you are here on a Friday, by all means order the *baccalà*—stockfish served with a fresh tomato sauce. On other days, it is a toss-up between the veal scaloppine with white wine and the savory beef stew. For your vegetable, the *gobbi alla fiorentina* (*gobbi* being a thistlelike plant with leaves and stalks that are eaten like celery), served here lightly braised in a butter sauce, is an interesting choice you seldom see. Saving room for dessert takes some willpower, but at least share a slice of the lemon cake or try the creamy coconut ice cream.

(59) NERBONE
Stand #292, Piazza del Mercato Centrale (next to the San Lorenzo Church)

TELEPHONE
055-21-99-49

OPEN
Mon–Sat

CLOSED
Sun, Aug (dates vary)

The Mercato di San Lorenzo, Florence's huge indoor market, is the main source of food for a region that takes food very seriously and is without peer for its wide variety and enormous selection. Be sure you allow yourself enough time to appreciate the magnificent displays of food, which serve as a quick study course in the fine points and ingredients of Italian cooking. You will see several Italian-style fast-food stalls, but the most famous, and unquestionably the best, is Nerbone, Stand #292, where hot meat sandwiches have been the major drawing card since 1872.

Nerbone, which is under the same ownership as Alla Vecchia Bettola (see page 33), appeals to those with hearty appetites who don't mind a noisy, no-frills setting. The menu lists bowls of beans, mashed potatoes, tripe, and pastas. Never mind any of these. The standard order here is a sandwich of boiled beef (*bollito*), sliced onto a crusty roll and then dipped into the meat juices (*bagnato*). After you are handed your food, take it to the tables across the way, or stand at the bar with a beer, and enjoy!

HOURS
7 A.M.–2 P.M.

RESERVATIONS
Not accepted

CREDIT CARDS
None

À LA CARTE
From L3,500

MENÙ TURISTICO
None

COVER AND SERVICE CHARGES
None

ENGLISH
None

(60) PALLE D'ORO
Via Sant' Antonino 43/45r

Sooner or later all Cheap Eaters in Florence learn about Palle d'Oro, which sits on a crowded shopping street midway between Il Duomo and the big Central Market. For lunch, you will be joining Florentines ordering freshly crafted sandwiches up front or quick and easy hot dishes in the back. In the evening, take a seat and order a brimming bowl of soup or pasta, a fragrantly roasted chicken with a green salad, or a piece of grilled fish seasoned with fresh lemon and a splash of olive oil.

This antiseptically clean spot, surgical in decor, reminds me of a coffee shop in a motel. Don't let this discourage you, because for over a hundred years this fourth-generation family-run jewel has provided dependable and good fast food *alla italiano*. It is so crowded at lunch you probably won't be able to see the walls, which means you will miss some interesting black-and-white family photos showing Lorenzo, the great-grandfather, bringing the country wine to Florence piled high on a horse-drawn two-wheeled cart.

TELEPHONE
055-28-83-83

FAX
055-35-48-11

OPEN
Mon–Sat

CLOSED
Sun, Aug

HOURS
Noon–2:30 P.M., 6:30–9:45 P.M.

RESERVATIONS
Not accepted

CREDIT CARDS
AE, DC, MC, V

À LA CARTE
Lunch: L30,000, sandwiches from L4,000, beverage extra. Dinner: L35,000, beverage extra

MENÙ TURISTICO
Lunch: L17,000, three courses plus mineral water; cover and service included, other beverages extra. Dinner: L20,000, three courses plus mineral water; cover and service included, other beverages extra

COVER AND SERVICE CHARGES
Cover L2,000, service included

ENGLISH
Yes, and menu in English

(61) RISTORANTE DE' MEDICI
Via del Giglio, 49–51r

TELEPHONE
055-21-87-78
OPEN
Daily
CLOSED
Christmas
HOURS
Noon–1 A.M., continuous service; pizza 6 P.M.–1 A.M.
RESERVATIONS
Not necessary
CREDIT CARDS
MC, V
À LA CARTE
L30,000, beverage extra; pizza from L8,000
MENÙ TURISTICO
None
COVER AND SERVICE CHARGES
Cover L3,000, service not included
ENGLISH
Yes

If you order a pasta, a wood-fired pizza, or one of the succulent grilled meats—and avoid the tiny, overpriced salads—you will do just fine at this large, rather formal restaurant only fifty meters from the Medici Chapel and the Basilica of San Lorenzo. I think it is a place to remember for several reasons.

First, it is open from noon until 1 A.M., and you can go in anytime for a full meal or a light snack, great advantages if you have children. Second, the wide selection of pastas and pizzas are offered at prices that won't send you and your budget into orbit. The grilled meats are all of the finest quality, and the house specialty is *bistecca alla fiorentina,* sold by the gram. Watch out . . . this can make your bill soar. Fine Chianti wines are featured, as are several beers that pair well with a pizza. The desserts are all made in-house.

(62) SNACK BAR ANNA
Via de Ginori, 26r

TELEPHONE
055-89-53-285
OPEN
Mon–Sat
CLOSED
Sun, major holidays, Aug (dates vary)
HOURS
8 A.M.–8 P.M., continuous service
RESERVATIONS
Not necessary
CREDIT CARDS
None
À LA CARTE
Sandwiches from L3,500
MENÙ TURISTICO
None
COVER AND SERVICE CHARGES
None
ENGLISH
Yes

Pastries, hot chocolate, and cappuccino in the morning; custom-crafted *panini* (sandwiches) on white or wheat focaccia at noon, and the two-for-one happy hour from 6 P.M. until closing keep Cheap Eaters coming back to this primo pit stop near the Central Market. It is an unassuming bar, run by Ugo and Anna, a friendly couple who keep everything happily humming along from 8 A.M. until 8 P.M. every day but Sunday. The tables in back fill up during the noon rush, but any other time hang out at the bar . . . that is where the action takes place.

(63) TRATTORIA DA SERGIO E GOZZI
Piazza San Lorenzo, 8r

TELEPHONE
055-28-19-41
OPEN
Mon–Sat, lunch only
CLOSED
Sun, major holidays, Aug

When in Florence, under no circumstances should you miss a trip to the Mercato Centrale de San Lorenzo, a nineteenth-century cast-iron landmark housing one of the largest and most interesting markets in Europe. Surrounding the market are hundreds of stalls with sellers hawking more than enough treasures to fill up that extra suitcase. For even the least committed Cheap Chic shopper, it is definitely worth a look, even though the prices are not always the bargains the setting suggests.

There are many places to eat around the market, some very good and others appallingly bad. One of the most authentic and tourist-free is this trattoria, a true worker's hangout where you can enjoy hearty Tuscan food with burly market men and women. The only menu is posted outside. When you are seated, the waiter will tell you what's cooking. You are expected to order a full meal—just a salad and a glass of wine is *out.* You can count on chunky minestrone and bean soups, roasted meats, and sturdy boiled brisket. Country bread and creamy desserts add to your pleasure. Follow the lead of fellow diners and order a bottle of the house Chianti while enjoying the friendly service and a lunch that will leave some lire in your pocket.

HOURS
Noon–4 P.M.

RESERVATIONS
Not necessary

CREDIT CARDS
None

À LA CARTE
L25,000–30,000, beverage extra

MENÙ TURISTICO
None

COVER AND SERVICE CHARGES
Cover L2,000, no service charge

ENGLISH
Yes, usually

(64) TRATTORIA MARIO

Via Rosina, 2r

Mario's boasts many avid regulars, all of whom seem to be on a first-name basis. Consequently, there is a great deal of good cheer and camaraderie, with everyone swapping tall tales and telling jokes. They all know to arrive early and order a glass or two of the house red while waiting for the lunch service to begin. Latecomers will have to wait, or worse yet, they won't get their favorite dish, since the kitchen often runs out early.

The daily menu is posted on a board by the open kitchen. Friday is *fish only* day, and on Thursday gnocchi is the dish to order. On any day smart choices include the vegetable soup, stewed tripe, or a slab of roast veal or beef. You don't need to save room for dessert because all they serve is fresh fruit or a glass of sweet wine with those wonderful, hard, almond-flavored dipping cookies called *biscotti.* No coffee is served either, but there are dozens of bars around the market where it is fun to merge in and stand for an after-lunch espresso that will recharge your batteries for the rest of the afternoon.

TELEPHONE
055-21-85-50

OPEN
Mon–Sat, bar and lunch only

CLOSED
Sun, Aug

HOURS
Bar 7 A.M.–5 P.M., lunch noon–3 P.M.

RESERVATIONS
Not accepted

CREDIT CARDS
None

À LA CARTE
L18,000–20,000, beverage extra

MENÙ TURISTICO
None

COVER AND SERVICE CHARGES
Cover L1,000, service included

ENGLISH
Yes

(65) TRATTORIA ZÀZÀ
Piazza del Mercato Centrale, 26r

TELEPHONE
055-21-54-11
FAX
055-21-07-56
OPEN
Mon–Sat
CLOSED
Sun, major holidays
HOURS
Noon–3 P.M., 7–11 P.M.
RESERVATIONS
Advised
CREDIT CARDS
AE, DC, MC, V
À LA CARTE
L35,000–38,000, beverage extra
MENÙ TURISTICO
L20,000, two courses; cover and service included, beverage extra
COVER AND SERVICE CHARGES
Cover L2,000, service included, but tips appreciated
ENGLISH
Usually

Trattoria Zàzà, on the corner of Via Rosina, offers a winning mix of accommodating service, atmosphere, and hearty Tuscan food. Wooden picnic tables with long benches and hard stools line both the upstairs and downstairs dining rooms. The walls are papered with framed newspaper clippings of famous trotting horses and film posters of vintage movie legends, including Ingrid Bergman and Humphrey Bogart in the famous *Casablanca* farewell scene. Overhead are three rows of shelves stacked high with the Chianti you will be drinking with your meal.

The wide-ranging menu offers a multitude of choices for every course. To start, order the trio of their best soups, which includes a bowl of *ribollita, pomodoro fresca* (fresh tomato), and *passato di fagioli con faro* (bean soup). The roast chicken or veal scaloppine are good entrées. Lighter eaters will appreciate their *insalate giganti*—six salads that are meals in themselves. These seem to appeal to just about everyone. The de rigueur dessert is Zàzà's own *torta di mele alla Zàzà,* an upside-down apple tart similar to the French *tarte Tatin*. Service can be irritatingly slow.

San Niccolò

From Piazzale Michelangelo and in front of the Romanesque church of San Miniato al Monte you will have a sweeping view of Florence that you will never forget. The winding road leads you through the old city gates to Via di San Niccolò and the church of the same name with its fifteenth-century frescoes.

(66) FUORI PORTA
Via del Monte alle Croci, 10r

TELEPHONE
055-23-42-483
FAX
055-23-41-408
E-MAIL
enos@ats.it
INTERNET
fuoriporta.it
OPEN
Mon–Sat

Fuori Porta romances patrons with attentive service, good food, and a fabulous selection of wines from around the world, with the emphasis on 350 vintages from Tuscany. Located just beyond the city walls, off Via di San Niccolò and Via San Miniato and below Piazzale Michelangelo, this wine bar, run for a dozen-plus years by knowledgeable wine connoisseur Andrea Conti, is considered one of the best, if not *the* best, in Florence.

While it is known for its fine wines, which are shipped around the world from their wine shop next to the restaurant and wine bar, you need not experience fiscal trauma from an evening spent sampling superior wines that sell from L3,000–10,000 a glass.

Patrons also come for the kitchen's simple take on regional foods that pair well with any of the six hundred wines available at any one time. Lunch and dinner both feature a daily menu of assorted pastas, fresh fish at night, carpaccio, sandwiches, cheese and meat plates, plus the usual *crostini* and *bruschettas* that go so well with wine. If you are a serious wine buff, contact them through their e-mail for a list of wines that can be shipped to your doorstep.

CLOSED
Sun (except in Dec), Aug 7–20 (dates can vary)

HOURS
12:30–3:30 P.M., 7–12:30 A.M.

RESERVATIONS
Suggested on weekends

CREDIT CARDS
AE, MC, V

À LA CARTE
L10,000–20,000, wine extra

MENÙ TURISTICO
None

COVER AND SERVICE CHARGES
None

ENGLISH
Yes

(67) OSTERIA ANTICA MESCITA
Via di San Niccolò, 60r

Bench seating along exposed stone walls in what was once the crypt of the San Niccolò Church sets the rough-hewn tone of this pleasant osteria in a quiet, non-tourist-plagued section of the Oltrarno. Curious carnivores will be dizzy with the assortment of decisions, with wild boar sausage or a plate of smoked meats followed by tripe, pork entrails, and oxtail. Tamer tastes will be content with a slice of the artichoke torte or a bowl of bean and lettuce soup, vegetable couscous, or a plate of roast beef. The house wines are adequate, the prices fair, and the service friendly, which adds up to a nice meal just far enough from the hub of tourist Florence to keep it local and appreciated.

TELEPHONE
055-23-42-836

OPEN
Mon–Sat

CLOSED
Sun, Aug

HOURS
Noon–3 P.M., 7:30 P.M.–midnight

RESERVATIONS
Suggested

CREDIT CARDS
None

À LA CARTE
L25,000–30,000, beverage extra

MENÙ TURISTICO
None

COVER AND SERVICE CHARGES
Cover L1,000, no service charge

ENGLISH
Yes

Train Station

All long-distance trains arrive at the Santa Maria Novella railway terminal that joins Piazza di Santa Maria Novella and the great church of the same name. The station is a comfortable ten- or fifteen-minute walk from the center. Almost all buses in and out of Florence stop nearby, as do taxis and pickpockets who work the area on a twenty-four-hour basis.

(68) ANTICHI CANCELLI
Via Faenza, 73r

TELEPHONE
055-21-89-27

OPEN
Tues–Fri; Sat–Sun, continuously

CLOSED
Mon

HOURS
Noon–2:45 P.M., 6–10:45 P.M.

RESERVATIONS
Absolutely essential

CREDIT CARDS
AE, DC, MC, V

À LA CARTE
L30,000–35,000, beverage extra

MENÙ TURISTICO
L20,000, three courses; beverages, cover, and service included

COVER AND SERVICE CHARGES
Cover L2,000, 10% service added

ENGLISH
Yes, and *menù turistico* in English

Trattoria Antichi Cancelli, which means "the old gate," is under the same ownership as Trattoria Guelfa (see page 73). With its hanging peppers and garlic braids, potted plants, and tiny paper-covered marble-topped tables set under a brick ceiling, it looks like something from a movie. The difference, of course, is that the great food and jovial ambience are real. It does not take newcomers long to blend in and to quickly catch the mood of the place. As with Trattoria Guelfa, do not even *think* of arriving without reservations, and even then you can count on having to wedge yourself into the crowd and wait for a table.

It is important that you come prepared to eat. Management, especially Romeo and Erico, takes a dim view of dieters or anyone else not ordering at least a pasta, main course, and dessert. The daily menu is based on what is best at the market during each season and is handwritten on a scrap of paper stapled to the regular menu. The dishes of Tuscany are well prepared, and everything from the antipasti and pasta to the sauces and desserts is made here. The filling portions promise that no one will be thinking about the next meal for a long time.

NOTE: Especially appealing to many Cheap Eaters are the hours. Dinner is available at the unheard-of hour of 6 P.M., and on Saturday and Sunday, the restaurant serves continuously from noon until 10:45 P.M.

(69) L'ANGOLO DEL GELATO
Via della Scala, 2r

TELEPHONE
055-21-05-26

OPEN
Tues–Sun

CLOSED
Mon

HOURS
Summer 9:30 A.M.–1 A.M.; winter 11 A.M.–midnight

RESERVATIONS
Not accepted

CREDIT CARDS
None

À LA CARTE
Gelato from L1,500–8,000

MENÙ TURISTICO
None

Italians are addicted to gelato, and nowhere is this more evident than in Florence, where *gelaterias* seem to be a dime a dozen. For the best ice cream near Santa Maria Novella, drop by L'Angolo del Gelato, a corner store owned by a friendly man named Fabrizio and his mother. Everything they serve is made here from fresh ingredients and seasonal fruits. It is all sold by the size of the cup and you can have as many flavors as you want in whatever cup you select. The most popular flavors are chocolate and, in summer, lemon. In winter, look for creamy *semifreddo* flavors and the *fiesta*, an almost illegally rich chocolate ice cream laced with Grand Marnier. In summer, indulge to your waistline's content with their fat-free fruit *sorbettos* or fruit-based yogurt ice cream.

The servings are generous. Those in the know always ask for their gelato with some *panna montana* on top . . . or freshly whipped cream.

COVER AND SERVICE CHARGES
None

ENGLISH
Yes

(70) TRATTORIA ENZO E PIERO
Via Faenza, 105r

Enzo and Piero's trattoria is very simple, with rough stuccoed walls and lots of well-fed habitués sitting at the yellow linen–clad tables. On each table is a bottle of Chianti wine vinegar and another of good olive oil so you can dress your own salad or, as the Italians do, sprinkle olive oil on just about everything but dessert.

Both Enzo and Piero are on hand each day to ensure that all runs well. They greet their guests at the table, suggest what is best to order, and check back periodically to see that everyone has everything needed for a fine meal. They also keep an eagle eye on the kitchen, where their high standards ensure absolutely fresh ingredients prepared with care. Whenever you come, be sure to ask for the daily specials, often they are not offered with the regular menu. If you are here on a Friday, try the *baccalà alla livornese,* salt cod cooked in a nippy red sauce with liberal doses of garlic; on Wednesday, order the osso buco cooked in a tomato sauce. Other flavorful options are the *tortellini alla cardinale* (with cream, tomatoes, and ham), one of the better *pasta al pomodoros* in Florence, or the stuffed and baked breast of turkey and ham. For dessert you want the *panna cotta,* a cooked custard surrounded by fresh strawberries and chocolate. The *menù turistico* is a Cheap Eat if ever there was one, even though it does not include a beverage. For a few lire more, you can add a quarter or a half carafe and still walk away for under L30,000 per person.

TELEPHONE
055-21-49-01

OPEN
Mon–Sat

CLOSED
Sun, Sat–Sun from July–Aug, 10 days at Christmas, Aug (3 weeks, dates vary)

HOURS
Noon–3 P.M., 7–10 P.M.

RESERVATIONS
Advised for dinner

CREDIT CARDS
AE, DC, MC, V

À LA CARTE
L35,000, beverage extra

MENÙ TURISTICO
L22,000, three courses; cover and service included, beverage extra

COVER AND SERVICE CHARGES
Cover L3,000, service included

ENGLISH
Yes

(71) TRATTORIA GUELFA
Via Guelfa, 103r

The Trattoria Guelfa is a hands-down favorite, and regulars fill it every day for lunch and dinner. Reservations are crucial, but even with them, be prepared to wait up to half an hour, especially on weekends. Service can be irritatingly slow, but when you consider that only two waiters, including hardworking Claudio, the owner, are on duty to serve the congenial crowd, it is amazing anyone gets anything, let alone having it always arrive piping hot. Under the same ownership is Antichi Cancelli (see page 72).

TELEPHONE
055-21-33-06

OPEN
Mon–Tues, Thur–Sun

CLOSED
Wed

HOURS
Noon–3 P.M., 7–11 P.M.

RESERVATIONS
Essential

CREDIT CARDS
AE, MC, V

À LA CARTE
L35,000–40,000, beverage extra

MENÙ TURISTICO
L18,000, three courses; beverage, cover, and service included

COVER AND SERVICE CHARGES
Cover L3,000, service included

ENGLISH
Yes

The key to success here is the wonderful back-to-basics food—all of it lovingly prepared Italian home cooking. If you stay with the chef's specialties, or daily offerings, you cannot go wrong. Depending on the day and time of year, expect to find fat green and white tortellini stuffed with ham and mushrooms, spaghetti with fresh crab, or *cappellacci,* three big pasta tubes stuffed with cheese and spinach and served in a white mushroom cream sauce. Other standouts include roast pork, grilled veal chops served with rosemary-roasted potatoes, and a delightful *pinzimonio di verdure crude* (a selection of seasonal raw vegetables served with oil for dipping). All the desserts remind me of home, especially the *panna cotta con cioccolato,* a cold pudding with hot chocolate poured over it, and the rich chestnut pudding, *budino di castagne.*

Food Shopping in Florence

Probably the Cheapest Eat you will have in Florence is the one you prepare yourself. It may be an ambitious three-course meal cooked in your apartment kitchen or a snack purchased from the market and eaten on the run or on a pretty piazza. Even if you just wander through an Italian outdoor market or cruise the aisles of a supermarket, you will get a good look at the everyday Italian way of life. In Florence, here are the places where I like to shop for food.

Indoor/Outdoor Markets

MERCATO DELLA CASCINE
Cascine Park (edge of Florence)

This weekly outdoor market on Viale Lincoln along the Arno River is a cross between an outdoor food market and cheap clothing stalls pitching everything from aprons to underwear. It is very local, as most tourists don't venture out this far. Go early for the best selection. Watch your wallets and purses and take your own shopping bags. The English spoken here is very limited.

HOURS Tues 7 A.M.–1 P.M.

(72) MERCATO CENTRALE DE SAN LORENZO
Piazza del Mercato Centrale (San Lorenzo Central Market)

A *must* for every visitor to Florence. Inside on two levels are stalls selling every sort of meat, fish, cheese, fruit, and vegetable imaginable. This is the best in Italy, and the largest covered market in Europe. Outside are hundreds of stalls with hawkers selling a variety of fake Gucci scarves and bags, plus T-shirts for everyone on your list, Florentine paper products, leather goods, and more. Not much bargaining in the prices, so pick the seller with the best attitude. No one has a monopoly on any item . . . dozens of sellers all sell the same things at the same prices. Very touristy, but fun and worth at least an hour or so.

HOURS Indoor food market: Mon–Sat 7 A.M.–1 P.M. Outdoor stalls: winter Tues–Sat 9 A.M.–6 P.M.; summer daily 9 A.M.–9 P.M.

(73) MERCATO SANT' AMBROGIO
Piazza Sant' Ambrogio

A lively indoor/outdoor neighborhood market selling to the locals. If you patronize a stall three or four times, you will be treated just like one of the natives. Here you will find all the same meats, fish, dairy products, fruits, and vegetables found at the Mercato Centrale, but at slightly better prices. The Tavola Calda da Rocco (see page 56) across from the coffee bar is a great place for lunch. The dry-goods stalls outside have some worthwhile buys in cotton underwear and socks. Best day to go: Saturday.

HOURS Mon–Sat 7 A.M.–1 P.M.

Supermarkets

ESSELUNGA
Via Pisana, 130 (edge of Florence)

This American-style supermarket has free parking, but avoid Saturdays. There is a second branch at Viale de Amicis, 89, also on the edge of Florence.

HOURS Mon–Sat 9 A.M.–7 P.M.; closed Wed afternoons

CREDIT CARDS None

(74) STANDA
Via Pietrapiana, 42/44 (Piazza Santa Croce)

This is the K-Mart of Italy, with a food, bakery, deli, meat, and liquor section in back. The other locations are: Via de' Panzani, 31 (near the train station), and Via dei Mille, 140 (at the edge of town).

TELEPHONE 055-28-30–71

HOURS Mon 2–9 P.M., Tues–Sat 8:30 A.M.–9 P.M.

CLOSED Sun

CREDIT CARDS MC, V

Health Food Stores

(75) SUGAR BLUES HEALTH FOOD STORE
Via Ventisette Aprile, 46/48 (Piazza della Indipendenza)

The only large health food game in town, this store carries vitamins, packaged foods, a small selection of deli items, cereals, juices, teas, honey, yogurt, and cosmetics. The produce leaves something to be desired unless you happen to be there when it arrives. Otherwise it sits out and after a day or two goes limp. There is a second storefront at Via dei Serraglia, 57, near Piazza Santo Spirito.

TELEPHONE 055-48-36-66

HOURS Mon–Tues, Thur 9 A.M.–1:30 P.M., 4–7:30 P.M.; Wed 9 A.M.–1:30 P.M.

CREDIT CARDS None

ROME

Every road does not lead to Rome, but every road in Rome leads to eternity.

—*Arthur Symons,* Cities, *1903*

When thou art at Rome, do as they do at Rome.

—*Cervantes,* Don Quixote

In the eternal city of Rome, antiquity and history are taken for granted as part of normal life. A leisurely stroll or a bus ride can take you past some of Western civilization's greatest monuments, piazzas, and landmarks. This city, teeming with humanity and choked with traffic jams and crazy drivers, happily thrives amid these testimonies to the past.

Romans originated the first developed cuisine in the Western world, and are famous to this day for their passion for eating. While Rome cannot claim to be the gastronomic capital of Italy, it is the city where food is most pleasurably consumed. The cooking is rich in flavors and aromas, but there is nothing fancy about it. In fact, some may think it almost primitive, because many of the famous dishes, such as *coda all vaccinara* (oxtail stew with vegetables), *trippa all roman* (tripe cooked with meat sauce, mint, and pecorino cheese), and *cervella fritta* (fried calves' brains), are based on the head, the tail, and the innards. The Jewish community in Rome favors deep-frying and has raised this cooking method to a delicate art form. Consider *carciofi alla giudia* (artichokes flattened and fried until brown and crisp) and zucchini blossoms stuffed with ricotta cheese and anchovies and quickly deep-fried. Other vegetables have a starring role, especially green leafy vegetables cooked in water and served *all'agro,* with lemon juice and olive oil. *Puntarella,* an interesting light green leafy vegetable, is served as a salad with an unforgettable dressing made from pounded garlic and anchovies.

In Rome there are literally thousands of dining choices, from the elegant citadels of fine cuisine to the rapidly vanishing little family owned and run trattorias. As in every major world capital, fast-food chains have invaded the city. The good news is that serious chefs are sticking with regional standbys and the basic *cucina* everyone wishes Mama still had the time and desire to prepare. Roman restaurants of all types are noted for serving the same specialties on the same days of the week. Tuesday and Friday, look for fresh fish. On Thursday, it is gnocchi, and on Saturday, tripe. For a traditional Sunday lunch with the extended family, plan on rich lasagna. Pizza is the light meal of choice in the evening. As an appetizer, *pinzimonio* is a healthy choice of celery, fennel, carrots, radishes, and cucumber served with a side of oil for dipping. Other favorite starters and pastas are *stracciatella* (chicken broth with egg

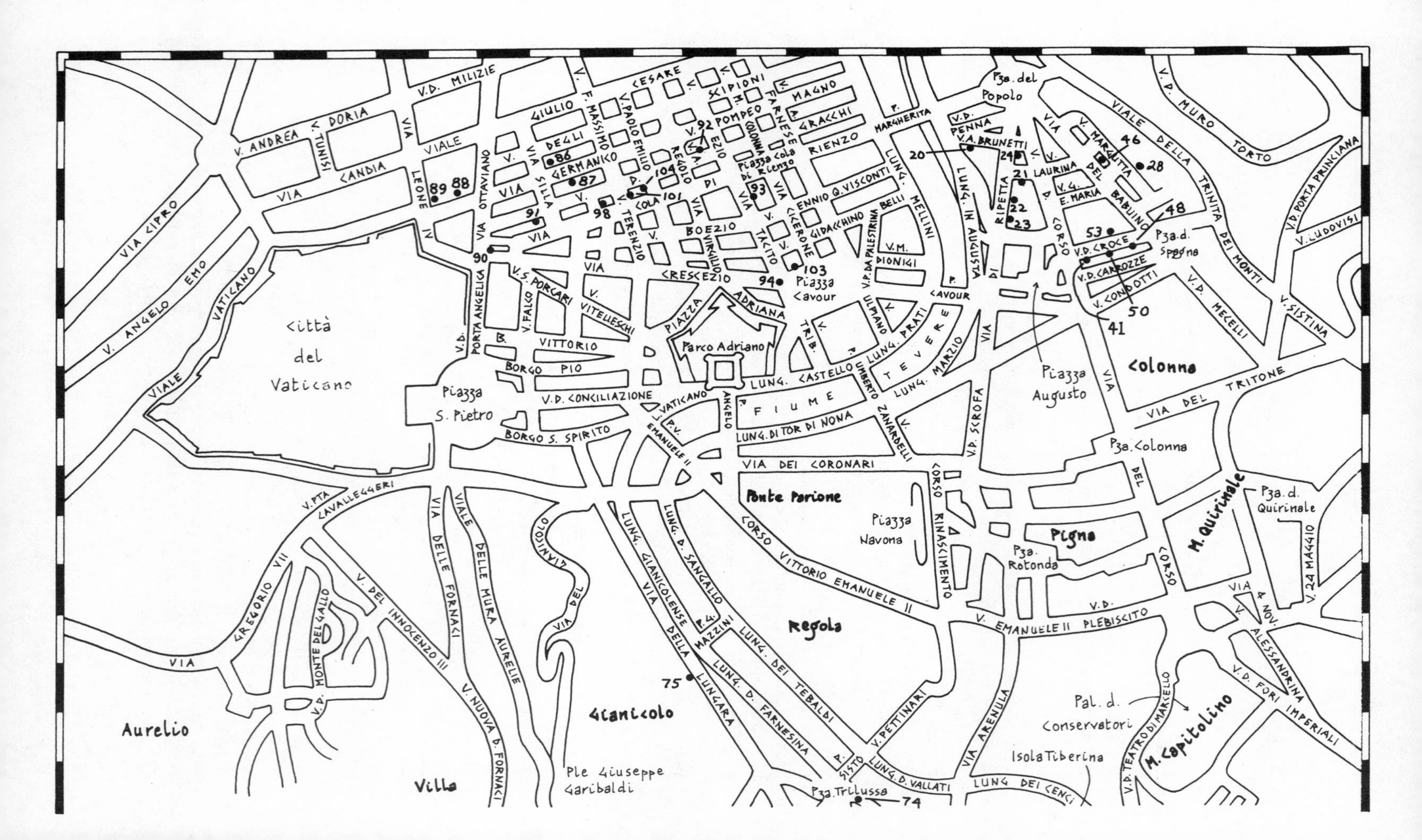

Città del Vaticano
Piazza S. Pietro
Parco Adriano
Piazza Cavour
Piazza Augusto
Colonna
Pza. del Popolo
Pza. d. Spagna
Pza. Colonna
Pza. d. Quirinale
M. Quirinale
Pigna
Pza. Rotonda
Piazza Navona
Ponte Parione
Regola
Gianicolo
Ple Giuseppe Garibaldi
Aurelio
Villa
Pal. d. Conservatori
M. Capitolino
Isola Tiberina
Pza. Trilussa
Piazza Cola di Rienzo
V. D. Milizie
V. Andrea Doria
V. Tunisi
Via Candia
Viale Giulio Cesare
Via Leone IV
Via Cipro
V. Angelo Emo
Viale Vaticano
Via Ottaviano
Porta Angelica
Via Crescenzio
Piazza Adriana
Borgo Pio
Borgo S. Spirito
V. D. Conciliazione
Lung. Castello
Lung. di Tor di Nona
Via dei Coronari
Corso Vittorio Emanuele II
Corso Rinascimento
Lung. Mellini
Lung. in Augusta
Via di Ripetta
Via del Babuino
Via Margutta
V. d. Croce
V. d. Carrozze
V. Condotti
Viale della Trinità dei Monti
V. d. Muro Torto
V. d. Porta Pinciana
V. Ludovisi
V. Sistina
V. d. Mercede
Via del Tritone
Via del Corso
V. 24 Maggio
Via 4 Nov.
V. Alessandrina
V. d. Fori Imperiali
V. d. Teatro di Marcello
V. d. Plebiscito
Via Arenula
Lung. dei Cenci
Lung. d. Vallati
Lung. dei Tebaldi
Lung. d. Farnesina
Lung. Gianicolense
Via della Lungara
Via del Gianicolo
Viale delle Mura Aurelie
Via delle Fornaci
V. Nuova d. Fornaci
V. del Innocenzo III
V. Pta Cavalleggeri
Via Gregorio VII
V. d. Monte del Gallo
20 21 22 23 24 28 41 46 48 50 53 74 75 86 87 88 89 90 91 92 93 94 98 101 103 104

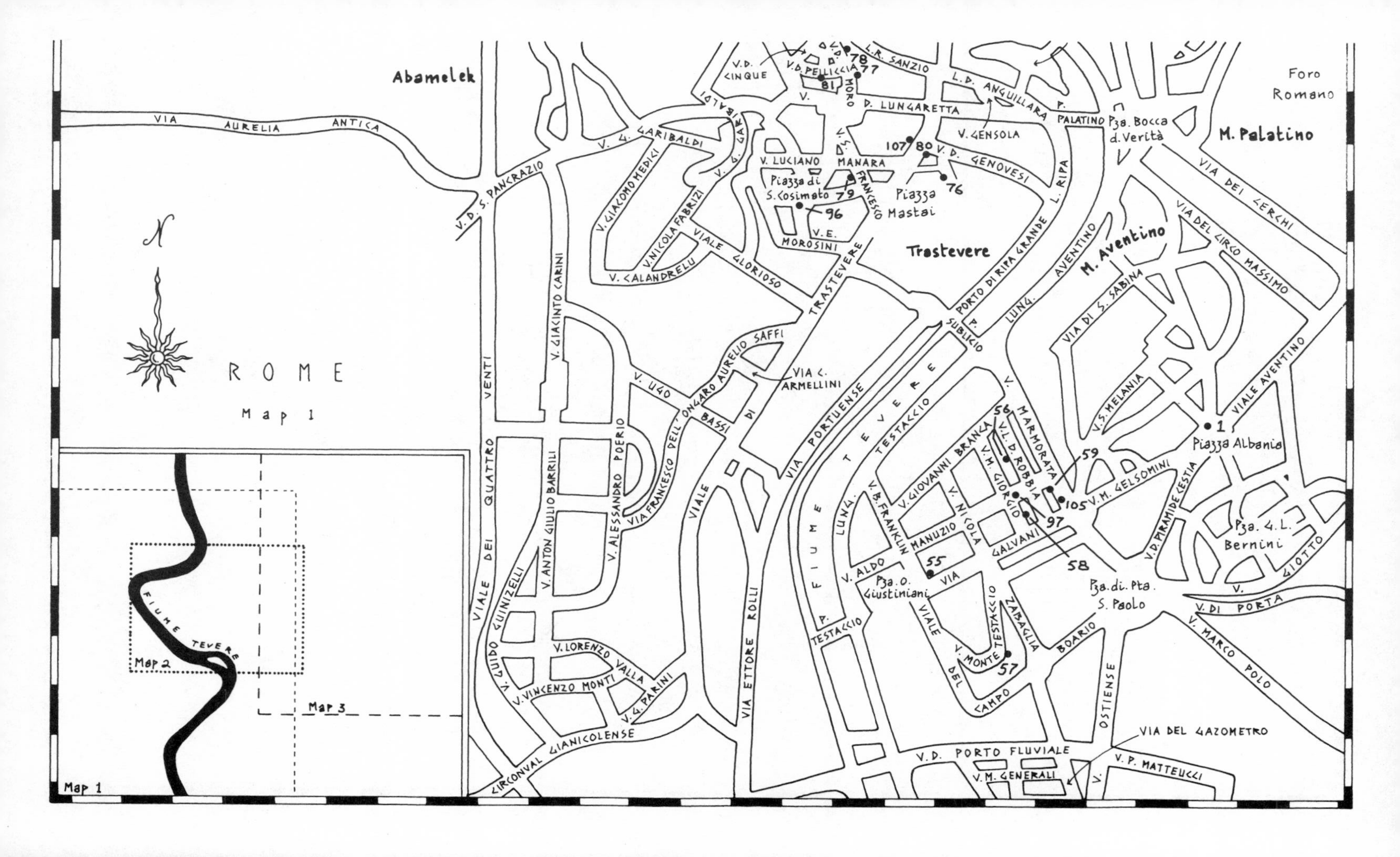
ROME
Map 1
N
Abamelek
Foro Romano
M. Palatino
M. Aventino
Trastevere
Via Aurelia Antica
V. D. S. Pancrazio
V. 4. Garibaldi
V. Giacomo Medici
V. Nicola Fabrizi
V. Calandrelli
Viale Glorioso
V. Giacinto Carini
Viale dei Quattro Venti
V. Anton Giulio Barrili
V. Alessandro Poerio
Via Francesco Dell'Ongaro
V. Ugo Bassi
Aurelio Saffi
Via C. Armellini
Viale di Trastevere
Via Portuense
Viale Ettore Rolli
V. Guido Guinizelli
V. Lorenzo Valla
V. Vincenzo Monti
V. 4. Parini
Circonval Gianicolense
V. D. Cinque
V. D. Pelliccia
Moro
L. R. Sanzio
L. D. Anguillara
D. Lungaretta
V. Gensola
Palatino
Pza. Bocca d. Verità
V. Luciano Manara
Francesco
V. D. Genovesi
Piazza di S. Cosimato
Piazza Mastai
V. E. Morosini
Porto di Ripa Grande
L. Ripa
Lung. Aventino
Via dei Cerchi
Via del Circo Massimo
Via di S. Sabina
V. S. Melania
Viale Aventino
Piazza Albania
P. Sublicio
Fiume Tevere
Lung. Testaccio
P. Testaccio
V. Marmorata
V. L. D. Robbia
V. Giovanni Branca
V. M. Giorgio
V. B. Franklin
V. Nicola
Manuzio
Galvani
V. Aldo
Pza. O. Giustiniani
Via
Viale del Campo
V. Monte Testaccio
Zabaglia
Boario
V. M. Gelsomini
V. D. Piramide Cestia
Pza. 4. L. Bernini
Giotto
V. di Porta
V. Marco Polo
Pza. di. Pta. S. Paolo
Ostiense
Via del Gazometro
V. D. Porto Fluviale
V. M. Generali
V. P. Matteucci
1
55
56
57
58
59
76
77
78
79
80
81
96
97
105
107
Fiume Tevere
Map 2
Map 3
Map 1

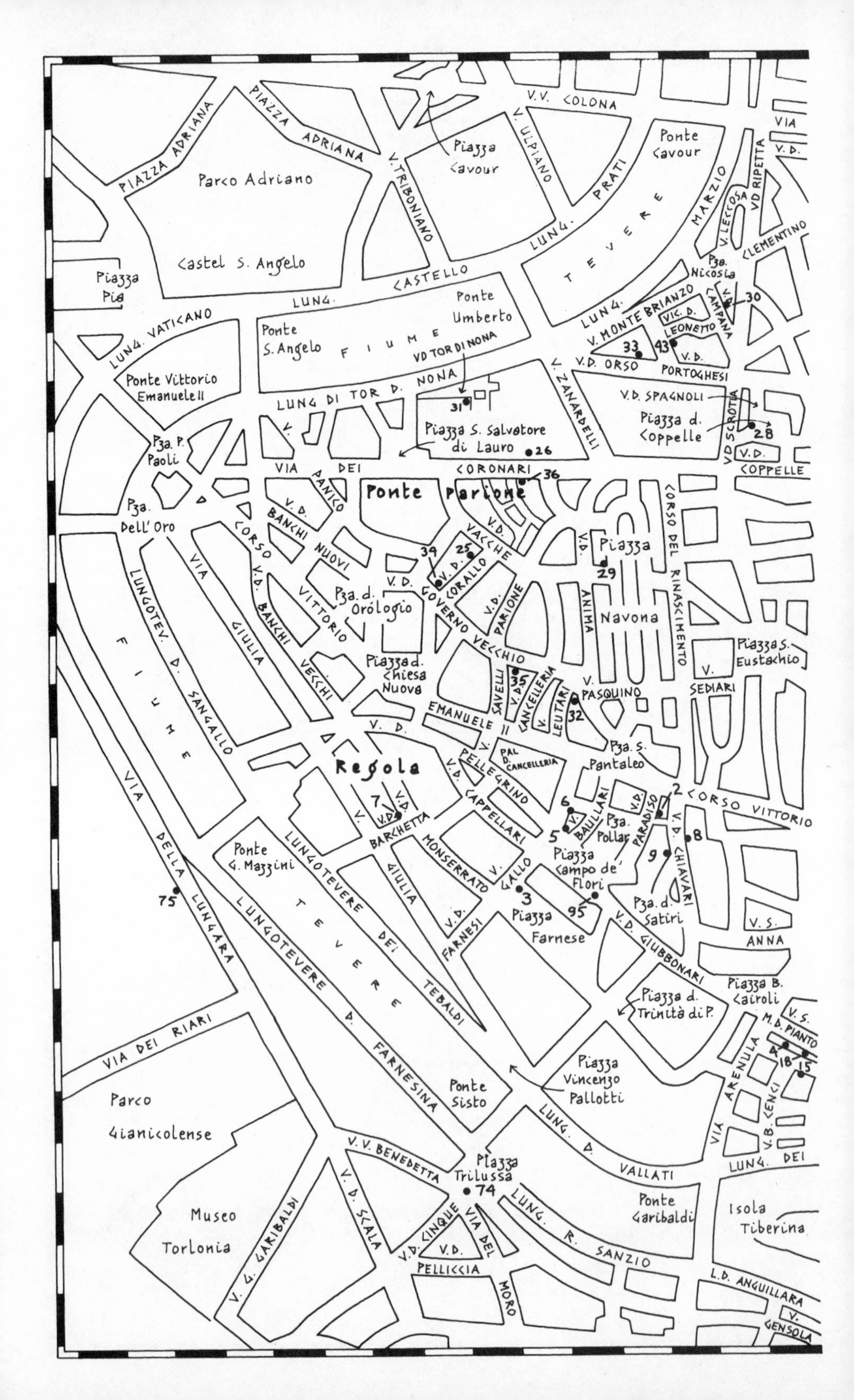
Piazza Adriana
Parco Adriano
Castel S. Angelo
Piazza Pia
Lung. Vaticano
Lung. Castello
V. Tribboniano
Piazza Cavour
V. V. Colona
V. Ulpiano
Lung. Prati
Ponte Cavour
Tevere
Marzio
Ponte S. Angelo
Ponte Umberto
Fiume
VD Tor di Nona
Lung di Tor D. Nona
Ponte Vittorio Emanuele II
Pza. P. Paoli
Pza. Dell' Oro
Piazza S. Salvatore di Lauro
Via dei Coronari
V. D. Banchi Nuovi
Ponte
Parione
V. D. Vacche
V. D. Corallo
V. D. Governo Vecchio
Pza. d. Orologio
Corso V. D. Banchi Vecchi
Vittorio
Via Giulia
Lungotev. D. Sangallo
Fiume
Via della Lungara
Piazza d. Chiesa Nuova
Emanuele II
V. D. Pellegrino
Regola
V. D. Barchetta
V. D. Cappellari
V. Monserrato
V. Gallo
Piazza Farnese
Ponte G. Mazzini
Lungotevere dei Tebaldi
Lungotevere D. Farnesina
Via dei Riari
Parco Gianicolense
Museo Torlonia
V. V. Benedetta
V. G. Garibaldi
V. D. Scala
V. D. Cinque
Via del Moro
V. D. Pelliccia
Piazza Trilussa
Lung. R. Sanzio
Ponte Sisto
Piazza Vincenzo Pallotti
Lung. D. Vallati
Ponte Garibaldi
Isola Tiberina
Lung. dei
L. D. Anguillara
V. Gensola
Via Arenula
V. B. Cenci
M. D. Pianto
V. S.
Piazza B. Cairoli
Piazza d. Trinità di P.
V. D. Giubbonari
Pza. d. Satiri
V. D. Chiavari
V. S. Anna
Corso Vittorio
Piazza Campo de' Fiori
Pza. Pollar
V. Baullari
V. D. Paradiso
Pal D. Cancelleria
Pza. S. Pantaleo
V. Savelli
V. D. Cancelleria
V. Leutari
V. Pasquino
V. D. Parione
V. D. Anima
Piazza Navona
Corso del Rinascimento
Piazza S. Eustachio
V. Sediari
V. Zanardelli
V. D. Orso
V. Monte Brianzo
Lung.
Vic. D. Leonetto
V. D. Portoghesi
V. D. Campana
Pza. Nicosia
V. Leccosa
VD Ripetta
Clementino
Via
V. D.
V. D. Spagnoli
Piazza d. Coppelle
VD Scrofa
V. D. Coppelle
2
3
4
5
6
7
8
9
15
18
25
26
28
29
30
31
32
33
34
35
36
43
74
75
95

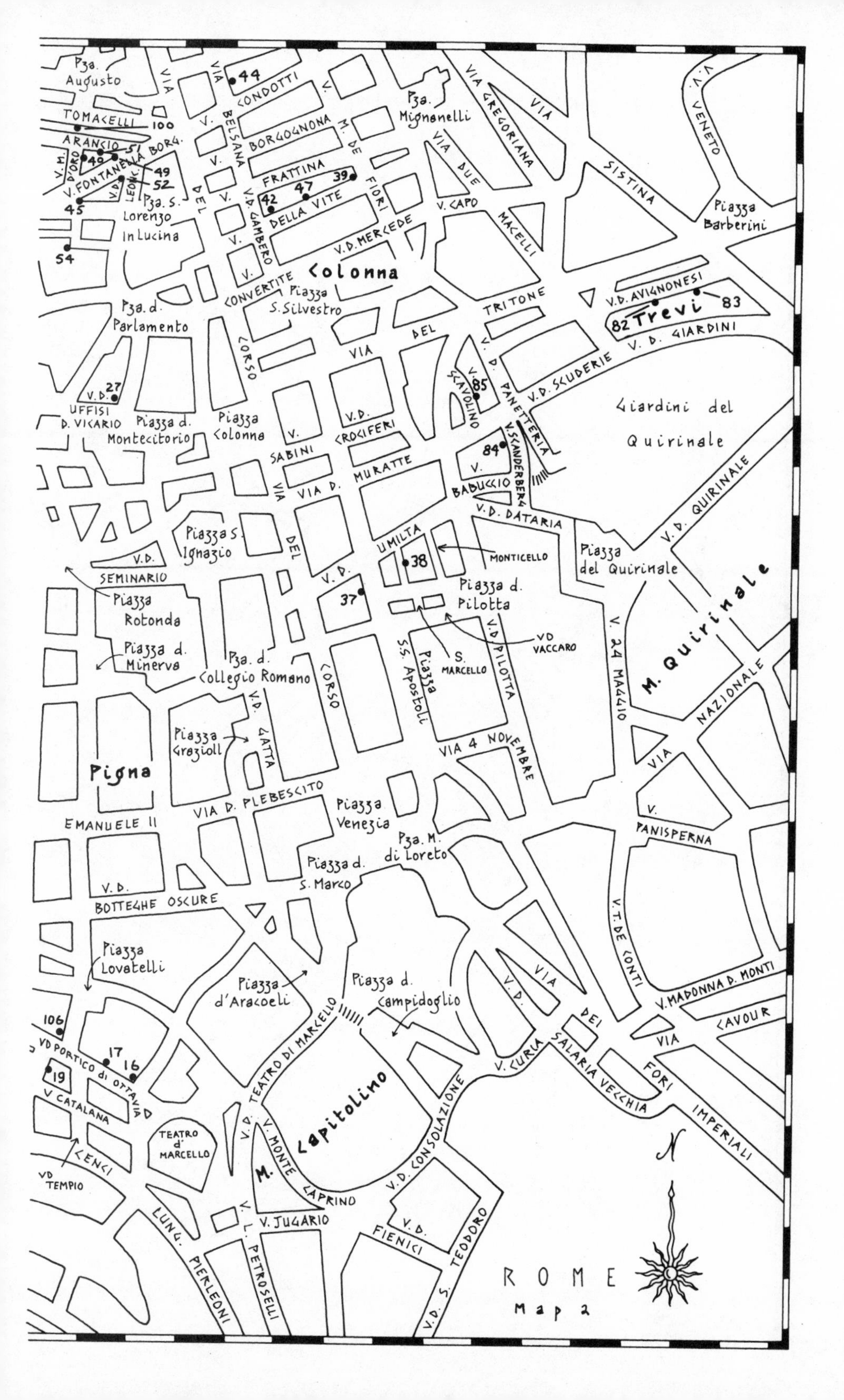

ROME
Map 2
Colonna
Trevi
Pigna
M. Quirinale
M. Capitolino
Giardini del Quirinale
Pza. Augusto
Pza. Mignanelli
Piazza Barberini
Pza. S. Lorenzo In Lucina
Piazza S. Silvestro
Pza. d. Parlamento
Piazza d. Montecitorio
Piazza Colonna
Piazza S. Ignazio
Piazza Rotonda
Piazza d. Minerva
Pza. d. Collegio Romano
Piazza Grazioli
Piazza del Quirinale
Piazza d. Pilotta
Piazza SS. Apostoli
Piazza Venezia
Pza. M. di Loreto
Piazza d. S. Marco
Piazza Lovatelli
Piazza d'Aracoeli
Piazza d. Campidoglio
Teatro d' Marcello
Via Condotti
V. Borgognona
V. Frattina
V. della Vite
V. D. Mercede
Via Gregoriana
Via Sistina
V. V. Veneto
Via Due Macelli
V. Capo
Via del Tritone
V.D. Avignonesi
V.D. Giardini
V.D. Scuderie
V.D. Panetteria
V. Scanderberg
V. Baduccio
V.D. Dataria
V.D. Quirinale
V. 24 Maggio
Via Nazionale
V. Panisperna
V.T. De Conti
V. Madonna D. Monti
Via Cavour
Via dei Fori Imperiali
Salaria Vecchia
V. Curia
V.D. Consolazione
V. Monte Caprino
V. Jugario
V.D. Fienici
V.D.S. Teodoro
V.L. Petroselli
Lung. Pierleoni
V.D. Teatro di Marcello
Via 4 Novembre
V.D. Pilotta
Monticello
VD Vaccaro
S. Marcello
V.D. Umiltà
V.D. Crociferi
Via D. Muratte
V. Sabini
Via del Corso
Via D. Plebescito
V.D. Gatta
V.D. Seminario
Uffisi D. Vicario
Emanuele II
V.D. Botteghe Oscure
VD Portico di Ottavia
V Catalana
Cenci
VD Tempio
Tomacelli
Arancio
V. Fontanella Borg.
V.M. D'Oro
Leonc.
V. Belsana
V.D. Gambero
V. del Convertite
M. de Fiori
Via Schiavolino
Via
Dei
N
100 44 40 51 49 52 45 54 42 47 39 27 85 84 82 83 38 37 106 17 16 19

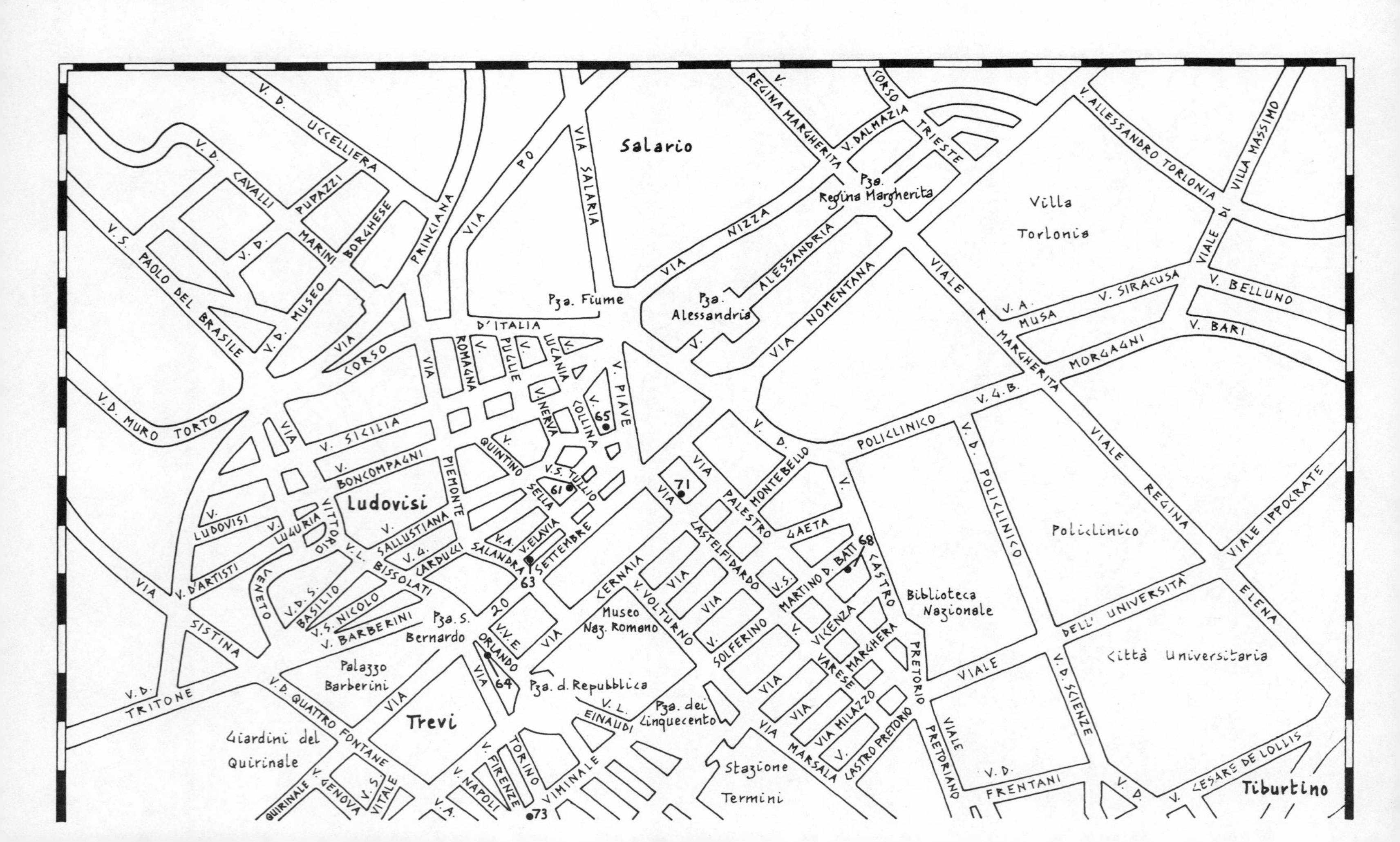
Salario
Villa Torlonia
Policlinico
Città Universitaria
Biblioteca Nazionale
Ludovisi
Trevi
Tiburtino
Pza. Fiume
Pza. Alessandria
Pza. Regina Margherita
Museo Naz. Romano
Pza. d. Repubblica
Pza. dei Cinquecento
Stazione Termini
Pza. S. Bernardo
Palazzo Barberini
Giardini del Quirinale
Via Salaria
Via Po
Via Nizza
Via Alessandria
Via Nomentana
Viale R. Margherita
Viale Regina Elena
Viale Ippocrate
V. Alessandro Torlonia
Viale di Villa Massimo
V. Belluno
V. Bari
V. Siracusa
V. A. Musa
Morgagni
V. G. B. Morgagni
V. d. Policlinico
Viale dell' Università
V. d. Scienze
V. d. Frentani
V. Cesare de Lollis
Viale Pretoriano
Via Castro Pretorio
Via Milazzo
Via Marsala
Via Varese
Via Vicenza
Via Solferino
Via Palestro
V. Gaeta
Via Montebello
V. Volturno
Via Castelfidardo
V. S. Martino d. Batt.
Via Cernaia
Via XX Settembre
V. Piave
V. Collina
V. S. Tullio
V. Sella
V. Quintino
V. Nerva
V. Lucania
V. Puglie
V. Romagna
Corso d'Italia
Via Piemonte
V. Sicilia
V. Boncompagni
V. Sallustiana
V. G. Carducci
V. Salandra
V. Flavia
V. L. Bissolati
V. Ludovisi
V. Lucullo
V. d'Artisti
Via Vittorio Veneto
V. S. Nicolo
V. S. Basilio
V. Barberini
V. V. E. Orlando
V. L. Einaudi
Via Torino
V. Firenze
V. Napoli
Viminale
V. Genova
V. S. Vitale
Quirinale
V. d. Quattro Fontane
V. d. Tritone
Via Sistina
V. d. Muro Torto
V. S. Paolo del Brasile
V. d. Uccelliera
V. d. Cavalli
Pupazzi
V. Marini
V. d. Museo Borghese
Via Principiana
Via Corso
Corso Trieste
V. Dalmazia
V. Regina Margherita
61
63
64
65
68
71
73

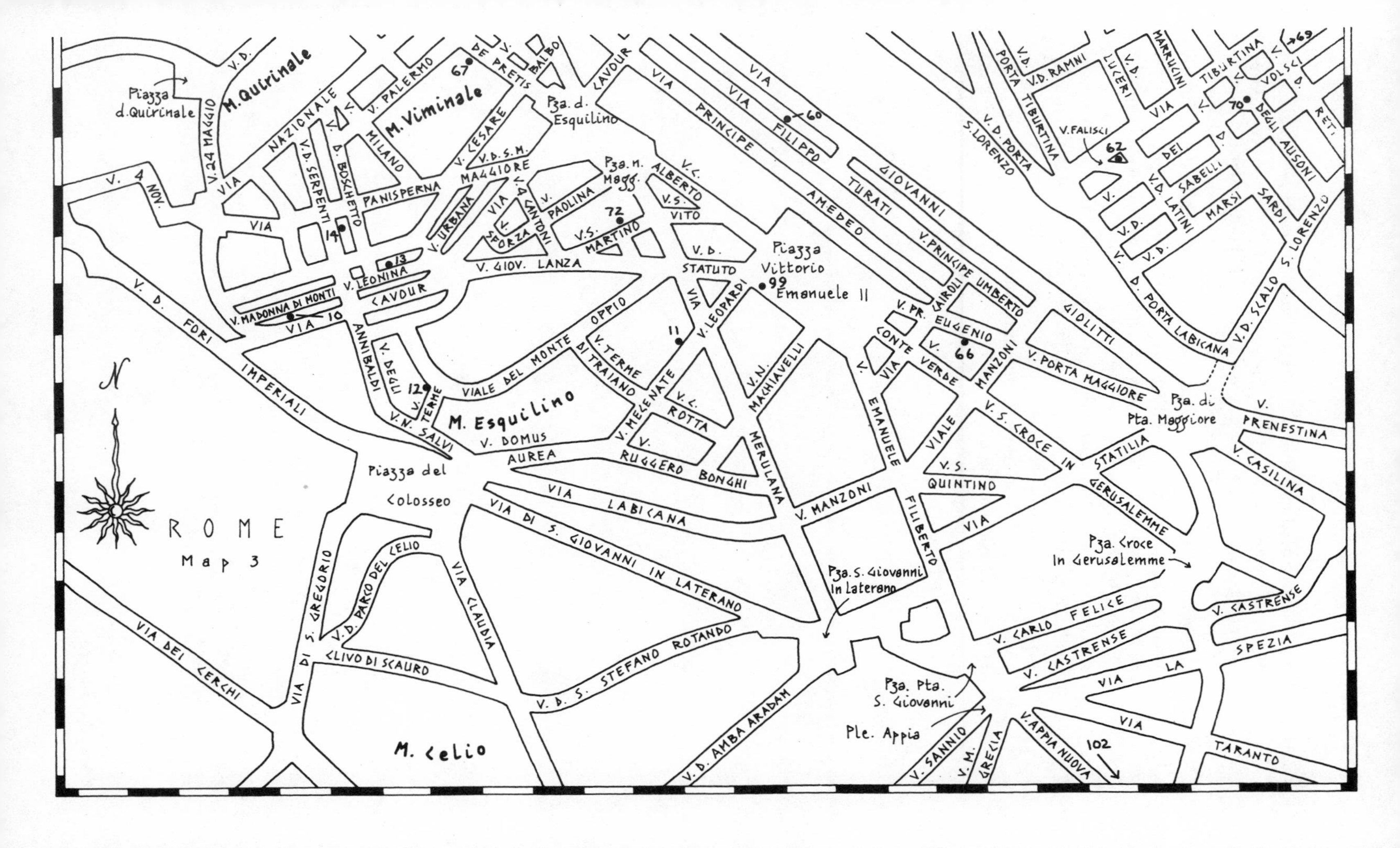

ROME
Map 3
N
M. Quirinale
Piazza d. Quirinale
M. Viminale
M. Esquilino
M. Celio
Pza. d. Esquilino
Pza. M. Magg.
Piazza Vittorio Emanuele II
Piazza del Colosseo
Pza. S. Giovanni In Laterano
Pza. Croce In Gerusalemme
Pza. di Pta. Maggiore
Pza. Pta. S. Giovanni
Ple. Appia
V. D. Fori Imperiali
Via dei Cerchi
Via di S. Gregorio
V. D. Parco del Celio
Clivo di Scauro
Via Claudia
V. D. S. Stefano Rotando
V. D. Amba Aradam
Via di S. Giovanni in Laterano
Via Labicana
V. Domus Aurea
Viale del Monte Oppio
V. Terme di Traiano
V. Mecenate
V. Ruggero Bonghi
V. C. Rotta
Via Merulana
V. Manzoni
V. Emanuele Filiberto
V. N. Machiavelli
V. Leopardi
Via Statuto
V. D. Statuto
V. Giov. Lanza
V. Leonina
Cavour
V. Madonna di Monti
Via
V. D. Serpenti
V. D. Boschetto
Panisperna
Via Milano
Via Nazionale
V. 24 Maggio
V. 4 Nov.
V. D.
V. Palermo
De Pretis
Balbo
Cavour
V. Cesare
V. D. S. M. Maggiore
V. Urbana
Via 4 Cantoni
V. Sforza
V. Paolina
V. S. Martino
V. C. Alberto
V. S. Vito
V. Annibaldi
V. degli Terme
V. N. Salvi
Via Principe Amedeo
Via Filippo Turati
Via Giovanni Giolitti
V. Principe Umberto
V. Pr. Eugenio
Cairoli
Via Conte Verde
Manzoni
Viale V. S. Quintino
V. S. Croce in Gerusalemme
Statilia
V. Porta Maggiore
V. Prenestina
V. Casilina
V. Castrense
V. Carlo Felice
V. Castrense
Via La Spezia
Via Taranto
V. Appia Nuova
V. M. Grecia
V. Sannio
V. D. Porta Labicana
V. D. Scalo S. Lorenzo
V. D. Porta S. Lorenzo
Porta Tiburtina
V. D. Ramni
V. D. Luceri
Marrucini
Via Tiburtina
V. Volsci
Degli Ausoni
Reti
Via dei Sabelli
V. D. Latini
Marsi
Sardi
V. Falisci
10
11
12
13
14
60
62
66
67
69
70
72
99
102

and cheese stirred in just as it is served), *penne all'amatriciana* (pasta with tomatoes, onions, bacon, and hot pepper), *spaghetti alla carbonara* (pasta with bacon, onion, eggs, cheese, and wine), and mouthwatering displays of vegetable, meat, and seafood antipasti laid out with the precision of a fine jeweler. Not to be forgotten is *bruschetta,* made of thick slices of bread toasted on the grill, rubbed with garlic, and sprinkled with oil and a dash of salt and pepper. Popular entrées are *saltimbocca* (which means "hop into the mouth" and consists of thin slices of prosciutto and veal sautéed in butter and wine), *abbacchio* (milk-fed baby lamb roasted, or the chops grilled to perfection over an open fire), and *baccalà* (dried salt cod, usually dipped in butter and fried in olive oil). Desserts are kept simple: a piece of fruit or a dish of fresh fruit. If something more is desired, there is the ever-present *dolci* darling of the decade, *tiramisù* (which means "pick me up"), a rich mix of coffee, cake, chocolate, and mascarpone cheese liberally laced with liqueur.

Restaurants in Rome

The number in parentheses before each restaurant corresponds to a number that marks the restaurant's location on the Rome map (an entry with no number before it is located outside the parameters of the map); a dollar sign ($) indicates restaurants in the Big Splurge category.

RESTAURANTS

Aventine

The Aventine is the most elegant of the seven hills in Rome and the address of embassies. It is also an ideal vantage point for views of the Tiber River and the Palatine Hill.

(1) L'INSALATA RICCA IV
Piazza Albania, 3, 4, 5

TELEPHONE
06-57-43-877
OPEN
Mon–Tues, Thur–Sun
CLOSED
Wed
HOURS
12:30–3 P.M., 7:30–11:30 P.M.

L'Insalata Ricca is a small chain of popular, casual trattorias strategically located around Rome. Several are in the tourist boonies and not listed here, but in addition to this one in Aventine, you will find another close to Campo de' Fiori, near Piazza Navona, another in Aventine, and the newest addition near the Vatican.

All are bustling with families and foreign residents and offer great value and variety, conforming to Cheap Eating budget concerns admirably. For both lunch and dinner, plan to arrive early, because within ten minutes of opening, there is a crowd standing outside waiting for a seat. Once there's room, everyone sits at closely packed tables or on the outside terraces, delighting in the mammoth helpings of their specialties: antipasti, pastas, pizzas, and huge salads. They also have a short list of frozen fish and beef, but these are dishes to be avoided here. Anytime you go, you can always plan on selecting from at least seven or eight regular pastas, plus several daily specials and a tempting list of pizzas in several of the locations. In addition, there are twenty enormous main-course salads, ranging from a basic green to corn, tuna, shrimp, and walnut or cheese and pears. Dense chocolate cake, fruit tarts, mousses, and *tartufo* round out the successful meal. The house wines, including organic varieties, are good. Other pluses included an English menu and a nonsmoking policy that is enforced.

NOTE: The other establishments include L'Insalata Ricca (06-68-80-3656; Largo dei Chiavari, 85—a Campo de' Fiori address spotted as 8 on the map),

L'Insalata Ricca II (06-68-30-7881; Piazza Pasquino, 72—a Piazza Navona address spotted as 32 on the map), L'Insalata Ricca III (06-57-51-76; Via del Gazometro, 62/64/66—an Aventine address that is outside the parameters of this book's map of Rome), and L'Insalata Ricca VI (06-39-73-0387; Piazza Risogimento, 5/6—a Vatican area address spotted as 90 on the map).

Campo de' Fiori and Piazza Farnese

The name Campo de' Fiori means "field of flowers," but the flower market has moved to the outskirts of Rome (see page 144), and now there are only a few flower stalls open during the morning market, which is the most colorful in Rome. Around the market is a maze of cobblestone alleys, fading *palazzos,* crumbling churches, and pretty fountains. Not far from Campo de' Fiori is the serenely elegant Piazza Farnese, with its Michelangelo-designed Palazzo Farnese, now the French Embassy.

(2) COSTANZA ($)
Piazza del Paradiso, 63/65

TELEPHONE
06-68-61-717, 68-80-1002

OPEN
Mon–Sat

CLOSED
Sun, Aug

HOURS
12:30–3 P.M., 8–10:30 P.M.

RESERVATIONS
Essential

CREDIT CARDS
AE, DC, MC, V

À LA CARTE
L50,000, beverage extra

MENÙ TURISTICO
None

BREAD AND SERVICE CHARGES
Bread L4,000, service included

ENGLISH
Yes

Costanza is almost buried in a hidden corner of this tiny piazza a minute or two away from Campo de' Fiori. The rather anonymous exterior masks the warmth of this multiroom *hostaria,* which sits on part of the ruins of the Theater de Pompeo, sections of which are displayed inside behind glass. The attractive interior is a mix of stuccoed walls, low ceilings, and long beams with the expected roundup of wine bottles, paintings, candles at night, and other bric-a-brac. This dark, cozy atmosphere makes it the perfect place for a romantic meal with a special person.

The wide-ranging menu, which holds few disappointments, is admittedly for diners with more flexible budgets. On the pasta front, the *pasta e fagioli Costanza,* a carbohydrate festival of white beans and pasta in a broth with onions, bacon, and tomato sprinkled with grated cheese, is delicious. So are any of the risottos, the seasonal ravioli with artichokes, crepes with spinach and cheese, or the *tagliolini* with salmon and radicchio. From here, you move on to a number of main-course dishes, ranging from steak tartare, grilled or roasted veal, pork, baby kid, and beef to fresh fish and vegetables. The ever-present *dolci, tiramisù,* is featured and is especially rich, as are most of the other homemade desserts. I love the *torta di mirtilli* (blueberry tart) or, for a lighter choice, the zabaglione mousse.

(3) DA GIOVANNI AR GALLETTO
Piazza Farnese, 102

TELEPHONE
06-68-61-714

OPEN
Mon–Sat

CLOSED
Sun, 1 week mid-Aug (usually Aug 15–21, but dates can vary)

HOURS
Noon–3 P.M., 7:30–11:30 P.M.

RESERVATIONS
Advised, especially for outside tables

CREDIT CARDS
AE, DC, MC, V

À LA CARTE
L35,000–40,000, beverage extra

MENÙ TURISTICO
None

BREAD AND SERVICE CHARGES
Bread L2,000, service included

ENGLISH
Yes

Da Giovanni ar Galletto is a perennial favorite because it is a family owned place where every member plays a part. Mama, the *real* boss, runs the kitchen. Papà holds court in the dining room, seating and serving guests who swap stories about their favorite soccer teams. One of the sons-in-law, a colonel in the Italian army, jokes that he ate here as a young man and loved the restaurant so much he married the owner's youngest daughter. After one meal you will understand his enthusiasm. The inside is charming, with its wood-beamed ceiling festooned with hanging hams, hunting murals, and bright orange linen on the well-spaced tables. On warm days, reserve a table outside on the Piazza Farnese, a beautiful Baroque square with fountains at either end, an ideal place to lose touch with everything but what is on your plate and who is across the table.

A full meal can creep into the Big Splurge category if you are not watchful, but with a little care and a liter of the house wine you should be fine. I recommend going easy on the appetizers, thus saving room for a bowl of Mama's homemade ravioli, gnocchi, or fettuccine noodles tossed with zucchini. If you like fish, be sure to order the special *fritto misto Italiano* when you reserve your table. Meat eaters lean toward the *saltimbocca alla Romana,* thin slices of veal seasoned with fresh sage, covered with ham, and sautéed in butter with a splash of white wine. The beef, slowly cooked in red wine with carrots and fresh mushrooms, is another favorite. The desserts are all homemade, but I have never had any room for more than the *fragole con gelato,* fresh strawberries spooned over vanilla ice cream.

(4) DAR FILETTARO A SANTA BARBARA
Largo dei Librari, 88

TELEPHONE
06-68-64-018

OPEN
Mon–Sat, dinner only

CLOSED
Sun, Aug, Dec 24–Jan 3

You need only remember one thing about this hidden Cheap Eat (near the cinema, off Via dei Giubbonari): *filleto di baccalà,* or deep-fried codfish, their specialty. All the fast-food-fish fanciers in this section of Rome flock here. Their version is batter-dipped and quickly deep-fried, leaving the inside moist and the outside crisp. Add a glass of wine and maybe a salad and you should be ready for the next round of sightseeing.

HOURS
5–11 P.M.
RESERVATIONS
Not accepted
CREDIT CARDS
None
À LA CARTE
L10,000, beverage extra
MENÙ TURISTICO
None
BREAD AND SERVICE CHARGES
Bread L1,500, service included
ENGLISH
Limited

(5) GRAPPOLO D'ORO
Piazza della Cancelleria, 80/81

The tourists eat early and the Italians late at this exceptionally popular location on the edge of Campo de' Fiori, so time your visit accordingly. Please note the address carefully so you will not confuse this with two other restaurants in Rome bearing the same name.

Predictable trattoria decor, prices, and traditions prevail, down to the old-time white-jacketed headwaiter managing an overworked staff that has only a nodding acquaintance with English and offers distracted service when the rush is on. However, the excellent food, the warm plates, the good-size servings, and the eclectic crowd make up for the few shortcomings of the service. *Fettuccine con trote* (with trout) or risotto with truffles and mushrooms are delicious first courses. Veal kidneys with polenta, brains cooked in butter, or grilled liver may appeal to some. Less adventurous diners will like the scalloped veal in wine sauce, the *saltimbocca,* or the grilled lamb chops. The *insalata mista* is full of designer greens, radicchio, and tomatoes. For dessert, the *tartufo nero* (chocolate ice cream rolled in dark chocolate) is my choice. Otherwise, there is the usual *tiramisù, torta del giorno* (daily cake or tart), or *panna cotta.*

TELEPHONE
06-68-64-118, 68-97-080
OPEN
Mon–Sat
CLOSED
Sun, Aug (dates vary)
HOURS
Noon–3 P.M., 7:15–11 P.M.
RESERVATIONS
Strongly advised
CREDIT CARDS
AE, DC, MC, V
À LA CARTE
L40,000, beverage extra
MENÙ TURISTICO
None
BREAD AND SERVICE CHARGES
Bread L2,000, service included
ENGLISH
Limited

(6) HOSTARIA FARNESE
Via dei Baullari, 109

At the Hostaria Farnese, you will enjoy homemade food served in a pleasant family atmosphere. The inside hasn't many froufrous, just black bentwood chairs, tables with green tablecloths, and a few outside tables during the summer months.

Everyone gets into the act with the food and service: Mama cooks while Papa and their three daughters and

TELEPHONE
06-68-80–1595
OPEN
Mon–Wed, Fri–Sun
CLOSED
Thur, Aug
HOURS
Noon–3 P.M., 7 P.M.–midnight
RESERVATIONS
Advised

CREDIT CARDS
AE, DC, MC, V

À LA CARTE
L35,000–40,000, beverage extra

MENÙ TURISTICO
None

BREAD AND SERVICE CHARGES
Bread L2,000, 10% service added

ENGLISH
Yes

one son serve. The menu is one of utmost simplicity, featuring healthy minestrone, spinach ravioli, roast lamb, grilled meats, veal scaloppine, pizza for lunch and dinner, and a few desserts. The portions will not overwhelm you, and neither will your bill.

(7) HOSTARIA GIULIO
Via della Barchetta, 19

TELEPHONE
06-68-80–6466

OPEN
Mon–Sat

CLOSED
Sun, Aug (dates vary)

HOURS
12:30–3 P.M., 7 P.M.–midnight

RESERVATIONS
Advised for terrace

CREDIT CARDS
AE, MC, V

À LA CARTE
L45,000, beverage included

MENÙ TURISTICO
L30,000, two courses; bread and service included, beverage extra

BREAD AND SERVICE CHARGES
Bread L2,500, service included

ENGLISH
Yes, also Spanish and Portuguese

Hostaria Giulio is in a wonderful old building that dates back to the early 1400s. Fiorella and Giulio, the charming owners, are into their fourth decade of serving and pleasing their guests. The small dining room has arched ceilings, a beautifully tiled floor, and stone walls lined with black-and-white prints of old Rome and an interesting collection of Sicilian provincial plates. The fifteen tables are covered with light yellow linens and bouquets of fresh flowers. During the steaming summertime, be sure to reserve one of the sought-after tables on the streetside terrace.

The menu features a parade of seasonal dishes. Depending on the time of your visit, you will find good renditions of homemade ravioli filled with spinach and ricotta cheese, fettuccine with garlicky pesto or topped with truffles in a white sauce, and *orecciette* (ear-shaped *semolina* pasta) tossed in winter with broccoli and in summer with fresh tomatoes and mozzarella cheese. Gnocchi is served every Thursday year-round, while veal and fresh fish are always on, along with vegetables, assorted cheeses, and the usual desserts, including wild strawberries in season. When all is said and done, you will not have spent much more than L40,000 or L45,000 per person, including a glass or two of the drinkable house wine.

(9) RISTORANTE DER PALLARO
Largo del Pallaro, 15

TELEPHONE
06-68-80-1488

OPEN
Tues–Sun

CLOSED
Mon, Aug 10–25

HOURS
1–3 P.M., 8 P.M.–12:30 A.M.

Ristorante der Pallaro will not thrill you with a glitzy location or a snappy interior design, but it reflects the loving attention of a chef-owner husband-and-wife team who really care about what is put on your plate—and, after all, that is still the bottom line when it comes to eating out. The cast of characters in the three-room, knotty-pine *ristorante* usually includes a lively mix of families, spry senior citizens, a yuppie or two, and anyone else on the prowl for a satisfying Cheap Eat in Rome.

When you arrive, look a little to the right of the beaded curtains covering the entry and you will see Paolo Fazi busily working in her tiny kitchen. Her husband, Mario, and Carlo, the waiter who has been here a decade and is considered "almost a son," help out front. They offer no à la carte menu . . . whatever Paolo cooks is what you eat, and the portions are so large that even a veteran coal miner after a ten-hour shift would have trouble finishing. You will start with an antipasto, then be served the pasta of the day, which might be spaghetti or *pappardelle* with tomato sauce and cheese. Next comes the main course, which is always veal served with potatoes. Finally there is a piece of homemade peach marmalade cake, all washed down with tangerine juice, mineral water, *and* wine. Coffee is not available.

RESERVATIONS
Advised, especially on Sunday and holidays

CREDIT CARDS
None

À LA CARTE
None

MENÙ TURISTICO
L30,000, four courses; beverages, bread, and service included

BREAD AND SERVICE CHARGES
All included

ENGLISH
Enough

Colosseum/Forum

The main archaeological ruins are concentrated between Piazza Venezia, down Via dei Fori Imperiali to the Forum, around the Colosseum to the Circus Mazimus, and south toward the Baths of Caracalla.

(10) ENOTECA CAVOUR 313
Via Cavour, 313

For a light lunch or dinner accompanied by a few glasses of fine wine, it will be hard to beat the Enoteca Cavour 313, one of the most complete wine bars in Rome. This appealing location features over six hundred different wines and champagnes from every wine-growing region in Italy, as well as wines from France, California, and Australia. The casual atmosphere, with wooden tables and booths, draws everyone from workers in dusty shoes on their way home from the job site to socialites dressed to the nines. Angelo, one of the owners, speaks English and knows his wines. He will be happy to make suggestions about the one thousand–plus wines he always has in stock, or to discuss whatever special wines he is featuring at the time. Lingering is encouraged, and you are free to order as much or as little as you want to eat. Don't expect pizza, pasta, or three-course meals. Instead you will be tempted by beautiful salads, smoked fish, cold meats, cheeses, pâtés, rich desserts, and fruits filled with special ice cream from Southern Italy.

TELEPHONE
06-67-85-496

OPEN
Mon–Fri; Sat–Sun, dinner only

CLOSED
Sun during July and Aug

HOURS
12:30–2:30 P.M., 7:30 P.M.–12:30 A.M.

RESERVATIONS
Advised in the evening

CREDIT CARDS
AE, DC, MC, V

À LA CARTE
L20,000–25,000, beverage extra

MENÙ TURISTICO
None

BREAD AND SERVICE CHARGES
Bread L1,500, service included

ENGLISH
Yes

(11) IL RE DEL TRAMEZZINO
Via Mecenate, 18A

TELEPHONE
None
OPEN
Mon–Sat, bar and lunch only
CLOSED
Sun, Aug
HOURS
Bar: Mon–Fri 7:30 A.M.–8 P.M., Sat 7:30 A.M.–3 P.M. Lunch: 12:30–3 P.M.
RESERVATIONS
Not accepted
CREDIT CARDS
None
À LA CARTE
Sandwiches L4,000–5,000; full meal L15,000–18,000, beverage extra
MENÙ TURISTICO
None
BREAD AND SERVICE CHARGES
No bread charge at the bar, L500 at a table; service included at bar, 10% added at table
ENGLISH
Minimal

There is no telephone number to call for reservations in this residential neighborhood bar within walking distance of the Colosseum and the Forum. Management does not stand on ceremony either. They only care about providing good food and lots of it to hungry eaters in search of a big lunch at a decent price. When you go, check the menu written on a board by the bar or in the front window. You can sit at the bar that wraps around a colorful antipasti display or, in summer, nab one of the sidewalk tables. The typical menu at this lunch-only establishment should put you in fine spirits, especially when it results in such dependable standbys as gnocchi, eggplant *alla parmigiana,* and pasta *all'amatriciana* (bacon, garlic, tomatoes, hot red peppers, and onion). In addition to the daily hot specials, they offer different salads, cold meat plates, sandwiches, and a homemade dessert to wrap up the meal. Because it is a Cheap Eat in a pricey area, this is a very popular destination. You must time your visit to beat the rush because they often run out of the best dishes early.

(12) OSTARIA DA NERONE ($)
Via delle Terme di Tito, 96

TELEPHONE
06-47-45-207, 48-17-952
OPEN
Mon–Sat
CLOSED
Sun, Aug
HOURS
12:30–3 P.M., 7–11 P.M.
RESERVATIONS
Advised
CREDIT CARDS
AE, DC, MC, V
À LA CARTE
L40,000–45,000, beverage extra
MENÙ TURISTICO
L25,000, two courses; beverage, bread, and service included
BREAD AND SERVICE CHARGES
Bread L2,500, 10% service added
ENGLISH
Enough, and menu in English

This classic restaurant is a smart choice for a leisurely lunch between sightseeing rounds near the Colosseum and the Forum. The emphasis is firmly on old-fashioned value, as is evidenced by the many regulars who have been eating here for decades. Some Cheap Eaters have also said that once they found the restaurant, they have never eaten anyplace else during their stay in Rome. The interior is mighty basic: whitewashed walls with a picture or two, white linens on the tables, uniformed waiters who came with the building, hard chairs, and a pay phone by the front door. In warm weather, tables are set up outside so you can dine with a view of the Colosseum.

Before ordering, be sure to take a long look at the beautiful antipasti display and the lovely desserts and plan the rest of your meal accordingly. For lunch, you may want to concentrate solely on these two courses. Otherwise, for the first course, hope that the homemade ravioli stuffed with ricotta cheese and sage in a butter sauce is on the menu. On Thursday, you can depend on gnocchi, and every day you can order their specialty, *fettuccine alla Nerone,* a creamy dish with salami, ham, peas, mushrooms, and eggs. As your main course, order roast lamb, the chicken with tomatoes and peppers in a wine sauce, or the roast rabbit. If you are in a more daring culinary mood, try the calves' brains sautéed with mushrooms and butter, or oxtail. The desserts are worth every calorie. To ease your pangs of guilt, remember, you can walk back to your hotel or spend the afternoon strolling around the Forum and the Colosseum.

(13) PIZZERIA LEONIA
Via Leonina, 84

One of the best slices of pizza you will have in Rome will be at the Werner family stand-up pizza bar within walking distance of the Colosseum and the Forum. It is run by Pietro Werner, his wife, two daughters, and maybe by now with the help of his smiling little grandson, Lorenzo. Every week they feature one kind of pizza at a special price. If you arrive any day between 9 and 10 A.M., there will be a 30 percent discount on your order. It is a virtual mob scene around lunchtime, when the wait for your number to be called seems endless and the crowd ahead of you seems to multiply, not move on. The big trays of piping-hot pizzas are brought from the oven every ten to fifteen minutes, so early or later you will still be guaranteed a delicious choice. The pizzas are cut into pieces as big or as small as you want. I suggest trying two or three varieties, saving plenty of room for a healthy sampling of their apple pizza, replete with warm apple slices and raisins under a light dusting of cinnamon; a taste of the sweet cream and mixed fruit; and at least a few bites of the double-crusted chocolate pizza. There are usually as many as twenty-three other choices you can eat here or munch as you go. On the back wall are another ninety-two possibilities, and if you still don't see the combination you want, ask. If possible you will be accommodated.

TELEPHONE AND FAX
06-48-27-744

OPEN
Mon–Fri

CLOSED
Sat, Sun, last half of July, Aug

HOURS
8:30 A.M.–10 P.M., continuous service

RESERVATIONS
Not accepted

CREDIT CARDS
None

À LA CARTE
From L2,000 per slice

MENÙ TURISTICO
None

BREAD AND SERVICE CHARGES
None

ENGLISH
Yes

(14) TRATTORIA L'ALBANESE
Via dei Serpenti, 148

There is nothing overly glamorous about the Trattoria l'Albanese, but it is a clean and hospitable family-run choice near the Colosseum. There is a garden dining area in back and a plain front room that fills quickly at lunch with committed followers, who indulge in the rich food that is much more familiar to a working farmer than to those who are health-conscious diners.

TELEPHONE
06-47-40–777

OPEN
Mon, Wed–Sun

CLOSED
Tues, July 25–Aug 25

HOURS
Noon–3 P.M., 7–11 P.M.

RESERVATIONS
Not necessary

CREDIT CARDS
AE, MC, V

À LA CARTE
L30,000–35,000, beverage extra

MENÙ TURISTICO
L28,000, two courses; bread, beverage, and service included

BREAD AND SERVICE CHARGES
Bread L2,000, service included

ENGLISH
Limited, but friendly

Dieters need not apply for their pasta specials, especially the *bombolotti alla Norcina* (an egg-rich pasta laden with sausage, mushrooms, and peas in a Parmesan cream sauce) or the cannelloni (fat pasta tubes stuffed full of ground meat, cheese, and vegetables and covered with a thick tomato sauce). The *menù turistico* is a Cheap Eat pleasure that includes several choices of soup or pasta, a meat main course, vegetables, and wine. A slice of the decadent Dominican chocolate cake is extra, but worth it to those of us who consider chocolate to be a daily requirement. To make this even more popular, it is open on Sundays and serves low-cost pizzas and *crostini* in the evening.

Jewish Quarter

It is said that when St. Peter came to Rome, he stayed in the Jewish Quarter in Trastevere, where there were some thirty thousand fellow Greek-speaking Jews and fifteen synagogues. Europe's oldest surviving Jewish community was moved in 1555 to its present location by Pope Paul IV, who ruled that the Jewish Quarter was the only place where all Rome's Jews could live and work. Today, the Jewish population in all of Italy is what it was in Nero's time, and the Rome community is the largest. The Via del Portico di Ottavia, behind the synagogue, is the Jewish Quarter's main street and has some of the best Jewish restaurants in Rome.

(15) AL POMPIERE ($)
Via S. Maria del Calderari, 38

TELEPHONE
06-68-68-377, 68-80-3142

OPEN
Mon–Sat

CLOSED
Sun, July 20–Aug 31

HOURS
12:30–3 P.M., 7:30–11:30 P.M.

RESERVATIONS
Advised

CREDIT CARDS
V

À LA CARTE
L45,000, beverage extra

The Jewish Quarter in Rome is a maze of tiny piazzas, cobblestone streets, small shops, restaurants, and ancient ruins. In the heart of this (off Via Arenula) you will find Al Pompiere, a charming restaurant located on the second floor of the Cenci Bolognetti Palace, which dates from the 1600s. The three simple dining rooms have dark ceilings, frescoes, rustic wooden tables and chairs, and not much else. The emphasis here is on real food for real people.

This is the place to sample Roman Jewish cooking at its best. For the antipasti, *do not miss* the *carciofo alla giudia,* a flattened, fried artichoke that looks like a pressed flower. Another must, whenever they are in season, are the *fior di zucca ripieni,* zucchini blossoms stuffed with mozzarella and anchovies, then deep-fried. Other house specialties include daily homemade pastas, succulent roast baby lamb, *baccalà* (salt-dried cod), and *fritto vegetale,* a plate of crisply fried vegetables. The desserts to order include ricotta cheesecake and the *gran misto del Pompiere,* a taste of everything.

Cheap Eaters will want to know that at lunch *only* they can order from the *menù turistico*, but are relegated to a separate dining room where paper cloths, paper napkins, and lower tabs replace the linens, slightly fancier fare, and much higher tabs that the sprinkling of high rollers are getting in the adjoining room. This popular Cheap Eat lunch deal changes daily and allows you to order as much or as little as you want. In other words, you can get a two-course meal with vegetables, dessert, and coffee, or be happy with a main course and a piece or two of bread.

MENÙ TURISTICO
Lunch only, served in a separate dining room, each course priced individually or L28,000 for everything (two courses, vegetable, dessert, coffee, and bread)

BREAD AND SERVICE CHARGES
Bread L3,000, service included

ENGLISH
Yes

(16) DA GIGGETTO AL PORTICO D' OTTAVIA ($)
Via del Portico di' Ottavia, 21/a

Any trip to Rome would be incomplete without sampling Roman-Jewish cuisine. Nowhere will it be more authentic than in this family-owned trattoria next to the ruins of the Theater of Marcellus. Out front is a large seating area shaded by umbrellas. The inside consists of four rooms done in the usual rustic style with terra-cotta floors, ropes of garlic hanging from the ceiling, and white linens covering light green tablecloths. The ambitious menu is thankfully translated into English.

For your appetizer course, you must try one of their specialties: crisp, tender fried artichokes, fried zucchini flowers filled with mozzarella and anchovies, fried codfish fillets, rice balls filled with mozzarella and covered with a tomato sauce, or potato croquettes. If I order meat, I usually like to stay light on the *primo* course, selecting a simple spaghetti with butter and Parmesan cheese. When I skip the meat and fish dishes, I order something more substantial, say the *spaghetti carbonara* or the *spaghetti con vongole veraci* (with fresh clams). If you are having meat, the osso buco with mushrooms and peas is a filling choice, as is the roast lamb or veal. True to Roman tradition, many unusual cuts of meat are featured. If you're not careful, the beef tongue in parsley sauce, lamb sweetbreads, or the fried brains with mushrooms, artichokes, and zucchini will make a convert out

TELEPHONE
06-68-61-105

FAX
06-68-32-106

OPEN
Tues–Sun

CLOSED
Mon, last 2 weeks of July

HOURS
12:30–3 P.M., 7:30–11 P.M.

RESERVATIONS
Advised, especially on weekends

CREDIT CARDS
AE, DC, MC, V

À LA CARTE
L55,000–60,000, beverage extra

MENÙ TURISTICO
None

BREAD AND SERVICE CHARGES
Bread L3,000, service included

ENGLISH
Yes, and menu in English

of you. The pace doesn't let up with dessert, which offers fresh fruit, ice cream, or a sinfully fattening delicacy from La Dolceroma, an American-Austrian bakery next door run by the owner's son (see below).

(17) LA DOLCEROMA

Via del Portico di' Ottavia, 20/B

TELEPHONE
06-68-92-196
OPEN
Tues–Sun
CLOSED
Mon, July and Aug
HOURS
8 A.M.–1:30 P.M., 3:30–8 P.M.
RESERVATIONS
Not accepted
CREDIT CARDS
None
À LA CARTE
From L2,200 per pastry
MENÙ TURISTICO
None
BREAD AND SERVICE CHARGES
None
ENGLISH
Yes

Stefano Ceccarelli's family has owned the restaurant next door for generations (see "Da Giggetto al Portico di' Ottavia," above). But Stefano wanted to do something on his own. Since he has always been interested in baking, it was natural for him to open La Dolceroma, which sells American and Austrian delicacies and is now one of Rome's most popular and well-known bakeries.

In this tiny place you can see directly into the kitchen from the front room, which has a display case and a table with chairs. Stefano does all of the baking himself, listing the ingredients so you will know exactly what you are eating. And what will you be eating? The list is endless: perhaps chocolate or blueberry muffins or one of several types of cookies, including chocolate chip, peanut butter, and oatmeal raisin. He makes brownies, cheesecake, carrot cake, chestnut cake, pecan pie, and *Sacher torte.* At Christmastime you will find *stollen* and *Linzertort.* If you are not in the mood for any of these, try his hand-dipped chocolates. Everything is sold by weight and packaged to go. If you are here from late spring until October, American coffee and cappuccino will be served.

(18) L'ENOTECA DI ANACLETO BLEVE

Via S. Maria del Pianto, 9A/11

TELEPHONE
06-68-65-970
OPEN
Mon afternoon: bar and *enoteca,* Tues–Sat: bar, *enoteca,* and lunch
CLOSED
Sun
HOURS
Enoteca: 9 A.M.–1 P.M., 5–8 P.M., lunch 12:30–3 P.M.
RESERVATIONS
Advised for lunch
CREDIT CARDS
AE, MC, V

Rising prices for food and services have forced many small restaurants and trattorias out of business in Italy. Coming along in their place are *enoteche* (wine bars) that sell wine by the case, bottle, or glass. In addition, many of these places offer lunch and light snacks geared to complement the wines as well as your pocketbook.

Whenever I am in the Jewish Quarter in Rome, I head for this *enoteca,* where I can depend on having a nice lunch and a glass of good wine. On display are artistically arranged salads and vegetables, assorted cheeses and cold meats, and several hot daily specials.

No one speaks much English on the restaurant side, but it won't matter because you can let your eyes guide you to whatever looks most appealing. Seating is on tables in the *enoteca* and in a back room.

À LA CARTE
L8,000–16,000, beverage extra
MENÙ TURISTICO
None
BREAD AND SERVICE CHARGES
Bread L1,500, service included
ENGLISH
Limited

(19) SORA MARGHERITA
Piazza della Cinque Scole, 30

TELEPHONE
06-68-64-002
OPEN
Mon–Fri, lunch only
CLOSED
Sat, Sun, Aug 7–15
HOURS
Noon–3 P.M.
RESERVATIONS
Not accepted
CREDIT CARDS
None
À LA CARTE
L25,000–28,000, beverage extra
MENÙ TURISTICO
None
BREAD AND SERVICE CHARGES
Bread L1,000, service included
ENGLISH
None

For those who wear sunglasses at night and would not be caught dead without a cellular telephone, Sora Margherita will have no appeal. But for Cheap Eaters, it is very appealing. The menu is handwritten in red and black felt-tip pen on a piece of grid paper ripped out of a notebook. Wine is served in juice glasses, which are placed on paper overlays covering formica tables. In this basement hideaway behind a green door with no sign, chef Margherita Tomassini turns out some of the heartiest and simplest Jewish cooking in the Quarter. She wears slippers to work and stands on tradition, never changing her time-worn menu, which is served only for lunch.

She always fixes fettuccine with cheese, black pepper, and tomatoes or cream sauce, and her specialty—*agnolotti*—a type of meat ravioli. On Thursday she adds gnocchi with tomato sauce. Grilled fish is the Friday highlight, but before ordering, be sure you check the price: is it sold by the gram or the piece? Meatballs are a daily dish, as are the fried artichokes and the veal chops. However, Margherita doesn't bother with dessert.

Piazza del Popolo

The Piazza del Popolo, which means the "people's square," is at the northern entrance to the city. Today the piazza serves as a general meeting and assembly place for celebrations, strikes, or political demonstrations. Standing here you can see the Piazza Venezia at the end of Via del Corso; the Via di Ripetta, which served as a throughway to the Vatican; and Via del Babuino leading to the Spanish Steps. In the center of the piazza is the 3,200-year-old obelisk of Pharaoh Ramses II, the largest in Rome, brought by Augustus from Egypt around 10 B.C.

(20) AL 59 RISTORANTE DA GIUSEPPE ($)

Via Angelo Brunetti, 59

TELEPHONE
06-32-19-019

OPEN
Mon–Sat

CLOSED
Sun, Aug

HOURS
1–3 P.M., 8–11 P.M.

RESERVATIONS
Essential

CREDIT CARDS
AE, MC, V

À LA CARTE
L50,000–60,000, beverage included

MENÙ TURISTICO
None

BREAD AND SERVICE CHARGES
Bread L4,000, service included

ENGLISH
Yes

The food at Al 59 Ristorante da Guiseppe is a triumph of Bolognese cooking and a good reason to make a pilgrimage across Rome. If you can stretch your budget only once or twice for a special meal in Rome, this is a worthy choice. The clean and classic interior is elegant and so is the superb food, passionately prepared by master chef and owner Giuseppe, who is, naturally, from Bologna. Everything from start to finish is made in-house. If you walk by before lunch, you will see several gray-haired men sitting around a large table hand-rolling the tortellini, which is the trademark pasta of Bologna. The meal could begin with antipasto or soup, but I always start with the tortellini with pumpkin or the heaven-sent spinach ravioli filled with ricotta cheese and lightly sauced with fresh tomatoes. Next consider the *bolliti misti*, which is served from a special cart rolled to your table. With a side of vegetables or a mixed salad, you will have a very filling meal. The sheer culinary bliss continues with the desserts, whether it be the plump baked apple or the *crostata* filled with jam.

Because this is so popular with the locals, reservations are absolutely essential, especially for dinner, which is still humming at 10:30 P.M.

(21) AL VANTAGGIO

Via del Vantaggio, 34

TELEPHONE
06-32-36-848

OPEN
Daily

CLOSED
Sun in summer

HOURS
Noon–3 P.M., 7–11 P.M.

RESERVATIONS
Advised, especially if you want to sit outside

CREDIT CARDS
AE, DC, MC, V

À LA CARTE
L35,000, beverage extra

MENÙ TURISTICO
L25,000, three courses; wine or mineral water, and bread and service charges included

BREAD AND SERVICE CHARGES
Bread L1,500, service included

ENGLISH
Yes, and menu in English

An interesting mixture of neighborhood locals and smart Cheap Eating visitors has been filling this family-owned and run restaurant for more than thirty-five years because it consistently offers good food and good value. During my last trip to Rome to do the research for this book, my flat was just around the corner, so I grew to know and enjoy this homespun spot whether I was eating there—again and again—or merely walking by, observing. The owner, Luigi, keeps his patrons well-served and well-fed at the filled tables either in the two rooms inside or on the streetside terrace.

The *menù turistico* is a worthwhile deal that includes several choices for the first and second courses, plus fruit for dessert and wine. If you are going à la carte, you can order a salad and a bowl of pasta without growls of complaint from the properly dressed waiters. The menu has all the popular icons of Roman cuisine, served in generous portions, and in the evening includes pizza. No matter what you are having to eat, be sure to ask for an order of the house pizza bread, which comes to the table in a puffy and hot round, and if you are not careful, will be gone before your first course appears. The house wine is fine, and the final bill will be Cheap Eater friendly.

(22) BUCCONE
Via di Rippeta, 19

The modest business card says "Buccone sells wine, liquors, champagnes, and regional foods." What it does not tell you is that inside this seventeenth-century *palazzo* is a fabulous *enoteca* filled with wines and spirits all clearly organized into region and prices to fit every pocketbook. In addition, they stock an amazing selection of olive oils and balsamic vinegars, and now have opened the back room to serve lunch. Their delicious buffet menu always includes soup, two or three pastas, vegetables, salads, cold meats and cheeses, and tortes, strudels, and lemon cake for dessert. Wine is served by the bottle or the glass, enabling you to sample as you go. It is important to know that you can also stop in any time during the day to have a glass or two of wine at the bar. Francesco Buccone speaks English and is very knowledgeable and proud of his wines. You will recognize his mother sitting at the cash register, holding court while keeping an eagle eye on all the proceedings.

TELEPHONE AND FAX
06-36-12-154

OPEN
Daily

CLOSED
3 weeks in Aug

HOURS
Wine shop: 9 A.M.–8:30 P.M., hot food: noon–3:30 P.M.

RESERVATIONS
Advised

CREDIT CARDS
AE, DC, MC, V

À LA CARTE
L8,500–17,000

MENÙ TURISTICO
None

BREAD AND SERVICE CHARGES
None

ENGLISH
Yes

(23) LA BUCA DI RIPETTA
Via di Ripetta, 36

An interesting neighborhood crowd reflecting the upscale neighborhood two blocks down from the Piazza del Popolo gathers daily for lunch and dinner at this popular whitewashed trattoria. The one-room restaurant, with banquette seating around the sides, is always crowded, a sure sign that the food is delicious and the prices affordable. It has been run by the same family for forty years and has the kind of warm atmosphere and comfortable service that puts you in a happy mood immediately. Service by three waiters and the owner is swift and efficient enough to somehow turn the tables every hour or so without making guests feel rushed.

A carafe of the house red or white wine will complement any of the daily pastas, perhaps *pesto alla genovese* or buttery linguine bathed in a lemon sauce. Don't overlook the roast lamb served with clouds of puréed potatoes, or any of the veal dishes. You can, however, skip the desserts, which tend to be heavy and overpriced.

TELEPHONE
06-68-95-78

FAX
06-32-19-391

OPEN
Tues–Sat; Sun, lunch only

CLOSED
Mon, Aug

HOURS
12:15–3 P.M., 7:30–11 P.M.

RESERVATIONS
Essential

CREDIT CARDS
AE, DC, V

À LA CARTE
L35,000–40,000, beverage extra

MENÙ TURISTICO
None

BREAD AND SERVICE CHARGES
Bread L2,500, service included

ENGLISH
Yes

(24) PIZZA RÉ
Via di Ripetta, 14

TELEPHONE
06-32-11-4468

OPEN
Mon–Sat; Sun, dinner only

CLOSED
Never

HOURS
12:30–3 P.M., 7:30 P.M.–midnight

RESERVATIONS
Essential for dinner

CREDIT CARDS
AE, MC, V

À LA CARTE
L20,000–25,000; pizza from L12,000, salads from L12,000, desserts from L7,000

MENÙ TURISTICO
Lunch only, L16,000, two courses, no pizza

BREAD AND SERVICE CHARGES
None

ENGLISH
Yes

Pizza Ré has been a hit from the get-go because it has its formula for success down pat and delivers what the Romans adore: huge Neapolitan wood-fired pizzas with enough toppings to keep the patrons coming back time and again. The location, a block or so from Piazza del Popolo, is open, airy, and pleasant. The floors are tiled with turquoise and yellow inserts, the yellow walls have murals and blue light accents, the tabletops are plain marble, and the food is served with dispatch. Even though every table is crowded to the point of sharing, and the waiting crowd spills ten deep into the street almost every night, you never feel squeezed in or given the bum's rush. On Sunday you will share your Pizza Ré experience with happy, boisterous families. On the weekends after 10 P.M., women will feel out of place unless they can fit into a strappy size-two minidress and can walk in whatever the shoe craze of the moment is, but the men will only need a dark shirt and a cell phone glued to their ear to feel part of the action.

If you decide to start your meal with a salad, let me advise you to share it because they arrive on a platter and are big enough for three. Two of the best are the *caprese,* made with *mozzarella di bufala,* and the *insalate mista,* with three types of greens, tomatoes, and carrots. All of the thirty-six pizzas almost fall off the plate—you will think you can't finish more than a slice or two, but you will be surprised. They are light and oh so easy to eat. At lunch they offer a *menù turistico,* but frankly, I would save that Cheap Eat for another place. When you come here, you come in the evening and you order a pizza.

Piazza Navona and the Pantheon

Piazza Navona is the most theatrical square of Baroque Rome. It is where the aristocracy rubbed shoulders with the populace at the games and celebrations held here on the site of Roman Domitian's stadium. In the center is Bernini's towering Fountain of the Rivers, and on the west side, Borromini's masterpiece, the Church of S. Agnese in Agone. Now the impressive piazza serves as a center stage in Rome, ringed with cafes and filled night and day with residents, tourists, and hawkers.

The Pantheon, with its majestic marble columns, bronze doors, and domed interior, is unchanged from the day it was erected two thousand years ago. It is the only perfectly preserved ancient building in Rome, and a reminder of the city's glorious past.

(25) DA FRANCESCO
Piazza del Fico, 29

"What are they giving away?" my friend asked as we strolled by this local favorite across the narrow street from a heavy-duty biker bar. At lunchtime it boasted wall-to-wall people inside and almost as many milling outside waiting to get in. What they do is prepare delicious food at fair prices in a lively atmosphere—proving that the public will still support a good thing. The food packs a punch, starting with fettuccine covered in a mushroom cream sauce, *penne all'arrabbiata,* or *tonnarelli* with artichokes. Meatballs in a gutsy tomato sauce, pork stewed in white wine, or ham and beans will keep you going for hours. At night, everyone is back for the self-service antipasti table and the pizza, bursting with tomatoes, mozzarella, and the usual toppings. It is all very informal, with paper table covers and wine poured into drinking glasses by prompt, if inelegant, waiters. Look for it at Via della Fossa, on the corner of Via del Corallo.

NOTE: Pizza is served for dinner only.

TELEPHONE
06-68-64-009

OPEN
Mon, Wed–Sun; Tues, dinner only

CLOSED
Aug (2 weeks)

HOURS
Noon–3 P.M., 7 P.M.–1 A.M.

RESERVATIONS
Preferred for dinner

CREDIT CARDS
None

À LA CARTE
L25,000–30,000, beverage extra; pizza L8,000–15,000

MENÙ TURISTICO
None

BREAD AND SERVICE CHARGES
Bread L2,000, service included

ENGLISH
Limited

(26) FIAMMETTA
Piazza Fiammetta, 8/9/10

The pizza chef in his white undershirt has the ovens stoked and ready to go when the first lunch and dinner guests begin to stream in. By 9:30 P.M., there is not an empty seat at this all-purpose pick near Piazza Navona, run since 1960 by members of the Christiani family. The rustic rooms have "Old West–style" chandeliers with wine carafes as lamp shades. There is a wall mural of the Ponte Vecchio in Florence, a collection of hanging pots, and the mandatory table displaying antipasti and desserts. When you order, look for the daily specials attached to the corner of the menu. Skip the boring salads and focus on one of the pizzas or a grilled meat or fish accompanied by a seasonal vegetable. For dessert, I would suggest the *cantuccini con vin santo,* a glass of sweet wine with *biscotti* to dip into it, or the *castagnaccio*, a chestnut flour cake.

TELEPHONE
06-68-75-777

OPEN
Mon, Wed–Sun

CLOSED
Tues, July 15–Aug 1 (dates can vary)

HOURS
12:45–3 P.M., 7–11:30 P.M.

RESERVATIONS
Advised, especially for dinner

CREDIT CARDS
AE, DC

À LA CARTE
L35,000, beverage extra; pizza L10,000–15,000

MENÙ TURISTICO
None

BREAD AND SERVICE CHARGES
Bread L2,000, service included

ENGLISH
Limited

(27) GIOLITTI

Via Uffici del Vicario, 40

TELEPHONE
06-69-91-243

OPEN
Daily

CLOSED
Never

HOURS
Gelateria 7–2 A.M.; Mon–Fri lunch noon–2 P.M.

RESERVATIONS
Not accepted

CREDIT CARDS
None

À LA CARTE
Ice cream L2,500–15,000; lunch, sandwiches from L2,300, hot and cold dishes from L8,000, beverage extra

MENÙ TURISTICO
None

BREAD AND SERVICE CHARGES
None

ENGLISH
Yes

When ice cream is mentioned in Rome, the hands-down favorite is Giolitti, an always-crowded Art Nouveau *gelateria* near the Pantheon where generations of the same family have been scooping their gelato since 1900. It is admittedly not an easy address to find unless you pay attention to the majority of people within a two-block radius eating ice cream . . . just go the opposite way from which they are coming and you will soon be there. In the early morning, fifteen flavors of ice cream are available, along with cappuccino and a counter full of waist-expanding pastries. On Tuesday through Saturday, light lunches of salads, omelettes, and a few hot dishes are served in an upstairs dining room. Standing at the bar you can order a quick sandwich or more pastries. By 2:30 in the afternoon, there is a three-deep crowd ordering cones or dishes from more than fifty-seven revolving varieties of pure gelato. First you pay for the size you want, then you take your order to the counter. There is no real place to sit while eating your ice cream, but it is fun to join the throng standing around outside and indulge in the premier people-watching this place always affords.

(28) IL BACARO ($)

Via degli Spagnoli, 27

TELEPHONE
06-68-64-110

OPEN
Mon–Sat, dinner only

CLOSED
Sun, Aug, Christmas (2 weeks)

HOURS
Seatings at 8 P.M. and 9:30 P.M.

RESERVATIONS
Required

CREDIT CARDS
AE, MC, V

À LA CARTE
L50,000–60,000, beverage extra

MENÙ TURISTICO
None

BREAD AND SERVICE CHARGES
Included

ENGLISH
Limited, but there is a menu in English

I am always happy to stumble upon places like Il Bacaro. Hidden on a back street, just far enough from tourist central to keep it locally based, it caters to a well-dressed, sophisticated clientele who know and appreciate good food. It is open only for dinner, with two reservation-only seatings. Diners can book for the 8 or the 9:30 P.M. seatings in either the umbrella-shaded terrace or inside the small, understated room, which has a bar in one corner and rather loud music playing over it all.

No matter what time of the year you are here, or where you sit, you can depend on an imaginative meal, well-executed and politely served. The only antipasto is fresh mozzarella with mullett eggs. If that isn't for you, then start with the house salad, which is a pretty array of thin slices of zucchini and fresh Parmesan on a bed of fancy greens, garnished with finely chopped carrots and fennel and dressed with a light vinaigrette. The pastas are all made here and presented in different combinations. I thought the *risotto radicchio e gorgonzola* (risotto with radicchio and gorgonzola cheese) was a creamy delight. The *bombolotti con broccoli e salsicce* combines small macaroni and broccoli with fat, slightly spicy sausages. The meat and fish dishes are prepared with simple respect and without sauces to mask the real flavor of the food. Try the *carpaccio alto di manzo,* tender beef slices cooked on one side and served with chicory and white truffle oil. Also delicious is the *scaloppe alle mele,* veal *escalopes* with apples in a cream sauce, and the smoked goose with kiwi sauce. The fish is as innovatively conceived as the rest of the menu. If you like salmon, try their smoked Canadian salmon with a spicy salsa.

And don't forget dessert! The winner here is the warm pear tart, dusted with powdered sugar and drizzled with hot dark chocolate sauce. The house wine is realistically priced by the bottle, or you can order other vintages by the glass. After-dinner coffee is not served.

(29) I TRI SCALINI

Piazza Navona, 28/32

For a *tartufo* (chocolate ice cream and cherries covered with a bittersweet chocolate casing and swathed in whipped cream) to die for, I Tri Scalini is *the* place. It is big and barnlike, with a long bar, a dreary tearoom upstairs, and lots of tables on the Piazza Navona. Dedicated Cheap Eaters will order their *tartufo* standing at the bar. It will cost double to have it served at a table. If you do sit outside, tell whoever seats you that you are just having a *tartufo,* or you could be seated in the dining section where ordering just dessert would not be acceptable. As noted, full lunches and dinners are served, but they are basically high-priced tourist fare that I cannot recommend.

A word of warning: Don't be fooled by imitations and mistakenly go to Al Tre Tartufi next door.

TELEPHONE
06-68-79-148

OPEN
Mon–Tues, Thur–Sun

CLOSED
Wed, Dec and Jan (dates vary)

HOURS
8 A.M.–midnight

RESERVATIONS
Not necessary

CREDIT CARDS
None

À LA CARTE
Tartufo at the bar L7,000, at a table L12,000

MENÙ TURISTICO
Not recommended

BREAD AND SERVICE CHARGES
None for *tartufo*

ENGLISH
Limited

(30) LA CAMPANA ($)

Vicolo della Campana, 18

It is nice occasionally to have starched linen tablecloths with proper table settings and polite service by accomplished Italian waiters in rooms filled with upmarket diners. You will find this, along with excellent-value-for-money food, at La Campana, one of Rome's oldest restaurants.

TELEPHONE
06-68-67-820, 68-75-273

OPEN
Tues–Sun

CLOSED
Mon, Aug (last 2 weeks)

HOURS
12:30–3 P.M., 7:30–11 P.M.

RESERVATIONS
Advised

CREDIT CARDS
AE, DC, MC, V

À LA CARTE
L40,000–50,000, beverage extra

MENÙ TURISTICO
None

BREAD AND SERVICE CHARGES
Bread L3,000, service included

ENGLISH
Limited

The servings are big and the food robust, so I suggest following the lead of the regulars and ordering as you go along. When ordering, pay attention to the paper menu with its daily and seasonal specials, not the plasticized one. Start with either the house red or white to sip with the *antipasti misto,* which is big enough to share. Next, try the spicy *spaghetti puttanesca* or the fettuccine with butter and mushrooms if you plan on ordering a second meat or fish course. Otherwise, the *pappardelle con salsa lepre* (wide noodles with hare sauce) or the Thursday special of gnocchi are heavy-duty enough to require only a salad or vegetable accompaniment.

The important thing is to save room for dessert. La Campana also wants to make sure you will not miss this course, and most of their offerings are seductively displayed on tables by the entrance, resulting in oohs and aahs of anticipation. Their version of *tarte Tatin* has a spongy base covered with glazed apples. It is not too sweet and is laced with just enough cream to give it an interesting edge. If that does not speak to you, surely one of the cakes, tarts, puddings, abundant fruit creations, or a simple dish of gelato will.

(31) LILLI
Via Tor di Nona, 26

TELEPHONE
06-68-61-916

OPEN
Mon–Sat

CLOSED
Sun, Dec 20–Jan 1

HOURS
1–2:45 P.M., 8–11 P.M.

RESERVATIONS
Not accepted

CREDIT CARDS
AE, MC, V

À LA CARTE
L30,000, beverage extra

MENÙ TURISTICO
None

BREAD AND COVER CHARGES
Bread L2,000, no service charged

ENGLISH
Limited

The Ceramicola family runs this Cheap Eat pick nestled alongside the river not too far from Piazza Navona. It is a good place to remember if you want a nice lunch or dinner in a small family restaurant that caters to the locals, not the tourists. Their pleasant outside terrace with tables and umbrellas is where you want to be when the weather is warm. The knotty-pine interior lined with pictures and photos seems dated, from a less sophisticated era, but the food is always delicious, there is more than enough on your plate, and the bottom line is reasonable . . . all important Cheap Eating criteria. The daily menu features pasta laced with clams, *penne all'arrabbiata* (short, thick pasta with a hot red sauce), several meat dishes, and the usual salads and veggies.

(33) L'ORSO '80 ($)
Via dell' Orso, 33

The same is true every year—all I want for Christmas besides a fiery red Jeep and a week at my favorite spa is another great meal at this wonderful trattoria in the heart of old Rome. The restaurant has been owned for two decades by brothers Alfredo and Memmo and their longtime friend Antonio, the talented chef. Here you will eat truly memorable food, served with gusto and guaranteed to ignite even the most jaded palate. Because the prices tend to be higher than most, reserve this dining experience for a Big Splurge.

The restaurant is justly known for its fabulous antipasti table, and I agree—it is one of the best I sampled in Italy. You name it and it is here, from seasonal vegetables prepared six different ways to dozens of bowls of fish and shellfish. If you are not careful, you could make this your entire meal. But save room, please, for one of the homemade pastas, such as the *papparadelle al salmone,* wide buttery noodles smothered in a creamy salmon sauce, or the spaghetti with fresh clams. Grilled meats are another specialty, as is the impressive lineup of fresh fish. In the evenings, the wood-fired pizza oven is roaring, turning out a limited but delicious selection of crisp-crusted pizzas. After a meal such as this one, dessert hardly seems possible, but I do recommend a bowl of sweet strawberries as the perfect finish.

TELEPHONE
06-68-64-904, 68-61-710

OPEN
Tues–Sun

CLOSED
Mon, Aug

HOURS
1–3:30 P.M., 7:30–11:30 P.M.

RESERVATIONS
Necessary, especially for dinner

CREDIT CARDS
AE, DC, MC, V

À LA CARTE
L55,000–60,000, beverage extra

MENÙ TURISTICO
None

BREAD AND SERVICE CHARGES
Included

ENGLISH
Yes

(34) PALLADINI
Via del Governo Vecchio, 29

There is no sign outside, no seating inside, positively no charm, and definitely no English spoken in this spartan deli, a great place for anyone whose lire are in danger of running out . . . or for those who appreciate a really great sandwich. Only sandwiches are available, made with freshly baked chunks of *pizza bianca* (pizza bread) brushed with olive oil and stuffed with fillings of your choice by two old men wearing undershirts and faded Levis. Surprisingly enough, these are sensational sandwiches, especially the *bresaola e rughetta,* smoked meat and arugula sprinkled with Parmesan and lemon juice. You can either join the lunch bunch and eat standing by the cases of soft drinks and beer that line the room or take your creation with you and eat it as you go. If you do eat here, you are admonished in nineteen different languages by a sign saying, "After using the cups, please throw them in the trash can!"

TELEPHONE
06-68-61-237

OPEN
Mon–Fri; Sat, lunch only

CLOSED
Sun, Aug

HOURS
7 A.M.–7 P.M.

RESERVATIONS
None

CREDIT CARDS
Sandwiches from L4,500

À LA CARTE
None

MENÙ TURISTICO
None

BREAD AND SERVICE CHARGES
None

ENGLISH
None

(35) PIZZERIA DA BAFFETTO
Via del Governo Vecchio, 114

TELEPHONE
06-68-61-617
OPEN
Daily, dinner only
CLOSED
Aug
HOURS
6:30 P.M.–1 A.M.
RESERVATIONS
Not necessary
CREDIT CARDS
None
À LA CARTE
Pizza L10,000–15,000
MENÙ TURISTICO
None
BREAD AND SERVICE CHARGES
Included
ENGLISH
Limited

In Rome, Pizzeria da Baffetto is synonymous with good pizza, and the line that forms at the front door of this matchbook-size spot attests to this. Expect to share your table in this tiny room, which is dominated by a pizza oven, a menu board on one wall, and a small cash desk. The seats are hard, and long stays are discouraged. The only things on the menu besides the sizzling pizzas are *bruschetta,* the traditional preparation of grilled bread covered with garlic, basil, and ripe red tomatoes, and *crostini,* toasted bread with mozzarella cheese and a variety of simple toppings.

(36) TRI ARCHI DA LORETO
Via dei Coronari, 233

TELEPHONE
06-68-65-890
OPEN
Mon–Sat
CLOSED
Sun, Aug
HOURS
Noon–3 P.M., 7–11 P.M.
RESERVATIONS
Advised for dinner
CREDIT CARDS
AE, DC, MC, V
À LA CARTE
L25,000–30,000, beverage extra
MENÙ TURISTICO
L20,000, three courses; beverage, bread, and service included
BREAD AND SERVICE CHARGES
Bread L1,000, service included
ENGLISH
Limited

Tri Archi is the sort of folksy place people frequent when no one is in the mood to cook. The prices are firmly in the Cheap Eat category, making this an address to remember if you want a glimpse of the average Romans and the food they thrive on. The clientele, which ranges from families with noisy children to gray-haired couples who have staked out regular tables, makes for some interesting people-watching. The inside is neat and utilitarian, with orange tablecloths, a few green plants, and a mural on one wall. The sole waiter is a study in efficiency and grace under pressure. The food is simple, standard fare: minestrone soup, pastas with the familiar *ragù,* daily specials, above-average salads, and desserts in the never-mind column. The house wine is perfectly adequate.

Near Piazza Venezia

The majestic Via dei Fori Imperiali links Piazza Venezia to the Colosseum in a six-way traffic circle that underscores Rome's insane driving. The commanding white Vittoriale was built to honor the first king of united Italy, and now houses a permanent museum of tapestries, medieval sculpture, silver, and ceramic works. In the front is an equestrian statue of Vittorio Emanuele, whose moustache is three meters long. This is also the home of the eternal flame, Italy's memorial to the unknown soldier.

(37) BIRRERIA PERONI
Via di San Marcello, 19

There is no spa cuisine at Birreria Peroni—only hearty, stick-to-your-ribs plates of pasta, beans, beef, pork, and veal that appeal to strong-hearted souls who have put in a hard day's work. With the unbeatable combination of enormous portions and reliable prices, all washed down with tall mugs of beer (no wine or coffee is served), it is no wonder that this restaurant has such a following. Unless you arrive early, or go late and run the risk of your favorite dish being sold out, you can expect to stand and wait for a table during the crowded lunch hour. The service is hectic at best, with waiters shouting orders to a harried cashier who somehow keeps it all straight while ringing up everyone's order. Things calm down somewhat at night, but you can still count on sitting mighty close to your neighbor or sharing a table in one of Rome's oldest and most atmospheric restaurants.

TELEPHONE
06-67-95-310

OPEN
Mon–Fri; Sat, dinner only

CLOSED
Sun, Aug

HOURS
12:30–2:45 P.M., 7–11:30 P.M.; Sat until midnight

RESERVATIONS
Not accepted

CREDIT CARDS
MC, V

À LA CARTE
L10,000–20,000, beverage extra

MENÙ TURISTICO
None

BREAD AND SERVICE CHARGES
Bread L350 per piece, 17% service added

ENGLISH
Limited, menu in English

(38) L' ARCHETTO
Via dell' Archetto, 26

An impressive selection of pastas served in mammoth portions, along with a full complement of pizzas, *crostini, bruschettas,* and meat dishes, make L' Archetto one of the restaurants most frequented by Cheap Eaters when they are between Piazza Venezia and the Trevi Fountain.

By all means, try not to be seated upstairs, a small area jumbled with posters, fringed lamp shades, garlic braids, and dried peppers hanging from the rafters along with a display of aging postcards sent by customers. There is just too much going on here, with waiters zipping around as if they are in training for the next Olympics and diners wandering by en route to better seating downstairs (the best tables are in the second room of the basement).

The *only* things to consider ordering are the pasta dishes, pizzas, *bruschetta,* or *crostini.* Pasta aficionados will have a delicious meal with any of the sixty-seven varieties. There is everything from a simple garlic, olive oil, and parsley rendition to fresh seafood (Tuesday and

TELEPHONE
06-67-89-064

OPEN
Daily

CLOSED
Never

HOURS
12:30–3 P.M., 7 P.M.–midnight

RESERVATIONS
Advised for dinner

CREDIT CARDS
AE, DC, MC, V

À LA CARTE
L20,000–30,000, beverage extra

MENÙ TURISTICO
None

BREAD AND SERVICE CHARGES
No bread charge, 15% service added

ENGLISH
Yes, and menu in English

Friday only) and the "Chanel," topped with tomato, garlic, lobster, brandy, cream, and pepper. Pizza eaters have twenty-five choices. For the antipasto course, order a simple *bruschetta* (toasted Italian bread covered with olive oil, garlic, and a variety of other toppings). *Primo* dessert temptations include homemade cakes, *tortas,* gelato, *tiramisù*, or *panna cotta.*

Spanish Steps (Piazza di Spagna) and Via Condotti

The 138 steps were built from 1723 to 1725 to join the piazza with the important places above it, including the Villa Medici and the Church of Santa Trinità dei Monti. In May the steps are banked by potted azaleas, and throughout the year, they serve as resting grounds for an international collection of lounge lizards, who hang out here hoping for some action. The view from the top over the roofs of Rome is worth the climb, but the view from Via Condotti looking up the steps is equally beautiful. The streets leading to the piazza are lined with expensive boutique shopping, especially the Via Condotti, the city's premier shopping street.

(39) AL 34 ($)
Via Mario de' Fiori, 34

TELEPHONE
06-67-95-091

OPEN
Tues–Sun

CLOSED
Mon, Aug (2 weeks)

HOURS
12:30–3 P.M., 7–11 P.M.

RESERVATIONS
Essential

CREDIT CARDS
AE, DC, MC, V

À LA CARTE
L50,000–60,000, beverage extra

MENÙ TURISTICO
Menu "Oscar" del Gambero Rosso or Menu "Roma," L55,000, include appetizer, three courses, salad, wine, water, coffee, and bread. Menu "Syrenuse," L68,000, features fish for every course, salad, sorbet, wine, water, coffee, and bread

Popular, crowded, and romantic, Al 34 was voted Best Value Trattoria in its price category by American Express cardholders in Rome. No wonder . . . it is a wonderful restaurant. Reservations are essential and recommended for 9 or 9:30 P.M. If you eat much earlier, you will be dining with other tourists, and any later could put you standing in the aisles waiting for your table to clear. The cozy, wood-beamed interior is illuminated at night with ceramic table lights. Both dried and fresh flowers add a nice touch, as does the collection of soup tureens and lids displayed near the entrance to the kitchen. The food is typically Roman, and for variety and sheer elegance of dishes offered, the three fixed-price menus are, without question, the best high-class Cheap Eating deals in Rome.

Waiters in bow ties and black vests serve guests big bowls of soup, the best spinach salad in the area, wonderful pastas with imaginative toppings, well-executed meat dishes, and fresh seasonal vegetables. For dessert, any of the homemade cakes can be recommended, especially the chocolate almond torte or the lemon cream, and the *tiramisù.*

BREAD AND SERVICE CHARGES
Bread L2,000, service included

ENGLISH
Yes, and menu in English

(40) ARANCIO D'ORO
Via Monte d'Oro, 17

Located near the daily antiques market on the Piazza Borghese, this typical trattoria is a popular lunchtime rendezvous for the many businesspeople who have offices nearby. In the evening, the mood slows down, and it fills with residents and a stray tourist or two. Arancio d'Oro and its cousins, Settimio all'Arancio (see page 117) and Piccolo Arancio (see page 137), are owned by the Cialfi family and are equally well-known for their friendly hospitality and good food at realistic prices. The only time I have seen them fall a little short is on major holidays (i.e., Christmas or New Year's Day), when other restaurants are closed but they choose to stay open. The help and the kitchen staff operate on a limited basis during these holiday times, and it is reflected in the food and service, which can be mediocre. At all other times, the cooking tempts you with pastas in creamy sauces, sizzling platters of grilled meats, fresh fish on Tuesday and Friday, and a lemon mousse dessert you wish was double in size. Pizzas are served in the evenings only.

TELEPHONE
06-68-65-026

OPEN
Tues–Sun

CLOSED
Mon, July–Aug

HOURS
12:30–3:30 P.M., 7:30–11 P.M.

RESERVATIONS
Advised

CREDIT CARDS
AE, DC, MC, V

À LA CARTE
L35,000, beverage extra

MENÙ TURISTICO
None

BREAD AND SERVICE CHARGES
Bread L2,000, service included

ENGLISH
Yes, and menu in English

(41) BELTRAMME DA CESARETTO FIASCHETTERIA
Via della Croce, 39

I cannot claim to have discovered this uncut Cheap Eat gem, because it has been a household name for over a century. It is now a declared national monument, and when you go, you will quickly see that not much has changed since it opened in 1879. There are still just seven tables with forty place settings. In the 1960s, it was the hangout of important painters, actors, and poets, as well as for the scriptwriters for *La Dolce Vita,* which was conceived over long lunches at the back tables. The restaurant is located on an interesting shopping street that has everything from fishmongers, flower stalls, and fancy bakeries to luxurious lingerie shops and trendy leather boutiques. It doesn't stand out as a flashy spot; in fact, the only name you will see at this address is the word *Fiaschetteria* positioned at the top of the building. The present mix of diners figures into the restaurant's continuing success. At lunchtime regulars sit at shared tables with napkins around their necks, downing their

TELEPHONE
None

OPEN
Mon–Sat

CLOSED
Sun, Aug

HOURS
12:30–3 P.M., 7:30–11 P.M.

RESERVATIONS
Advised, but they don't have a phone number!

CREDIT CARDS
None

À LA CARTE
L35,000–40,000, beverage extra

MENÙ TURISTICO
None

BREAD AND SERVICE CHARGES
Bread L3,000, service included, but tips accepted with a smile

ENGLISH
Yes

food and wine with earnestness. At night, it is mostly couples who live nearby and a few smart visitors who have been tipped off to some of the only affordable food in this expensive enclave of Rome.

No one has ever claimed that this is a health-food sanctuary for the calorie-conscious. There are no food puritans sitting at other tables rolling their eyes in horror as you delve into an outrageously rich fettuccine with veal sauce, a rabbit in white wine, or a filling pork chop. The basic menu stays about the same, but watch for the daily handwritten specials, which reflect the best foods of the season. Desserts fall into the "forget it" pile.

(42) CENTRO MACROBIOTO ITALIANO
Via della Vite, 14 (third floor)

TELEPHONE
06-67-92-509
OPEN
Mon–Sat
CLOSED
Sun, Aug
HOURS
10 A.M.–7:30 P.M.; hot lunch 12:30–3 P.M. (or until food is gone); 7 P.M.–midnight
RESERVATIONS
Preferred for dinner
CREDIT CARDS
None
À LA CARTE
L10,000–18,000, beverage extra
MENÙ TURISTICO
None
BREAD AND SERVICE CHARGES
Bread and service included; L2,000 surcharge for non-members
ENGLISH
Yes

Serious vegetarians in Rome all know about the Centro Macrobioto Italiano, the first macrobiotic center in Italy, which is reached by four long flights of steep stairs or via a white-knuckle trip in a creaking elevator. You can either eat at one of the red marble–topped metal tables or take your meal with you.

From appetizers to desserts, the food is made with organic products and uses no butter. The daily-changing menu offers something for every type of vegetarian, including vegans and fish eaters. You can have macrobiotic grain casseroles, steamed veggie plates, a variety of salads and interesting breads, yogurt shakes, natural ice creams, and fresh fruit, plus vegetable juices, biologic wines, and organic beer.

Because the center is a private organization, membership is required. Normally it costs L30,000 per year to "belong." Visitors are allowed to eat here for lunch or dinner by paying a L2,000 surcharge and showing their passport. If you plan to be in Rome for an extended period and think you will be a regular, it would pay to join. Show your copy of *Cheap Eats in Italy* and the L30,000 annual fee will be cut in half.

(43) FRATERNA DOMUS
Via dell' Cancello, 9 (at Via di Monte Brianzo, 62; close to Piazza Nicosia)

TELEPHONE
06-688-02727
OPEN
Mon–Wed, Fri–Sun
CLOSED
Thur
HOURS
Lunch seating 1 P.M., dinner seating 7:30 P.M.

For an inspiring Cheap Eat in Rome, consider communal dining, family style, at Fraterna Domus, a Holy Hotel run by nuns. In addition to providing very nice Cheap Sleep accommodations (see *Cheap Sleeps in Italy*), the exceptionally friendly and welcoming nuns serve lunch and dinner to both guests and nonguests every day but Thursday. Reservations are required, since each meal has only a single seating. Plan to pay cash, as credit is not part of the deal. The smells coming from the spotless kitchen tell you the simply prepared food is going to be wonderful, and you can trust me that it is. There is only one set-price menu, so make sure you ask what they are serving if you have dietary restrictions. The menu includes a pasta or soup, the main course, a garnish, salad, and dessert or fruit. Wine is extra. They also offer special student prices.

RESERVATIONS
Required
CREDIT CARDS
None
À LA CARTE
None
MENÙ TURISTICO
L22,000, three courses; bread and service included, beverage extra
BREAD AND SERVICE CHARGES
Included
ENGLISH
Yes

(44) I NUMERI
Via Belsiana, 30

Paper cups, napkins, and straw mats on bare tables along with a real popcorn wagon keynote this large informal choice close to upper-crust shopping near Via Condotti. The Italian-style fast food is surprisingly good and always fresh, thanks to the huge turnover for lunch. Everyone orders the pastas or the crepes in winter and their big salads when the heat rises. I like the fusilli tossed with barely cooked zucchini and the *tonarrelli all arancia,* square noodles in an orange-cream sauce. Other favorite orders are any of the daily specials and, of course, the sweet or savory crepes, which range from the house special, with mascarpone cream cheese and chocolate, to the "Honeymoon," filled with honey and nuts.

TELEPHONE
06-67-94-969
OPEN
Mon–Sat; Sun, dinner only
CLOSED
Sun lunch, usually
HOURS
12:30–3 P.M., 7:30–11:30 P.M.
RESERVATIONS
Not accepted
CREDIT CARDS
AE, DC, MC, V
À LA CARTE
L15,000–20,000, beverage extra
MENÙ TURISTICO
None
BREAD AND SERVICE CHARGES
Bread at lunch L2,000, dinner L3,000, service included
ENGLISH
Limited, but menu in English

(45) LA FONTANELLA ($)
Largo della Fontanella Borghese, 86

La Fontanella is a beautiful choice, whether you sit inside in the main room, with its shimmering gold mosaic tiled mural, or outside on the tree- and umbrella-shaded terrace. Heavy white damask table coverings, gleaming silver, and pretty china further enhance the appeal, as do the lighted hurricane candles and fresh flowers. This formal and dignified tone is maintained by owners Nicola and Bruno and their cast of polite waiters wearing maroon vests and black bow ties, unobtrusively serving the attractively clad clientele. Even though you are a visitor in Rome, the staff at La Fontanella never makes you feel that way. Everyone is treated with respect and great dignity.

Dinner begins with a flute of champagne and a plate of nibbles to enjoy while you read the menu. Be sure to

TELEPHONE
06-68-71-582
FAX
06-68-71-092
OPEN
Tues–Sun
CLOSED
Mon, Aug 7–21
HOURS
12:30–3 P.M., 7:30 P.M.–midnight
RESERVATIONS
Advised
CREDIT CARDS
AE, DC, MC, V
À LA CARTE
L60,000–65,000, beverage extra
MENÙ TURISTICO
None

BREAD AND SERVICE CHARGES
Bread L4,000, service included

ENGLISH
Yes

ask about the daily specials, which will reflect the season, and keep in mind as you decide on your courses that the food is rich and the portions generous. For a light antipasto, consider the fried artichoke, served slightly warm and crisply tender—not woody and greasy like the "pinecones," as I like to call them, that you often get. Another nice beginning is one of their salads, each of which is a little different. The *insalata Fontanella* has arugula, cheese, mushrooms, and prosciutto tossed in a light mustard vinaigrette. Serious mushroom lovers will like the raw mushrooms mixed with fresh slices of Parmesan cheese. There is also a baby leaf spinach salad and one made with hearts of palm.

The pastas recall the days when we did not feverishly count calories and fat grams. I found both the spinach and ricotta and the zucchini ravioli to be divine, as were the crepes filled with black truffles. Then there is the spaghetti with seafood and the gamey *paparadelle al sugo di lepre,* wide noodles in a robust hare sauce. Decisions, decisions. Perfectly roasted and grilled Danish and Chianti beef, tender veal, baby Abruzzi lamb, and fresh fish follow. The fish is expensive, but it is fresh and delicious, usually plainly grilled and served smelling fragrantly of olive oil and lemon.

For the dessert of their dreams, Cheap Eaters must treat themselves to the chef's signature creation: a warm vanilla soufflé draped in rich chocolate sauce and gilded with whipped cream. There is also a beautiful dessert trolley, and if it is available, one of you might try the fresh fruit tart for dessert, a lovely mixture of fresh raspberries, boysenberries, and cranberries with a layer of cream placed on a crisp cookie crust. The house wine is good and served by the bottle. You pay only for as much as you drink. While the final bill will be a Big Splurge in the Cheap Eats category, this will be a special meal you will long remember.

NOTE: If you go for lunch, be sure to take a few minutes to wander through the small antiques market held in the square in front of the restaurant.

(46) MARGUTTA VEGETARIANO RISTORARTE
Via Margutta, 118

TELEPHONE
06-32-65-0577

OPEN
Daily

CLOSED
Never

You will not find drab people munching brown rice cakes and thumbing through yoga manuals at this smart, stylish vegetarian restaurant and contemporary art gallery owned by Claudio Vannini. The innovative vegetarian food is served in a relaxed, open, California-style atmosphere with seating on silver metal chairs placed around well-spaced tables covered in yellow cloths. Multicolored lights and attractive plants accent the art exhibits, which change every two months. While ordering à la carte could come close to being a Big Splurge, Cheap Eaters who take advantage of the brunch served daily from noon until 4 P.M. will enjoy one of the best meal deals going, not to mention a healthy one.

The food keeps pace with the contemporary surroundings and is, in a word, wonderful. Using only the freshest ingredients, the chef creates an array of vegetarian dishes that even the most militant carnivore will appreciate and enjoy. The menu changes with the seasons, but some tried-and-true dishes always remain. For instance, the pumpkin pudding with broccoli and herbs, the wild rice salad garnished with artichokes and fresh Parmesan cheese, and the stuffed vegetables au gratin are three appetizers guests adore. All the pastas are made here. I always look forward to the ravioli with artichokes and black truffles in a cheese sauce or Sicilian pasta with eggplant and salted ricotta cheese for my second course. Other favorites include risottos, grilled or quick-fried vegetables, and the soy hamburger made with mushrooms, spinach, potatoes, and tomatoes. The salads are varied and enormous, and if you are not starving, they could be meals in themselves when accompanied with whole-grain bread and a fancy dessert. The desserts are worth seriously cheating on your diet, especially the *semifreddo,* made with toasted almonds and honey and served with chocolate sauce.

HOURS
Noon–4 P.M., 7:30 P.M.–midnight

RESERVATIONS
Required on weekends, important for dinner, advised for lunch

CREDIT CARDS
AE, V

À LA CARTE
L40,000–50,000, beverage extra

MENÙ TURISTICO
Brunch buffet, Mon–Sat, L12,000, for one trip to the buffet, includes wine and water; Sun L35,000 for as much as you can eat, includes water and American coffee. Menu Degustazione, L40,000, includes two appetizers, two first courses, two second courses, and dessert, beverage extra. Menù Turistico, lunch only, L20,000, includes two courses, vegetable, and mineral water

BREAD AND SERVICE CHARGES
Bread L4,000, service included

ENGLISH
Yes, and menu in English

(47) MARIO ($)
Via della Vite, 55

No one ever comes to pick and nibble at Mario's, a typical Tuscan-style trattoria with whitewashed walls, raffia-covered chairs, bottles of Chianti on the tables, and service that ranges from friendly and attentive to rather slow but no one cares. For forty years it has been run by the Mariani family, and it's a popular eating destination for both Romans and visitors. I think it is fine for lunch but best for dinner, when there is a crowded, happy atmosphere. Because of the crunch during this prime time, always arrive with a dinner reservation.

TELEPHONE
06-67-83-818

OPEN
Mon–Sat

CLOSED
Sun, Aug

HOURS
12:30–3 P.M., 7–11 P.M.

RESERVATIONS
Strongly advised

CREDIT CARDS
AE, DC, MC, V

À LA CARTE
L50,000, beverage extra

MENÙ TURISTICO
None
BREAD AND SERVICE CHARGES
Bread L3,000, service included
ENGLISH
Yes, and menu in English

This is definitely the place to sample classic Tuscan fare, including *ribollita,* a heavy bread-thickened soup, and the famous *bistecca alla fiorentina,* a big steak rubbed with olive oil and herbs and grilled until just pink. Other dishes to consider are the braised beef with polenta, any of the daily specials, and, when in season, the wild boar and pheasant. Your wine should be a bottle of the house Chianti Classico. For dessert, I recommend zeroing in on the *tiramisù,* a liqueur-soaked layering of cake, marsala wine, espresso coffee, and creamy mascarpone cheese.

(48) PASTICCERIA D'ANGELO
Via della Croce, 30

TELEPHONE
06-67-82-556, 67-83-924
OPEN
Daily
CLOSED
Never
HOURS
Bar 7:30 A.M.–9 P.M.; lunch 12:30–3 P.M.
RESERVATIONS
Not necessary
CREDIT CARDS
AE, DC, MC, V
À LA CARTE
L10,000–20,000, beverage extra; pastries from L1,800, sandwiches from L3,000
MENÙ TURISTICO
None
BREAD AND SERVICE CHARGES
None
ENGLISH
Limited

For power snacking or lunching, the Pasticceria d'Angelo in the heart of Rome's premier shopping district is a *must.* It is open from 7:30 A.M. until 9 P.M., with continuous service from the bar and pastry counter and lunch service from 12:30 P.M. until 3 P.M. It's a good place to start the day with a quick cappuccino and warm roll or other tantalizing delight made in their kitchen. Later on, between shopping sprints, you can order lunch from the cafeteria line, where the daily offerings include assorted antipasti, salads, soups, pastas, and meats.

The nice thing about eating here is that you can have just a bowl of soup or indulge in a four-course blowout if you are stoking up for heavy-duty afternoon shopping. Freshly made sandwiches are also available, but these must be eaten standing at one of the bar tables in front. If you are on the run, ask to have your order wrapped to go: *da portare via.*

(49) PIZZERIA AL LEONCINO
Via del Leoncino, 28

TELEPHONE
06-68-76-306
OPEN
Mon–Tues, Thur–Sun
CLOSED
Wed, Aug
HOURS
1–2:30 P.M., 7 P.M.–midnight
RESERVATIONS
Not necessary
CREDIT CARDS
None
À LA CARTE
Pizzas from L9,000–14,000

Look for pizza, pizza, and more pizza at Al Leoncino, a three-room knotty-pine pizzeria with formica tabletops and hooks around the walls to hold winter coats. The service is fast, the pizzas inexpensive, the ambience as informal as it gets, and the place popular. What more can any Cheap Eater ask? The hardworking pizza chefs cook crisp-crust creations in the wood-fired oven in full view of the diners. Romans know their pizza, so when it is good and cheap, expect to wait, especially here, as few other pizzerias in the area are open for lunch. Wine sells for L6,000 a half-liter, calzone wrapped around eggs, cheese, and ham for L11,000, and the meal-size pizza from L9,000 to L14,000. You will leave happily satisfied with this Cheap Eat.

MENÙ TURISTICO
None
BREAD AND SERVICE CHARGES
None
ENGLISH
No, but menu in English

(50) RE DEGLI AMICI ($)
Via della Croce, 33B

This five-room restaurant is a Roman institution—it has red-and-white tablecloths, murals on the ceiling, local artists' works lining the walls, and brash waiters racing about madly. People continue to come here for the classic trattoria cooking, which offers multiple-choice self-service antipasti, a full complement of pastas, succulent grilled meats, and wood-fired pizzas to hungry audiences. Re Degli Amici also upholds the long-standing Roman tradition of serving a particular dish on certain days of the week. On Tuesday and Friday fresh fish are the specials. On Thursday, you can count on gnocchi; Saturday is tripe. Pizzas are available every evening, and lasagna is baked daily. A big bonus for many Cheap Eaters is that you can select your entire meal from the beautiful antipasti buffet, or order just a first or second plate, along with maybe a salad to start or a dessert to finish, and not suffer from a grumpy waiter who expects you to order the works.

TELEPHONE
06-67-95-380, 67-82-555
OPEN
Tues–Sun
CLOSED
Mon, third week of Jan–Feb, July (first 2 weeks)
HOURS
12:30–3 P.M., 7:30–10:30 P.M.
RESERVATIONS
Advised for dinner
CREDIT CARDS
AE, DC, MC, V
À LA CARTE
L50,000, beverage extra; pizza L15,000
MENÙ TURISTICO
None
BREAD AND SERVICE CHARGES
Bread L3,000, service included
ENGLISH
Yes

(51) SETTIMIO ALL'ARANCIO
Via dell' Arancio, 50

Settimio all'Arancio is part of a trio of trattorias run by the Cialfi family. The other two are Arancio d'Oro (see page 111) and Piccolo Arancio (see page 137). The mood here is exactly right for a neighborhood dining establishment, with wholesome, well-prepared food served in two small whitewashed dining rooms with green-and-white table linens. In summer the dining moves to one of the tables on the street, shielded from traffic by a wall of planter boxes filled with trees and shrubs.

Go for the *misto fritto* of fried zucchini, olives, and artichokes for your appetizer, the *fusilli alla melanzana* or *farfalle ai fiore di zucca* for your pasta dish, and on Fridays always order the grilled fish. Dreamy desserts include the lemon mousse or *tiramisù.* The menus at all three places are virtually the same.

TELEPHONE
06-68-76-119
OPEN
Mon–Sat
CLOSED
Sun, Aug
HOURS
12:30–3 P.M., 7–11:30 P.M.
RESERVATIONS
Advised
CREDIT CARDS
AE, DC, MC, V
À LA CARTE
L35,000, beverage extra
MENÙ TURISTICO
None
BREAD AND SERVICE CHARGES
Bread L2,000, service included
ENGLISH
Some, and menu in English

(52) SUPERNATURAL BISTROT PIZZERIA VEGETARIANA

Via del Leoncino, 38

TELEPHONE
06-68-67-480

OPEN
Daily

CLOSED
Never

HOURS
Noon–3:30 P.M., 7–11 P.M.

RESERVATIONS
Not accepted

CREDIT CARDS
None

À LA CARTE
L30,000, beverage extra; pizzas from L11,000, large salads from L10,000

MENÙ TURISTICA
None

BREAD AND SERVICE CHARGES
Bread L1,500, service included

ENGLISH
Yes

Vegetarians do not need to worry for a minute about being well-fed in Italy, where they can find an abundance of dishes, from appetizer through main course and dessert, to satisfy even the most militant meatless diner. A case in point is this corner vegetarian haven about five minutes from the Spanish Steps. As you can see from the name of the place, they have left little to chance in terms of pleasing their patrons. Here you can check out the menu written on a white board and indulge in assorted pizzas; calzoni; soy-based dishes including a stew, hamburger, and wurst; a handful of salads and toasts; vegetarian pastas, strudels, and kebabs; plus carrot, coconut, or apple nut pie. Order the house red or white wine and a cup of barley coffee, if you must, to finish. The inside is small and laid-back, but with a certain air of sophistication that comes from the huge prints by Walasse Ting and the Chinese pots of fresh flowers on most of the tables. The menu has two pages of quotes about the virtues of being a vegetarian (in both Italian and English) from famous vegetarians including Leonardo da Vinci, Thomas Edison, and Albert Schweitzer.

(53) TRATTORIA OTELLO ALLA CONCORDIA ($)

Via della Croce, 81

TELEPHONE
06-68-91-178

OPEN
Mon–Sat

CLOSED
Sun, Jan–Feb

HOURS
12:30–3 P.M., 7:30–11 P.M.

RESERVATIONS
Recommended

CREDIT CARDS
AE, DC, MC, V

À LA CARTE
L40,000–50,000

MENÙ TURISTICO
L36,000, includes two courses, potato or salad, fruit or cheese, wine or water

BREAD AND SERVICE CHARGES
Bread L3,000, service included

ENGLISH
Enough, and a menu in English, but not for the specials

The off-the-street setting of the Otello alla Concordia consists of three inside rooms and a vine-covered garden with a dramatic vegetable display. The restaurant has long been a favorite because of its consistency and good value. The wide-ranging menu covers the bases of Roman cuisine nicely, listing a series of handwritten seasonal and daily specials that should be carefully considered because they reflect the best efforts of the kitchen that day. Unfortunately, the person writing the specials on the daily menu flunked penmanship, but if you concentrate, you can figure most of it out. In the early days of spring, start with prosciutto and fresh melon or a linguine tosssed with shrimp and arugula. The daily main courses include tripe, roast pork, veal, lamb, and sausage fixed almost any way you want. If you are in a hurry, look at the *piatti espressi,* which highlights grilled meats, quickly deep-fried vegetables that are not fattening unless you think they are, and brains in butter that are good *only* if you think they are. Fresh fish is served on Tuesday, Wednesday, Friday, and Saturday and wines from Castelli Romani and Tuscany are poured with your meal.

NOTE: There is a nonsmoking section.

(54) VINI E BUFFET
Piazza della Toretta, 60

"This is a place for people; I am here for the neighborhood," states Victorio, the hospitable owner who has indeed been here for his loyalists for better than a decade. Inside there are twelve white-tiled tables with grape-accented centers that seat thirty-eight patrons. The stark white walls carry the grape theme further with displays of prints of many varieties. A seasonal menu changes four times a year and lists appetizers, *crostini,* main-course salads, cheeses, and cold plates. Wine is sold by the bottle, and you pay only for what you drink, or if you want to experiment with several of Victorio's regional Italian wines, you can order by the glass. This is a good watering hole to keep in mind if you are between the Spanish Steps and Piazza Navona.

TELEPHONE
06-68-71-445

OPEN
Mon–Sat

CLOSED
Sun, 4–5 days around Aug 15

HOURS
12:20–3 P.M., 7–11 P.M.

RESERVATIONS
Dinner only

CREDIT CARDS
None

À LA CARTE
L10,000–20,000, beverage usually extra

MENÙ TURISTICO
None

BREAD AND SERVICE CHARGES
Bread L2,000, service included

Testaccio

The Testaccio is not known for its designer boutiques, dainty tearooms, or matrons who lunch. This was once the slaughterhouse area of Rome, and many butcher shops are still in full swing. As you can imagine, food was, and still is, geared toward burly workers who do not worry about cholesterol or their waistline. The area is now high on the trendy index, and it is well worth a meal foray, especially for those eager to add another cuisine experience to their roster. The morning market in Piazza Testaccio is one of Rome's best and a good view of how and what the locals are eating at any time of year.

(55) AL VECCHIO MATTATOIO
Piazza Orazio Giustiniani, 2

I think the best time to eat at Al Vecchio Mattatoio is for Sunday lunch, when the pine-paneled dining room is bursting with extended families enjoying themselves to the fullest. Name a body part and it is probably on the menu and ordered with gusto by the well-fed patrons who roar through heaping plates of tripe, *pajata* (veal

TELEPHONE
06-57-41-382

OPEN
Wed–Sun; Mon, lunch only

CLOSED
Tues, Aug 15–31

HOURS
12:30–3 P.M., 7:30–11 P.M.

RESERVATIONS
Advised
CREDIT CARDS
None
À LA CARTE
L40,000–45,000, beverage extra
MENÙ TURISTICO
None
BREAD AND SERVICE CHARGES
No bread charge, 12% service added
ENGLISH
None, but there is a menu in English

intestines), liver, sweetbreads, or the more recognizable oxtail stew. For the conservatives among you, there is roast pork or veal, a lamb dish, and often beef. But quite frankly, if you are going to venture into this corner of Rome, plan to order what the area is known for and what the chefs do best, otherwise it really is not worth the safari. Of course, there are plenty of antipasti, salads, vegetables, and desserts to round out the meal. Strong wines go well with this type of food, so if you go for lunch, you probably do not want to plan too active an afternoon.

(56) BUCATINO
Via Luca della Robbia, 84/86

TELEPHONE
06-57-46-886
OPEN
Tues–Sun
CLOSED
Mon, end of July to Aug 15
HOURS
Noon–3 P.M., 7–11 P.M.
RESERVATIONS
Advised
CREDIT CARDS
DC, V
À LA CARTE
L32,000, beverage extra; pizza L9,000–12,000
MENÙ TURISTICO
None
BREAD AND SERVICE CHARGES
Bread L2,000, service included
ENGLISH
Yes

Bucatino is a popular tavern with three main rooms: two upstairs and a large one downstairs. I like to sit in the big room upstairs because it is more central to the interesting action and not as claustrophobic or stuffy as the room downstairs. Avoid at all costs the closet-size anteroom to your left as you walk in the door.

For the most inexpensive meal in the evening, have a pizza or pasta with a salad and maybe a dessert. On Fridays, the *pasta e ceci*—pasta with garbanzo beans in an onion, garlic, and tomato sauce—is a wonderful choice. So is the *bucatini all'amatriciana,* spaghetti covered in a thick tomato and bacon sauce. Main-course standbys are the *trippa alla romana, coda all vaccinara* (oxtail stew), roast veal with potatoes, or any fresh fish. Those eager to engage in off-beat dining should be satisfied for a *long* time with the *coratella alla Veneta:* lamb's heart, lung, liver, and spleen cooked in olive oil and seasoned with lots of pepper and onion. You will need a strong red wine to get you through this one.

(57) CHECCHINO DAL 1887 ($)
Via Monte Testaccio, 30

TELEPHONE
06-57-46-318
TELEPHONE AND FAX
06-57-43-816
E-MAIL
checchino@usa.net
INTERNET
www.checchino-dal-1887.com
OPEN
Tues–Sat; Oct–May, Sun lunch also

I urge you: Please do not let the location or the many unusual specialty dishes this restaurant is famous for turn you off. Checchino dal 1887 is one of Rome's most elegant and sophisticated dining choices. When it opened in 1887, it was a place to drink wine. Today you can see the original wine license hanging on the wall next to a picture of the great-great-grandfather and -grandmother of the Mariani family, which is still firmly in command. In addition to its fine food, the restaurant is known for its diversity of wines, with over four hundred varieties housed in a naturally temperature controlled underground *cave* that dates back to 75 B.C. You can pay up to L800,000 for a museum-quality wine, but there are also scores of wines available for L12,000 to L25,000, as well as monthly featured wines that are affordably priced.

The dining room is beautiful, with original marble-topped tables accented by embroidered napkins and fresh yellow roses, the favorite flower of the owner's mother, who can usually be found sitting behind the cash register at the entrance. During warm weather, tables are placed outside on the front terrace of the restaurant.

The menu is not only translated into English, but each dish is explained so you will know exactly what you are eating. You will soon realize that this is *very* important. The Testaccio location means an emphasis on meats of all kinds, especially entrails, which most Americans would never consider trying. I can promise you that even though you think you would never *taste,* let alone *like,* veal kidneys, lamb's brains, oxtail stew, or pig's trotters . . . here they are raised to a gourmet level and are indeed delicious. I was wary, but after one meal, I was impressed and eager to return. To begin, there is head cheese, macaroni with calf's intestines, rendered pig's cheeks in ewe's milk cheese, or veal foot, boiled, boned, and served in salad with carrots, beans, celery, and dressing. Any one of these is wonderful, I promise you. To follow, you will find oxtail stew, tripe, veal intestines stewed or grilled, and the jackpot entrée: *arrosto misto,* which offers a sampling of roasted sweetbreads, calf's small intestines, and marrow. Tamer tastes need not stay away, as there are many other choices, including their specialty lamb dish: *abbacchio alla cacciatora,* bite-size pieces of lamb sautéed in white wine, white vinegar, rosemary, and red pepper. If you order this, you get a bonus: a pretty ceramic plate from the restaurant to take home as a souvenir.

To finish your meal, you can order from a long list of interesting cheeses, or homemade sweets, each served with a glass of an appropriate wine. From beginning to end, the service is impeccable, the food delicious, and the time memorable. Please do yourself a favor and try it as a special Big Splurge.

CLOSED
Sun from June–Sept, Sun dinner Oct–May, Mon, Aug, Christmas (1 week)

HOURS
12:30–3 P.M., 8–11 P.M.

RESERVATIONS
Required

CREDIT CARDS
AE, DC, MC, V

À LA CARTE
L60,000–70,000, beverage extra

MENÙ TURISTICO
None

BREAD AND SERVICE CHARGES
Included

ENGLISH
Yes, and menu in English

(58) DA FELICE
Via Mastro Giorgio, 29

TELEPHONE
06-57-46-800
OPEN
Mon–Sat
CLOSED
Sun, Aug
HOURS
12:30–2:30 P.M., 7:30–9:30 P.M.
RESERVATIONS
Not accepted
CREDIT CARDS
None
À LA CARTE
L20,000–28,000, beverage extra
MENÙ TURISTICO
None
BREAD AND SERVICE CHARGES
Bread L2,000, service included
ENGLISH
None

What a place! What a find! Don't look for a sign outside, a printed menu anywhere, English to be spoken, coffee to be served, credit cards to be accepted, or much charm, other than the mega-dose of local color provided by the other patrons. You will dine in a simple room amid roughcast laborers, rotund men mopping their plates with chunks of bread, and perhaps a teased bleached blond in spike heels who keeps the mix interesting. The gruff owner keeps a *riservato* sign on all the tables, not that anyone has booked them—it is just his way of looking you over and deciding if he wants to bother with you. The daily menu depends on the mood of the chef and what the market has to offer. The waiters rattle off the selections in rapid-fire, and you are expected to select from his first reciting, so if your Italian is rudimentary, this may not be your Cheap Eat. There is nothing dainty about the recipes or the servings. It is all he-man fare guaranteed to put hair on anyone's chest. When you are through, you will have been wined and dined for around L25,000.

(59) VOLPETTI PIÚ
Via Alessandro Volta, 8/10

TELEPHONE
06-57-44-306
OPEN
Mon–Sat
CLOSED
Sun
HOURS
9:30 A.M.–3:30 P.M., 5:30–9:30 P.M.
RESERVATIONS
Not necessary
CREDIT CARDS
AE, MC, V
À LA CARTE
Most dishes sold by 100 grams, three-course meal L15,000, beverage extra
MENÙ TURISTICO
None
BREAD AND SERVICE CHARGES
None
ENGLISH
Limited, but you won't need it

Volpetti Piú is a wonderful deli and self-service restaurant around the corner from the gourmet shop, bakery, and cheese shop of the same name (see "Food Shopping in Rome," page 144). At the restaurant, the service is swift and simple, as in most cafeterias: you look, select, pay, have it warmed if necessary, and then take it to your seat.

The *pizza bianca* is divine, and so are the daily dishes featuring the foods and fabulous cheeses from the gourmet shop. Everything you see can be packaged to go.

Train Station, San Lorenzo, and Santa Maria Maggiore

Most of the immediate area around the train station should be considered Tourist Trap Central. There are, however, always exceptions and of course *Cheap Eats* has found them for you.

San Lorenzo is in the center of the sprawling University of Rome. The streets, named for ancient tribes of the Italian peninsula, are undergoing renewed vigor and the area is now considered a contemporary place to live. The restaurants here are mostly of the pizza-and-students variety.

Four blocks down from the railroad station on top of the Esquiline, one of the seven hills of Rome, is the Basilica of Santa Maria Maggiore, one of the major basilicas of Rome and officially part of Vatican City.

(60) AL FAGIANETTO
Via Filippo Turati, 21

Restaurants near train stations tend to be overpriced tourist traps with uninspired chefs and bored waiters. Al Fagianetto is definitely not in this category, and it gets my vote for serving some of the best-priced and most satisfying fare in this difficult area.

The comfortable dining room is hospitable and justifiably busy, especially at lunch. For both the first and second courses there are more than twenty options. I like to start with the *tonnarelli alla ciociara* (pasta with mushrooms, ham, and tomatoes) or the *risotto con funghi porcini.* Popular main courses include the house specialty: *fiagiano alla casareccia,* pheasant cooked with olives and mushrooms. They also do roast lamb and veal marsala nicely, and serve pizza every night.

For a light, easy-on-the-wallet meal, try one of the pizzas (served only for dinner) and a salad. With the exception of the ice cream, all the desserts are made here, so go ahead and indulge in one of their cakes or a seasonal fruit tart.

TELEPHONE
06-44-67-306

OPEN
Tues–Sun

CLOSED
Mon, Aug

HOURS
12:30–3:30 P.M., 7–11 P.M.

RESERVATIONS
Advised for four or more

CREDIT CARDS
AE, DC, MC, V

À LA CARTE
L30,000, beverage extra; pizza for dinner only L10,000–12,000

MENÙ TURISTICO
L25,000, three courses and vegetable, includes bread and service, beverage extra

BREAD AND SERVICE CHARGES
Bread L2,000, cover, and service included

ENGLISH
Limited, but menu in English

(61) BOTTIGLIERA REALI
Via Servio Tullio, 8

Mario Paziani runs his lilliputian restaurant as if he believes you will be coming back, and believe me you will, just as all his other patrons do on a regular basis. In fact, many come back perfectly willing to stand

TELEPHONE
06-48-72-027

OPEN
Mon–Fri; Sat, lunch only

CLOSED
Sun, Aug (1 week)

HOURS
12:30–3 P.M., 7:30–10 P.M.
RESERVATIONS
Not accepted
CREDIT CARDS
None
À LA CARTE
L18,000–28,000, beverage extra
MENÙ TURISTICO
None
BREAD AND SERVICE CHARGES
Bread L1,500, service included
ENGLISH
Limited

patiently in line at 2 P.M. The atmosphere inside is chummy, with six tables on one side and six along the other. Paper table covers and napkins, coats hung by the door, and a portable heater rolled down the center aisle sum up the interior. Daily pastas, hearty soups, fresh fish, and a wide selection of meaty main courses headline a menu that brings back the tastes and smells of Mom's kitchen. The food is not delicate or approaching gourmet, but there is plenty of it and the prices must drive the competition crazy.

(62) DA FRANCO AR VICOLETTO
Via dei Falisci, 1A

TELEPHONE
06-49-57-675
OPEN
Tues–Sun
CLOSED
Mon, Aug 15–30
HOURS
12:30–3:30 P.M., 7:30–11:30 P.M.
RESERVATIONS
Advised
CREDIT CARDS
None
À LA CARTE
L35,000–40,000, beverage extra
MENÙ TURISTICO
None, but they do have a tasting menu that includes a trip to the antipasti table, a choice of three pastas, the mixed grill, deep-fried fish, and dessert, beverage extra
BREAD AND SERVICE CHARGES
Bread L2,000, service included
ENGLISH
Yes

Restaurant groupies would be happy to wait in the street for a table here if they could only *find* the place. Da Franco ar Vicoletto is accessible *only* to the determined first-time guest who is armed with a compass and a detailed street map. Since there is no sign or name over the door, follow these directions once you get to the neighborhood: if you enter from Largo Falisci, look for the second door on your left, with the number 6930 to the left of the glass doors with black metal frames. If you come by way of Via Latini, turn right at the first corner and the restaurant entrance will be on the right side after the barber shop (with no name). If you arrive around noon, take a few minutes to check the local outdoor market at the corner of Via dei Falisci and Via dei Latini.

Is the hunt worth the effort? You bet it is, *if* you love fresh fish. Yes, they have a steak and a veal offering, but they are unremarkable. Here, stay with fish for every course from appetizer to main. Start by helping yourself to the fish antipasti. My vote for pasta goes to the fettuccine with shrimp and artichokes or to the spaghetti with fresh clams. For the second course, order the mixed grilled seafood platter or whatever is touted on the daily special list. Most of the fish is priced for 100 grams, so watch out or your bill will climb. The way around this is to order the tasting menu, which you must ask for because it is not formally listed on the main menu. It is too much food for all but the starving, but it is a good value, even if you can only tackle half of it. The desserts are mundane: no need to plan on saving room.

(63) DA GIOVANNI
Via Antonio Salandra, 1

The section around the train station can be a dicey no-man's-land when it comes to dining. Many of the restaurants are either on unsafe streets, serve unsavory food, or both. Not so at Da Giovanni, founded over forty years ago by the Vittucci family, which runs it today. Seating is downstairs in two knotty-pine rooms lined with coat hooks; the entrance is graced with hanging meats, and fresh flowers accent the dessert and appetizer table. Sunny orange damask linens complete the picture.

The chef really struts his stuff when it comes to the pastas. One of his best is the *fettuccine alla giovanni,* a combination of butter, cheese, mushrooms, tomatoes, and peas that will go directly to your arteries, but what a delicious journey. The main-course plates range from *abbacchio alla cacciatora con funghi* (lamb gently stewed in a tomato-mushroom sauce) to grilled veal chops, fresh fish, and fried brains in butter. In addition to these regulars, there are three daily pastas, five main courses, and a vegetable special. For a finale, the top choices are a heady version of *tiramisù* or whole baked pears (in season). A very light alternative is the *frutta secca,* a serving of dried fruit and nuts that pairs well with an after-dinner espresso.

TELEPHONE
06-48-59-50

OPEN
Mon–Sat

CLOSED
Sun, Aug

HOURS
Noon–3 P.M., 7–10 P.M.

RESERVATIONS
Not necessary

CREDIT CARDS
MC, V

À LA CARTE
L30,000–33,000, beverage extra

MENÙ TURISTICO
L28,000, three courses; wine, water, bread, and service included

BREAD AND SERVICE CHARGES
Bread L2,000, 10% service added

ENGLISH
Yes

(64) DAGNINO
Galleria Esedra, Via Vittorio Emanuele Orlando, 75

When I first looked for this cafeteria/pastry shop in the Galleria Esedra arcade near Piazza della Repubblica and the railroad station I was pessimistic. Most restaurants in this area are simply terrible: either overpriced greasy spoons, dirty ethnic joints with questionable patrons, or total tourist traps serving lousy food to the unsuspecting. What a surprise was in store when I reached Dagnino, which bills itself as a bar, *pasticceria, gelateria,* and a cafeteria specializing in Sicilian pastries and ice cream. What an oasis!

Time stopped somewhere in the fifties in this two-level monument to mirrors, marble, fat grams, and sweets. You can stop in during the early morning cappuccino and *cornetto* rush; hit the cafeteria line around noon before the hot choices get too picked over; or drop by later in the day for a snack. I like to go in the late afternoon, look over the magnificent pastries displayed along one wall, pick several, and retire to a quiet table

TELEPHONE
06-48-16-660

OPEN
Daily

CLOSED
Sat from Oct–May

HOURS
7 A.M.–10 P.M., hot food noon–8 P.M., continuous service

RESERVATIONS
Not accepted

CREDIT CARDS
AE, MC, V

À LA CARTE
Pastries L3,000–6,000, ice cream L5,000–8,000, hot food L8,000–10,000

MENÙ TURISTICO
L25,000, three courses with vegetable and coffee

BREAD AND SERVICE CHARGES
None

with a pot of tea. I always think I will take a few of the pastries home with me, but I usually end up devouring them all right on the spot. If you have children in tow, the ice creams are wonderful, and the *granita di limone* (lemonade) is the best I have tasted.

ENGLISH
Yes

(65) FIASCHETTERIA MARINI
Via Rafaele Cadorna, 9

TELEPHONE
06-47-45-534
OPEN
Mon–Sat, lunch only
CLOSED
Sun, Aug
HOURS
Bar: Mon–Fri 9 A.M.–8 P.M., Sat 9 A.M.–3 P.M.; lunch: 12:15–2:45 P.M.
RESERVATIONS
Groups of 10 or more
CREDIT CARDS
None
À LA CARTE
L10,000–15,000, beverage extra
MENÙ TURISTICO
None
BREAD AND SERVICE CHARGES
Bread L1,500, service included
ENGLISH
Enough

Eating at an *enoteca,* or wine bar, is one of the smart Cheap Eating tactics in Rome, not only because of the lower cost, but because the wine is good and the food choices lighter. From Monday through Friday, the Fiaschetteria Marini serves lunches only to a packed house. In the afternoon you can always drop in for a ham and cheese sandwich. Please plan to go early for lunch, or be prepared to stand with the regulars gossiping at the bar while waiting for a table.

The setting is casual, with paper covers on tiny marble-topped tables set both inside amid crates of wine bottles and outside on the sidewalk when weather permits. The daily-changing choices are limited, but all are absolutely delicious, especially the *pasta e fagioli* or any of the special German dishes that appear when the owner's mother, who is Austrian, gets busy in the kitchen.

NOTE: Dinner for ten or more is by reservation only.

(66) GIOVANNI FASSI/PALAZZO DEL FREDDO
Via Principe Eugenio, 65/67A

TELEPHONE
06-44-64-740
OPEN
Tues–Sun
CLOSED
Mon, except holidays
HOURS
Tues–Fri, Sun 3 P.M.–midnight, Sat until 12:30 A.M., holidays 10 A.M.–midnight
RESERVATIONS
Not accepted
CREDIT CARDS
None
À LA CARTE
Gelato from L2,500
MENÙ TURISTICO
None
BREAD AND SERVICE CHARGES
None

It is said that modern-day Romans hold the nation's gelato consumption record at more than five gallons per person per year. Judging from the amount I saw consumed at this century-old *gelateria* near the train station, I think that is an extremely low estimate. Giovanni Fassi began in 1816 as a little shop in Piazza Navona, and in 1880 moved to its present location. It has been run by the same family since the beginning and is considered to be the gelato mecca by most connoisseurs in Rome.

The ice cream is displayed in glass cases with signs in English. Decide what size *cono* (cone) or *coppa* (cup) you want, pay the cashier, and give your receipt to a server. You can take your treat to one of the tables scattered around the cavernous room or eat it on the run. Prices start around L3,000 and climb according to how elaborate and involved your order gets.

NOTE: Now there is a second location not too far from the Vatican, at Via Vespasiano, 56 a/c—it is spotted as 88 on the map.

ENGLISH
Limited

(67) GRAN CAFFÈ STREGA
Piazza del Viminale, 27/31

Huge, brightly lit, and packed with animated Italians—that is the Gran Caffè Strega, a combination cafeteria, restaurant, and pizzeria catering to Ministry of the Interior workers and tourists at lunch and an eclectic crowd in the evening.

Smart lunch-munchers skip the ready-made sandwiches and head straight for the self-service cafeteria counter. They also bypass the diet-destroying display of desserts and concentrate on one of the twenty salads and ten or twelve hot daily specials. Seating is either in a room with the pizza ovens or on a large outdoor lighted terrace shielded from traffic and street noise by a ring of bushes and trees. Along the back wall is a waterfall with a picture in the middle of it of a woman wearing (depending on your age and point of view), either a black slip or an old-fashioned 1920s-style bathing suit.

If you want to avoid the sometimes frustratingly long cafeteria line, you can opt for a pizza, which is served for both lunch and dinner. The twenty-three wood-fired varieties run the gamut from a simple topping of tomato and cheese to "the works" with a fried egg on top.

In the evening, waiters serving only pizzas and salads replace the cafeteria line.

TELEPHONE
06-48-56-70

FAX
06-48-67-70

OPEN
Daily

CLOSED
Never

HOURS
Noon–3:30 P.M., 7 P.M.–midnight

RESERVATIONS
Not necessary

CREDIT CARDS
AE, DC, MC, V

À LA CARTE
Cafeteria L15,000–25,000, pizza L12,000–20,000

MENÙ TURISTICO
None

BREAD AND SERVICE CHARGES
Bread L1,500, service included at lunch, 10% added at dinner

ENGLISH
Usually

(68) LA REATINA
Via S. Martino della Battaglia, 17

Sunday night is never easy for dining out in Rome. But that is not a problem at this restaurant, where the promise of a Cheap Eat packs them in. For thirty years, six brothers and their wives and children have cooked for and served a weathered-looking neighborhood clientele at this typical *trattoria di quatiere* near the train station. Neither the exterior nor interior have any panache, but the bottom line, inexpensive food, is why you are here. They offer a *menù turistico* as well as one translated into four languages. Don't look at these unless you must. Ask instead for the handwritten Italian *menu del giorno,* which lists all the good stuff. The house pasta specialty is *farfalle impazzite,* a homemade bow-tie pasta tossed with

TELEPHONE
06-49-03-14

OPEN
Mon–Fri, Sun

CLOSED
Sat, Aug 15–30, Christmas (10 days)

HOURS
Noon–3 P.M., dinner 6:30–11 P.M.

RESERVATIONS
Not necessary

CREDIT CARDS
None

À LA CARTE
L30,000, beverage extra, pizzas from L9,000–12,000

MENÙ TURISTICO
L25,000, three courses; bread and service included, beverage extra
BREAD AND SERVICE CHARGES
Bread L2,500, service included
ENGLISH
Yes

cream and spinach that is a kissing cousin to fettuccine Alfredo.

Fresh fish is not on the kitchen's shopping list, but meat and potatoes, veal, and seasonal vegetables are. In the evenings they serve a few pizzas. I have never been able to do dessert, but if you can, be sure it is made here.

(69) PIZZERIA L'ECONOMICA
Via Tiburtina, 46

TELEPHONE
06-44-56-669
OPEN
Mon–Sat, dinner only
CLOSED
Sun, Aug
HOURS
6:30–11:30 P.M.
RESERVATIONS
Not accepted
CREDIT CARDS
None
À LA CARTE
L9,000–16,000, beverage extra
MENÙ TURISTICO
None
BREAD AND SERVICE CHARGES
No bread charge, 10% service added
ENGLISH
Yes

The name says it all. Pizzeria L'Economica is a bare-bones, family-run place with zero decor. Its wide-ranging claim to fame is that it serves the least expensive (and its fans claim the best variety of) pizzas in the San Lorenzo area of Rome, which is about a ten-minute bus ride east of the train station. The giant wood-burning pizza fires are lit in the evening only from 6:30 to 11 P.M. If you don't want one of their super pizzas, the only other options are *crostini,* pieces of toast covered with any combination of ham, anchovies, sardines, mushrooms, tomatoes, and cheese, or an unbeatable antipasti selection. The desserts are definitely in the ho-hum category, so pass them up for another time, another place.

(70) POMMIDORO ($)
Piazza d. Sanniti, 44

TELEPHONE
06-44-52-692, 44-52-652
OPEN
Mon–Sat
CLOSED
Sun, Aug
HOURS
12:30–3 P.M., 7:30 P.M.–midnight
RESERVATIONS
Advised
CREDIT CARDS
AE, DC, MC, V
À LA CARTE
L40,000–50,000, beverage extra
MENÙ TURISTICO
None
BREAD AND SERVICE CHARGES
Bread L3,000, service included
ENGLISH
Enough

Anna and Aldo Bravi run a remarkable trattoria in the university district of San Lorenzo behind the train station. Opened by Aldo's grandmother as a wine shop, it was expanded into a restaurant by his father. Aldo has been on the payroll since he was seven, and now his sons and daughters and their spouses all work here. The wonderful food is the creation of his wife, Anna. The clientele is a wide sampling of locals—professors and students, workers in overalls, ladies draped in mink, businessmen making deals—all of whom are welcomed with the same degree of friendliness.

In the main room, with its arched brick ceilings, is a large open-fire oven and grill where seasonal game and other meats are cooked to perfection. Tables set with yellow linens are crowded into several rooms, as well as outside on a raised terrace.

The value-packed menu is astonishing in its versatility, offering the kind of quality that brings diners back again and again. Order a liter of the house wine and a plate of the thinly sliced prosciutto with figs. Don't miss Anna's own fettuccini tossed with wild mushrooms or her *pappardelle* with wild boar sauce. If you appreciate wild game, nowhere in Rome is it prepared with more skill. The culinary curious can try another of their specialties, offal cooked over the open fire, which they claim removes most of the fat and "gamey" taste. Otherwise, the mutton stew is a smart alternative, as are any of the grilled chops or fresh fish selections. The desserts are all by Anna, and her repertoire is long and delicious. Just ask what she has made that day, and whatever you pick will be sweet and perfect.

(71) RISTORANTE DA VINCENZO ($)
Via Castelfidardo, 4/6

TELEPHONE
06-48-45-96

FAX
06-48-700-92

OPEN
Mon–Sat

CLOSED
Sun, Aug

HOURS
12:30–3 P.M., 7 P.M.

RESERVATIONS
Advised

CREDIT CARDS
AE, DC, MC, V

À LA CARTE
L55,000–60,000, beverage extra

MENÙ TURISTICO
None

BREAD AND SERVICE CHARGES
Bread L2,000, service included

ENGLISH
Yes, and menu in English

The menu is translated into English, German, French, and Japanese, but the clientele is usually local. The setting is simple, the service friendly yet professional, the plates warmed when they should be, and the food delicious. From appetizers to dessert, there are fifty-six possibilities. Still, if you do not see what you want, just ask and chances are it can be prepared for you. Fresh fish is the kitchen's strong suit, and it is cooked and served with pride. My dinner guests all agreed that it was one of the best fish meals they had had in Rome.

If you are going all the way with fish, the sautéed clams or mussels and the smoked swordfish are nice starters. The spaghetti with clams and prawns or the rice with seafood are well-executed first courses. Besides fish, the *penne a l'arrabiatta* (a hot combination of peppers, tomatoes, and garlic) is a reliable first course. The baked sea bass or flounder are served with potatoes and can be topped with a zesty tomato sauce. The *saltimbocca alla Romana* (veal and ham cooked in a wine sauce), grilled pork chops, or roast chicken will keep the carnivores in your party pleased. Fresh fruit tarts, gelatos, and lemon-flavored *sorbetto* splashed with vodka will not lead you too far astray from your dieting resolutions. A shot of Sambuca, served if you order a full meal, will add to your desire to dine again at this wonderful Roman restaurant.

(72) RISTORANTE LA MONTICIANA
Via San Martino ai Monti, 40

TELEPHONE
06-48-72-695

OPEN
Mon–Sat

In its earlier long life it was called Da Sor Giovanni, after the man who ran it. Now it is run by his son, Claudio, who since taking over a few years ago changed

CLOSED
Sun, Aug
HOURS
12:30–3:30 P.M., 7:30–11:30 P.M.
RESERVATIONS
Advised
CREDIT CARDS
MC, V
À LA CARTE
L30,000–35,000, beverage extra
MENÙ TURISTICO
L25,000, two courses plus salad or fruit and coffee
BREAD AND SERVICE CHARGES
Bread L2,000, service included
ENGLISH
Enough, and menu in English

the name, spiffed up the interior, upgraded the food, added an English menu, and still managed to keep the prices in the same Cheap Eat category—can't complain about these improvements. It is not an easy place to find, because other than a gold sign by the left side of the entrance, there isn't much to indicate it is a restaurant. If you go to the corner of Via Domenichino and Via San Martino ai Monti, 40, in the neighborhood around the Santa Maria Miaggiore Church, you will be there. Why bother? Because this is one place that has stayed purely local in food and character.

Do not expect the red-carpet treatment, especially at lunch, when exercise dropouts and neighborhood businesspeople fill the smoky room with their jolly laughter and social banter. To get really Roman, order the house pasta favorite, *tonnarelli alla Monticiana* (egg pasta tossed with peas and mushrooms). Follow with the tripe, osso buco, or maybe the *Parmigiana di melanzane* (baked eggplant and Parmesan cheese) if it is one of the specials. A carafe of the *vini della casa* and the basket of country bread keeps the meal going until dessert, when you can have *panna cotta* or a piece of fruit.

(73) TRATTORIA ABRUZZESE
Via Napoli, 3a/4

TELEPHONE
06-48-85-505
OPEN
Mon–Fri; Sat, lunch only
CLOSED
Sun
HOURS
Noon–3:30 P.M., 7–11 P.M.
RESERVATIONS
Not necessary
CREDIT CARDS
AE, DC, MC, V
À LA CARTE
L40,000, beverage extra
MENÙ TURISTICO
L30,000, three courses; beverage, bread, and service included
BREAD AND SERVICE CHARGES
Bread L2,000, service included
ENGLISH
Yes, and *menù turistico* in English

The generous cooking is more likely to please a hungry gourmand than a finicky gourmet at this two-room trattoria in the shadow of the opera. Red-coated waiters wearing black pants and bow ties serve a contented crew of diners who return again and again for straightforward food prepared with the best ingredients.

The best Cheap Eat is certainly the *menù turistico,* which includes everything from soup to service. The choices for each course are varied and include daily specials. The meat dishes are better than the fish, especially the soul-soothing osso buco or the roast lamb. Typical Roman specialties of tripe or brains fried with artichokes offer different choices you can't get back home. If you stray from the set-price meal, you will pay more, but you will be able to indulge in the house pasta—*rigatoni bohème,* a cholesterol festival of cream cheese and sausage blanketed with Parmesan cheese. For dessert, skip the prunes and the baked pears and go for the *mont blanc,* made with cream, whipped cream, and custard in a meringue covered with even more cream. Oh well, you won't have it every day!

Trastevere

Trastevere, which means "across the Tiber," is across the Tiber from the Jewish Quarter, and is famous for its nightlife, authentic neighborhood atmosphere, and many pizza palaces, where purists insist one has not been to Rome until he or she has had a baptism by pizza in Trastevere.

(74) AL FONTANONE

Piazza Trilussa, 46 (as you cross Ponte Sisto)

Naturally, I recommend every entry in this book. I should know, I have been to them all, and in many cases, more than a few times. Some stand out more than others, and in Trastevere, Al Fontanone has always been one of my favorites. Joseph Pino (or Pino as everyone calls him), his wife, Marisa, her sister Mariela, and her husband, Luciano, have been greeting guests at their popular restaurant for almost thirty years, practicing their winning "we're all friends here" philosophy with everyone who arrives, be it for the first or the fiftieth time. The rustic interior, with dried herbs and flowers hanging from the corners and along the wooden beams, the comfortable chairs placed around well-spaced yellow-clad tables, the gaily lit summer terrace, and the family's heartfelt hospitality continue to make this a top pick.

I like to start my meal with a small sampling from the antipasti table or the *fritto all'italiana,* a plate of quickly deep-fried vegetables, and then move on to the specialty of the house, *fettuccine alla Fontanone,* a rich pasta with mushrooms, tuna, garlic, tomato, and fresh parsley. The simple fettuccine with *funghi porcini* (wild mushrooms) and a liberal lacing of garlic, fresh parsley, and extra-virgin olive oil is another simple yet very satisfying first course from May through November, when the mushrooms are fresh. The noodles in these dishes and all the other pastas are made right here, and the ingredients for most of the other dishes come from their own vegetable gardens or from local producers near their country home outside Rome. If you are going for a meat course, stellar choices are the *abbacchio al forno* (pink-roasted baby lamb), the strapping osso buco (veal shank with mushrooms or peas), or, on a cold day, polenta served with spicy sausage or pork ribs with a pecorino cheese and tomato. In the late spring through summer, try their dish made with new potatoes,

TELEPHONE
06-58-17-312

OPEN
Mon, Wed–Sun

CLOSED
Tues, Aug 20–Sept 18, Christmas (1 week)

HOURS
12:30–2:45 P.M., 7:15–11:15 P.M.

RESERVATIONS
Advised

CREDIT CARDS
AE, MC, V

À LA CARTE
L35,000, beverage extra

MENÙ TURISTICO
None

BREAD AND SERVICE CHARGES
Bread L2,000, service included

ENGLISH
Yes, and menu in English

artichokes, fava beans, and green peas cooked with ham, butter, and onion. Demand is so high that they offer it for both lunch and dinner. In addition to the regular menu, wood-fired pizzas, *crostini,* and *bruschette* are available each evening. After two or three courses, the idea of dessert may seem almost impossible, but do order the house *tiramisù,* even if you share it or eat only a spoonful.

(75) DA GIOVANNI OSTERIA E CUCINA
Via della Lungara, 41A

TELEPHONE
06-68-61-514

OPEN
Mon–Sat

CLOSED
Sun, Aug

HOURS
12:30–3 P.M., 7:30–10 P.M.

RESERVATIONS
Not accepted

CREDIT CARDS
None

À LA CARTE
L20,000, beverage included

MENÙ TURISTICO
None

BREAD AND SERVICE CHARGES
Bread L1,200, service included

ENGLISH
Minimal

For local color, Cheap Eats, and few other tourists, check out this hole-in-the-wall on Via della Lungara, which runs along the Tiber River. It is definitely a family-run show. The *padrone,* Giovanni de Blasio, is a neighborhood fixture (his sister runs the *tabacceria* next door). Before opening at noon, grandchildren occupy some of the tables while their mothers hurry about getting ready and writing out the daily menu.

There are two rooms. The front one, with beads of plastic flapping in the entry, has only nine tables and is "decorated" with coat hooks, a clock, some dusty wine bottles, and copper pots with dried pasta sticking out of them. The green-and-white tablecloths are covered with butcher paper. The small room in back is where the many regulars come in early to get their favorite table and catch up on local gossip. Be prepared to be squeezed next to a young student couple busy falling in love, a table full of boisterous workers in paint-spotted overalls downing their fourth glass of Chianti, or relatives of inmates from the Regina Coeli prison, which is nearby.

No one is here for inspirational cuisine. People eat here for the kind of simple, satisfying peasant food their grandmothers and mothers stopped cooking years ago. The handwritten menu is *almost* possible to decipher. To start, everyone orders a bowl of homemade egg fettuccine, lightly bathed in olive oil with a sprinkling of fresh herbs. Ambitious portions of roast veal, chicken, fresh fish, and grilled steaks follow, with the usual seasonal vegetables and salads available as extras. The dessert choices are narrow, so it is best to stay with the fresh fruit or a slice of the chocolate or cream cake if your sweet tooth insists.

(76) FONTE DELLA SALUTE
Via Cardinale Marmaggi, 2/4

If you are in Trastevere, you are probably going to have pizza for dinner. For dessert, I can think of no better choice than a creamy gelato from Fonte della Salute. You can order yours in a cup, but I think the ice cream, especially their "After Eight," a minty rendition of the candy, tastes wonderful in a chocolate-dipped cone. Of course you will follow the gelato-loving Romans around you and gild the lily by asking for *panna* (whipped cream) on top. Dieters can order frozen yogurt, fruity *sorbettos*, or a soy-based ice cream, and skip the *panna*, but if you do, you will miss the real experience of gelato in Rome.

TELEPHONE
06-58-97-471

OPEN
Daily

CLOSED
Never

HOURS
9–2 A.M., continuous service

RESERVATIONS
Not accepted

CREDIT CARDS
AE, DC

À LA CARTE
From L3,000

MENÙ TURISTICO
None

BREAD AND SERVICE CHARGES
None

ENGLISH
Depends on scooper

(77) MARIO'S
Via del Moro, 53/55

For serious bottom-of-the-budget dining in Trastevere, Mario's is a place discovered long ago by hard-core Cheap Eating desperados of all nationalities. Here you can forget all about imaginative dishes served with exotic sauces in elegant surroundings populated by beautiful people. Mario's is a remarkably plain family-run restaurant where the waitresses wear slippers and the cook hasn't had a new idea in years. The prices not only reflect this, but have not kept pace with spiraling inflation.

For those who have not mastered the finer points of the Italian menu, it is printed in English. The *menù turistico* is a deal when you consider that it includes three courses, wine, mineral water, and the bread and service charges. For not much more, you can select from uncomplicated à la carte dishes such as spaghetti with ricotta cheese and black pepper, osso buco, *scamorza ai ferri con prosciutto* (fried cheese with ham), or daily specials of gnocchi on Thursday, *baccalà* on Friday, and tripe on Saturday. In winter, look for the apple cake made by Mario's sister-in-law. And always avoid the dishes on the menu with an asterisk (*) next to them, unless you are willing to eat frozen food.

TELEPHONE
06-58-03-809

OPEN
Mon–Sat

CLOSED
Sun, Aug

HOURS
Noon–4 P.M., 7 P.M.–midnight

RESERVATIONS
Not necessary

CREDIT CARDS
AE, DC, MC, V

À LA CARTE
L20,000–28,000, beverage included

MENÙ TURISTICO
L18,000, three courses; beverages, bread, and service included

BREAD AND SERVICE CHARGES
Bread L1,500, service included

ENGLISH
Yes, and menu in English

(78) PANIFICIO ARNESE
Via del Moro, 15/16

TELEPHONE
06-58-17-265
OPEN
Daily
CLOSED
Never
HOURS
8 A.M.–9 P.M.; Fri and Sat until midnight
RESERVATIONS
Not accepted
CREDIT CARDS
None
À LA CARTE
From L1,500 per 100 grams
MENÙ TURISTICO
None
BREAD AND SERVICE CHARGES
None
ENGLISH
Depends on server

You are going to have to depend on your nose to lead you to this insider bakery in Trastevere. Even though there is an address, there is no sign outside. As you are walking along Via del Moro, look for The Corner Bookshop, which is across the street at number 48.

Any bakery that sells one thousand loaves of bread and five hundred pizzas *daily* is a rousing success. The breads and pizzas are baked in a 150-year-old wood-fired oven. When you go, take a number and you will make your way to the counter. Waiting a few minutes to be served works in your favor, allowing you time to look and decide what you want. There is not much room for dallying once your number is up! If you are buying a slice of zucchini and cheese, potato rosemary, or plain tomato pizza to eat here, ask to have it heated, then it will be handed to you wrapped in wax paper, sitting on a tray. Other eat-in choices are big pieces of focaccia bread, slit, and then filled with tomato, mozzarella, and arugula, and dashed with pure olive oil. They cannot make these wonderful sandwiches fast enough to keep up with the demand. Once you have been served, take your tray to a stool at the bar along the wall, buy a soft drink from the machine nearby, and enjoy one of the best Cheap Eat snacks in Rome.

(79) PIZZERIA IVO
Via di San Francisco a Ripa, 157

TELEPHONE
06-58-17-082
OPEN
Mon, Wed–Sun
CLOSED
Tues, Aug
HOURS
7 P.M.–1 A.M.
RESERVATIONS
Not accepted
CREDIT CARDS
None
À LA CARTE
L18,000–20,000, beverage included
MENÙ TURISTICO
None
BREAD AND SERVICE CHARGES
Bread L2,000, service included
ENGLISH
Yes

Pizzeria Ivo is an evening place, full of thirty-somethings who like a lively, chaotic atmosphere with high-speed waiters and noisy elbow-to-elbow dining (and who do not mind waiting in line to get in). Inside, the walls are papered with photos of Italian soccer teams and the tables are jammed together. In summer, tables are placed not only on the street but between parked cars. As you can imagine, the service out here is not brilliant.

So, what about the pizza? Not bad . . . and neither are the pastas. I would skip over the two or three meat dishes and plan on dessert elsewhere. A pizza along with a glass of wine or beer and a salad will get you out the door for not much more than L18,000. While it won't have been a restful or romantic evening meal, you will have sampled a typical Cheap Eat favorite.

(80) PIZZERIA PANATTONI
Viale di Trastevere, 53/59

The place may not look like much—in truth, it is known as *l'obitorio,* or "the morgue," because the tables are made of marble slabs. But despite the cold interior, it is the loudest, most crowded, and above all, cheapest pizzeria in Trastevere. If you time it right on a weekend night, you will be able to witness the pizza chefs turning out more than a hundred pizzas per hour to a loyal corps of young-at-heart diners. As you can guess, service is casual, and the tables are smashed together in the interest of squeezing in as many people as possible. If pizza does not appeal, there are several bean dishes that are really good. Try the *fagioli di fiasco* (beans cooked in wine over an open fire) or the white beans with tuna, onions, or cabbage. Here is all the fiber and roughage you will need for a week! The uninspired antipasti should be passed on, as should the tired desserts.

TELEPHONE
06-58-00-919

OPEN
Mon–Tues, Thur–Sun

CLOSED
Wed, Aug 8–28

HOURS
6 P.M.–2 A.M.

RESERVATIONS
Not accepted

CREDIT CARDS
None

À LA CARTE
L17,000, beverage included

MENÙ TURISTICO
None

BREAD AND SERVICE CHARGES
None

ENGLISH
Enough

(81) TRATTORIA DA AUGUSTO
Piazza de' Renzi, 15

Trattoria da Augusto, a Trastevere institution, has been serving basic Roman food to legions of committed Cheap Eaters for decades. The spirited place has been owned for fifty-plus years by Augusto; his wife, Leda, who is in charge of desserts; their daughter, Anna, who cooks; and their son, Sandro. It has no sign outside, absolutely no decor inside other than a ceiling fan and a poster of Charlie Chaplin, and certainly no pretense anywhere. The menu (carbon-copied daily) is handwritten in an Italian script that takes some detective work to decode. The locals know it by heart and thrive on the filling and predictable fare—big bowls of lentil soup on Monday, bean or vegetable soup on Wednesday, gnocchi on Thursday, and fish on Tuesday and Friday. Everything is washed down with large amounts of the rough house wine, and a good time is had by all.

TELEPHONE
06-58-03-798

OPEN
Mon–Fri; Sat, lunch only

CLOSED
Sun, Aug

HOURS
Noon–3 P.M., 8–11 P.M.

RESERVATIONS
Not accepted

CREDIT CARDS
None

À LA CARTE
L25,000, beverage extra

MENÙ TURISTICO
None

BREAD AND SERVICE CHARGES
Bread L1,500, service included

ENGLISH
Yes

Trevi Fountain

To ensure a return visit to Rome, Frank Sinatra advised in song that all visitors toss a coin into the Trevi Fountain—that is, of course, if they can get close enough to hit the water. This tourist site seems to be on the top of everyone's A-list and it is jam-packed day and night.

The fountain, a magnificent rococo of sea horses, craggy rocks, and Tritons, is worthy of the attention and hundreds of rolls of film used every day by those wishing to preserve their trips in a scrapbook of memories.

(82) COLLINE EMILIANE ($)
Via degli Avignonesi, 22

TELEPHONE
06-48-17-538
OPEN
Mon–Thur, Sat–Sun
CLOSED
Fri, Aug
HOURS
12:30–2:45 P.M., 7:30–10:45 P.M.
RESERVATIONS
Essential
CREDIT CARDS
MC, V
À LA CARTE
L50,000–60,000, beverage extra
MENÙ TURISTICO
None
BREAD AND SERVICE CHARGES
Bread L3,000, service included
ENGLISH
Yes, and menu in English

In Rome, as in any world-famous city, quality has its price. To enjoy a fine meal in subtly stylish surroundings during your stay in the Eternal City, follow the lead of savvy locals and reserve a table at Colline Emiliane.

The decor takes its cue from the countryside, pairing yellow walls with yellow floral tablecloths, and accenting the two rooms with food posters and fruit and vegetable prints. The Bolognese food is hearty and served with style. All of the pastas are made by the owner's wife, and I'm sure you will agree that they are superb. The *tagliatelle con asparagi e prosciutto* (homemade noodles with asparagus and ham) and the *tortelli di zucca* (pumpkin dumplings) are both worth a trip across town. To go all out, treat yourself to one of their truffle specialties, which range from a salad with truffles to veal cutlet and cheese fondue. All is fit for a king and priced accordingly. For the *secondi piatti* (main course) stay with any veal preparation or the mixed boiled meats served with green sauce. Don't leave without trying the pear tart with raisins and pine nuts or the *budino al cioccolato,* a chocolate custard.

(83) GIOIA MIA
Via degli Avignonesi, 34

TELEPHONE
06-48-82-784
OPEN
Mon–Sat
CLOSED
Sun, Aug
HOURS
12:15–3 P.M., 7–11 P.M.
RESERVATIONS
Advised
CREDIT CARDS
AE, DC, MC, V
À LA CARTE
L40,000, pizza L10,000–11,000, beverage extra
MENÙ TURISTICO
None

Gioia Mia has a well-deserved reputation for consistently good food, service, and prices. When you arrive, the tantalizing smells and the happy crowd tell you this will be good, and it is. The only flaw seems to be the service from one or two brusque waiters who are sometimes in dire need of attitude adjustments. The inside is typical trattoria, with hanging sausages and peppers, bowls of seasonally fresh fruits and vegetables in the window, wines displayed on high shelves, and, for fun, a stuffed boar's head sporting a yellow party hat and a clothesline with baby clothes clipped to it.

Smart diners often skip the antipasti table and begin their feast with one of the twenty-five or thirty pasta offerings. There is something here for everyone, from gnocchi, crepes, cannelloni, risotto, and ravioli to their rich signature pasta—*pappadelle all Gran Duca,* ham, mushrooms, tomatoes, cognac, and cream. Carnivores will be hard-pressed to choose between the beautifully grilled baby lamb chops and the *cuscinetto alla Gioa Mia,* veal and ham wrapped around cheese and served in a white wine cream sauce topped with mushrooms. Those with trencherman appetites can attack the one-pound *bistecca alla fiorentina,* an enormous grilled steak that is almost enough for three people. At night, nineteen different pizzas tempt from a simple concoction sprinkled with tuna or sausage to a pie with the works, including an egg.

The two desserts to keep in mind, if you can possibly do it, are the *mille foglie della casa* (a flaky pastry layered with thick cream, chocolate, and whipped cream) and the *pera alla Gioia* (a pear cake covered with whipped cream and chocolate). No one said this would be a meal for someone on Weight Watchers!

BREAD AND SERVICE CHARGES
Bread L1,000, 15% service included

ENGLISH
Yes

(84) PICCOLO ARANCIO
Vicolo Scanderbeg, 112

Many restaurants near the Trevi Fountain have given in to the temptation to feed as many tourists as possible, serving barely adequate food at prices as high as the traffic will bear. You will find none of this at Piccolo Arancio, a popular location off Via del Lavatore where Romans mix happily with the tourists. The Cialfi family also owns Settimio all'Arancio (see page 117) and Arancio d'Oro (see page 111). The menus are almost the same at all three locations, but for my Cheap Eating lire in Rome, this is the most friendly of the three and has the edge on food as well.

From the outside, it looks just like dozens of other establishments: white walls, beamed ceilings, a bouquet or two of flowers, and a posted menu. If you arrive early, you will see the family in action. One of the daughters-in-law will be minding a baby or two, while another will be helping in the kitchen. Grandfather usually sits at a table shelling peas or stuffing zucchini flowers with mozzarella and anchovies, which will later be dipped in bread dough and deep-fried to order. If you have never had one of these decadent appetizers, they are especially well-done here.

The food is substantial. The *pappardelle al sugo di lepre* (fettuccine with rabbit sauce) and the pasta with zucchini flowers in a light curry cream sauce are still my

TELEPHONE
06-67-86-139, 67-80-766

OPEN
Tues–Sun

CLOSED
Mon, Aug

HOURS
Noon–3 P.M., 7 P.M.–midnight

RESERVATIONS
Advised for dinner and holidays

CREDIT CARDS
AE, DC, MC, V

À LA CARTE
L35,000, beverage extra

MENÙ TURISTICO
None

BREAD AND SERVICE CHARGES
Bread L2,000, service included

ENGLISH
Yes, and menu in English

favorites. On Tuesday and Fridays the menu is devoted entirely to fish. The delicate sole with a lemon and wine sauce is always a sure bet. For a light dessert, order the vanilla ice cream with strawberry sauce or the lemon mousse.

(85) TRATTORIA SCAVOLINO
Vicolo Scavolino, 72/74

TELEPHONE
06-67-90-974
OPEN
Daily
CLOSED
Sat from Oct–May
HOURS
Noon–3 P.M., 6 P.M.–midnight
RESERVATIONS
Recommended for dinner
CREDIT CARDS
AE, MC, V
À LA CARTE
L25,000, beverage extra
MENÙ TURISTICO
None
BREAD AND SERVICE CHARGES
No bread, 10% service added
ENGLISH
Yes

A meal at Trattoria Scavolino will be pleasing to the eye, fulfilling for the stomach, and easy on the wallet. Tucked away on Vicolo Scavolino near the Trevi Fountain, it is owned by a hardworking couple, Antonio and Epifani, who open early for dinner year-around. If you are here during the summer months, there is music on the terrace starting at 8:30 P.M.

When you arrive, look for the daily specials written on a blackboard by the door. A plus for many is that you can feel free to order as little as you want from this daily menu or the regular one without incurring the wrath of snooty waiters or grumbling management. The *fettuccine with funghi porcini* or the ravioli *di ricotta e spinaci* are two reliable beginnings. An almost guilt-free meal is the vegetable antipasti plate and, for a change of dessert pace, the assortment of typical Italian cheeses. When accompanied by a basket of fresh bread, a glass of wine, and your favorite person across the table . . . who could ask for anything more on a Roman holiday?

The Vatican/Piazza Cavour

St. Peter's Basilica, the Sistine Chapel, and the Vatican Museums and Gardens are all within a 108-acre area known as Vatican City in the Vatican State, the world's smallest independent sovereign state. No one leaves Rome without seeing the splendors of the holiest shrine of Roman Catholicism, and one of the world's greatest art collections. An important side note is that mail sent from Vatican City goes much faster than from any other location in Rome.

Piazza Cavour holds nothing much for a visitor other than its proximity to Castel Sant' Angelo. The Castel was originally built by Emperor Hadrian in A.D. 135 as his tomb, and was used as a fortress in A.D. 271 during the building of the Aurelian Wall. Now visitors can see a chapel designed by Michelangelo for Pope Leo X, military paraphernalia, beautiful frescoes, and tromp l'oeil paintings. The views from the top of the Vatican to the heart of Rome are wonderful.

(86) DA MARCO FORMICHELLA
Via Silla, 26

The sign in front says, "Ristorante Ragno d'Oro," but this establishment is really Da Marco Formichella. It is just one of those go-figure oddities about Rome. Because it is far enough from the mainstream of Rome's tourist beat, it has remained a genuine neighborhood trattoria catering to regular diners who appreciate the consistently high quality of the food, from first to last course.

The white interior is decorated with a mixture of this and that—a collection of lighted Greek and Roman busts, mirrors, and painting. Black-panted waiters zoom from one table to another, and never miss an order.

The food is a bracing blend of Roman favorites that have real star appeal. Start by sharing the *antipasti assortiti,* a plate of quickly fried zucchini, shrimp, stuffed olives, and cheese and potato puffs. Lighter appetites can start with the tossed tomatoes and salad greens, but frankly it is not as interesting as the antipasti mix. There are sixteen pastas, ranging from a plain spaghetti with *ragù* to a heady *linguine all'astice* (with lobster), several risottos, and, for the undecided, a sampling of several of their pastas. A smattering of pizzas is available as well as a full roster of meats and vegetable sides. The best dessert is not listed, but ask for the dessert *misto,* a large assortment of bite-size pieces of cheesecake, macaroons, various *biscotti,* and shelled nuts. It is just the right ending to a meal in a place you will want to keep to yourself so that it will be just the same every time you return.

TELEPHONE
06-32-12-362

OPEN
Mon–Sat

CLOSED
Sun, Aug, Christmas, New Year's

HOURS
12:30–3:30 P.M., 8–11 P.M.

RESERVATIONS
Essential, especially for dinner

CREDIT CARDS
AE, MC, V

À LA CARTE
L40,000, beverage extra

MENÙ TURISTICO
None

COVER AND SERVICE CHARGES
None

ENGLISH
Limited

(87) GIRARROSTO TOSCANO ($)
Via Germanico 58/60

The area around the Vatican has been declared a dining wasteland by many because of all the tacky and overpriced tourist joints, which charge their one-time diners top dollar for bottom quality. You need not despair—there is a bright star on the horizon at Girarrosta Toscano. This is a marvelous find where the tables are packed with boisterous, gesticulating Italians, many of whom look like they have been firmly planted at the same table discussing the same gossip or politics for years.

TELEPHONE
06-39-72-5717, 39-72-3373

OPEN
Tues–Sun

CLOSED
Mon, Aug 10–31

HOURS
12:30–3 P.M., 8 P.M.–midnight

RESERVATIONS
Essential, as far in advance as possible

CREDIT CARDS
DC, MC, V

À LA CARTE
L55,000–70,000, beverage extra
MENÙ TURISTICO
None
BREAD AND SERVICE CHARGES
Bread L3,000, 15% service added
ENGLISH
Yes

The restaurant is so popular that reservations are required at least one day in advance. Seating is in a large two-room space dominated by a huge exhibition kitchen and open grill. The specialties are the foods and wines of Tuscany.

I think it is best to get started by ordering the hand-cut prosciutto or a light soup to save room for a bracing veal or beef steak grilled over the coals. As a garnish, consider forgoing the usual vegetables and ordering the *fagioli toscani all'olio,* white beans cooked in olive oil with a liberal lacing of garlic. They are so creamy and wonderful . . . I dream of having them right this minute. If you add a small salad and a bottle of Chianti Classico, you are bound for the land of happiness. Another strong recommendation is the house dessert, which has been served since the day they opened. It is a cream cake with hot chocolate sauce poured over it at the last minute. This is the perfect cap on your Big Splurge in Rome.

(89) HOSTARIA DEI BASTIONI
Via Leone IV, 29

TELEPHONE
06-39-72-30-34
OPEN
Mon–Sat
CLOSED
Sun, July 15–31
HOURS
Noon–3 P.M., 7–11:30 P.M.
RESERVATIONS
Advised for dinner
CREDIT CARDS
AE, DC, MC, V
À LA CARTE
L32,000, beverage extra
MENÙ TURISTICO
None
BREAD AND SERVICE CHARGES
No bread charge if you show your copy of *Cheap Eats in Italy,* otherwise, L2,000, service included
ENGLISH
Yes, and menu in English

Due to the constant influx of tourists to the Vatican, finding a decent meal at a fair price can become almost a mission here. All Cheap Eating hope is not lost, however, thanks to the Hostaria dei Bastioni, found through a tiny doorway below street level on the busy Via Leone IV. Inside, the basement dining room is nicely turned out in pink: on the walls, as underskirts for the white table covers, and on the cloth napkins. There is also a sidewalk dining terrace where you can relax in comfort and thank your lucky stars that you are not standing in the queue across the street that wraps itself around the block with pilgrims waiting to get into the Vatican Museums.

The appreciative diners are made up largely of businesspeople, neighborhood regulars, and smart visitors. At this homey, hospitable eatery, you will find moderately priced seafood and a host of other familiar Roman dishes. The antipasti selection is limited. Just have a peek at the display and see what looks best—it changes constantly—or ask Antonio, the hands-on owner who never seems to stop meeting, greeting, and serving his guests. You can't go wrong with the house specialty—*fettuccine alla Bastioni,* made with cream, bacon, fresh tomato, and a hint of orange. The risotto with seafood, the veal with potatoes, or the assorted roast meats, also served with potatoes, are safe bets if you do not go for the other house specialty—fish. The house *panna cotta* or a seasonal fruit make the best ending.

(91) L'ABRUZZESE
Via Catone, 18

This is a simple place on Via Catone at Via dei Gracchi, with pine walls and pink and white cloths covering tables filled by 12:45 P.M. for Saturday lunch. On one wall you will see a bulletin board with photos and postcards from many contented international guests who consider themselves part of a family circle who have come to appreciate this neighborhood restaurant. It is run by the Carloni family, which provides hearty Abruzzi food from a menu that holds something for everyone, from the daring to the daunted.

To the uninitiated, Abruzzi dishes are based on the pig and its interiors. With this in mind, consider the *papparadelle di cinghiale,* long, fat noodles with a dense sauce made with a savory wild boar sauce if you yearn for something you probably will not see on the menu of your favorite trattoria back home. Another, their *tagliatelle all'abruzzese,* flat ribbon pasta with mushrooms, cream, ham, and peas, is as soothing a soul-food dish as you will sample. The ravioli pillows stuffed with ricotta and spinach and blanketed with a tomato sauce is another comforting choice.

Fresh fish is served daily, wood-fired pizzas come out only at night, and the cream-based desserts are probably as sinful as you and your cardiologist would think they are. But you could always split a *charlotte* (cream-filled cake laced with liqueur) or the *dolce* darling of the decade, *tiramisù.*

TELEPHONE
06-39-73-3290

OPEN
Tues–Sun

CLOSED
Mon, Aug 15–26

HOURS
Noon–4 P.M., 7 P.M.–1 A.M.

RESERVATIONS
Advised

CREDIT CARDS
AE, MC, V

À LA CARTE
L30,000, beverage extra; pizzas from L9,000

MENÙ TURISTICO
None

BREAD AND SERVICE CHARGES
Bread L1,500, service included

ENGLISH
Yes, and menu in English

(92) PIZZA RUSTICA AL GRACCHI
Via dei Gracchi, 7

The pizza ovens work overtime at this take-out pizza stand, with the chefs turning out big trays of lip-smacking pizza as fast as they can sell it. Also available is rotisserie chicken. The food prices along this strip of real estate near the Vatican tend to reach the outer limits, so it is nice to find a convenient pit stop for refueling before or after tackling the Vatican's "D" plan: a five-hour walking tour. When you order, you choose the type and size of your slice from twelve to fifteen varieties, which are then cut and sold by the weight, or decide how much

TELEPHONE
06-37-23-733

OPEN
Mon–Sat

CLOSED
Sun, Aug

HOURS
10 A.M.–8 P.M., continuous service

RESERVATIONS
Not accepted

CREDIT CARDS
None

À LA CARTE
L1,500–2,500 per 100 grams

MENÙ TURISTICO
None
BREAD AND SERVICE CHARGES
None
ENGLISH
Limited to none

chicken you can consume. You will probably not snag either of their two red plastic chairs, so plan to take this one with you.

(93) TRATTORIA DINO
Via Tacito, 80

TELEPHONE
06-36-10-305
OPEN
Mon–Sat, lunch only
CLOSED
Sun, Aug
HOURS
12:45–4 P.M.
RESERVATIONS
Not necessary
CREDIT CARDS
None
À LA CARTE
L20,000–25,000, beverage extra
MENÙ TURISTICO
None
BREAD AND SERVICE CHARGES
Bread L2,500, service included
ENGLISH
Sometimes

For lire watchers in search of home cooking near the Vatican and Piazza Cavour, the Marrocu's family-run jewel is a smart choice. Once I looked inside the eight-table room and smelled the wonderful aromas floating from the tiny kitchen in back, I knew this was where I would eat lunch as often as possible. The whitewashed, rough stucco walls are hung with wood carvings, braids of garlic, dried herbs, old cooking pans, and pretty baskets. Each day a new menu is handwritten on pieces of scratch paper with a little drawing in the corner and placed on the tables. The food appeals to those who love to tackle a serious meal, anchored by a filling bowl of gnocchi or lasagna, followed by roast chicken or rolled beef stuffed and served with peas, and accompanied by a glass or two of the house Chianti. If this is not enough, there is always dessert—meringue cookies with lemon or a *crostata* with jam—and all for a final tab every Cheap Eater can appreciate.

(94) TRATTORIA MEMMO
Piazza Cavour, 14/15

TELEPHONE
06-68-75-065
OPEN
Tues–Sun
CLOSED
Mon, Aug
HOURS
12:30–3 P.M., 7:30–11:30 P.M.
RESERVATIONS
Not necessary
CREDIT CARDS
DC, MC, V
À LA CARTE
L35,000, beverage extra
MENÙ TURISTICO
None
BREAD AND SERVICE CHARGES
Bread L2,000, service included
ENGLISH
Yes

Hearty cooking speaks to us all, and you can always find it at Memmo's, a busy neighborhood trattoria with basic Italian food and courteous service from Antonio Torretti, the pleasant owner, to his crew of timeless waiters in long white aprons.

The food is much more tempting than the plain surroundings. The menu boasts an appealing array of seasonal specialties, as well as tried-and-true favorites that keep the neighborhood regulars returning day after day. Everyone knows that on Tuesday and Friday the special will be *pasta alle vongole veraci,* spaghetti with fresh clams. On Wednesday, the chunky minestrone soup is the highlight, and on Thursday, of course, the most popular dish is potato gnocchi. On Saturday, tripe headlines the menu, and for the family Sunday lunch, big portions of lasagna and cannelloni are consumed. There are also delicious daily pastas and meat dishes and a guilt-laden selection of desserts.

Gourmet Dining in a Private Home

LA TORRE DEGLI ANNIBALDI-GRAZIELLA MELLO ($)

The Annibaldi Tower, located in the center of Rome, was built between 1200 and 1204 with stones from Emperor Nerone's Domus Aurea and from the Titus Baths. The purpose of the tower was to serve as a defensive fortification for Piero Annibaldi, the brother-in-law of Pope Innocent III. It is also said that St. Francis of Assisi stayed here while waiting to see the pontiff. Now the tower is the home of Graziella Mello, who restored it to its architectural and archaeological splendor, and opens it to guests for private cocktail parties, dinners, banquets, wedding receptions, and cooking lessons. The tower consists of two floors of rooms, a luxurious, partially covered garden, and a rooftop terrace with a view of St. Peter's, all of which she opens for entertaining.

Sra. Mello is a recognized Cordon Bleu chef who uses her love of fine food and cooking skills to create memorable dining experiences for her guests. She offers a choice of menus of either Italian or International cuisine, and personally shops for all the ingredients, oversees the cooking, and acts as a gracious hostess. No detail is overlooked, from the fresh flowers and live musicians to the lovely place settings of china, crystal, and flatware. Her cooking classes, which include the recipes and a meal of what has been prepared, are held in her own kitchen for small groups, and last for eight weeks.

If you are traveling to Rome with a small group, need to entertain business clients, or wish to host a special event for friends or family, please contact Graziella Mello as far in advance as possible to make your arrangements.

TELEPHONE AND FAX
06-48-18-121

OPEN
By advance reservation *only*

CREDIT CARDS
None, cash only

PRICES
Prices on request; they depend on the type and style of event planned.

ENGLISH
Yes

Food Shopping in Rome

Rome has many food markets of all types and sizes. The most central and interesting are listed here. Most districts also have their own local food markets, which usually operate from 7 A.M. until 12:30 P.M.

Indoor/Outdoor Markets

At these markets do not count on much English being spoken and plan to pay in cash.

(95) CAMPO DE' FIORI
Piazza Campo de' Fiori

Campo de' Fiori has been a focus of Roman life since the sixteenth century. Today the outdoor market attracts loads of tourists and is probably the most charming medieval square in the city.

HOURS Mon–Sat 8 A.M.–1 P.M.

MERCATO DEI FIORI
Via Trionfale, 47/49 (edge of Rome)

An indoor wholesale flower market with bargain prices that is open to the public on Tuesday morning only.

HOURS Tues 10:30 A.M.–1 P.M.

(96) PIAZZA DI COSIMATO
Three blocks west of Piazza Santa Maria (Trastevere)

A smaller market but with a good selection.

HOURS Mon–Sat 7 A.M.–1 P.M.

(97) PIAZZA TESTACCIO
Off Via Aldo Manuzio (Testaccio)

This is in a working-class neighborhood with market prices to match. There are also a few clothing stalls and a lot of shoe stalls.

HOURS Mon–Sat 8 A.M.–1 P.M.

(98) PIAZZA DELL' UNITA
Off Via Cola di Rienzo (Vatican)

There are wonderful selections, good prices, and underground parking in this indoor market not far from the Vatican.

HOURS Mon–Sat 8 A.M.–7 P.M.

(99) PIAZZA VITTORIO EMANUELE
A few blocks south of Santa Maria Maggiore (Train Station)

This big and busy market has everything from fish and produce to dairy products, meat, and dry goods that appeal to the wide selection of people from different nationalities who shop here regularly. Watch your money at all times, and especially watch out for gypsies who cruise through in packs about an hour before the market closes.

HOURS Mon–Sat 6:30 A.M.–1:30 P.M.

(100) VIA DELL' ARANCIO
Off Via Tomacelli at the end of Via di Ripetta (Spanish Steps)

This small market in a high-end neighborhood makes up for in quality what it lacks in size. The few stalls sell *only* prime produce. If you keep going back to the same stall, after four or five visits you will be treated like a regular.

HOURS Mon–Sat 8 A.M.–1 P.M.

Gourmet/Wine Shops

(101) CASTRONI
Via Cola di Rienzo, 190, 196, 198 (Vatican)

Castroni is Rome's answer to Fauchon in Paris. The two stores (there is a second location at Via OttaViano, 55, at the corner of Via Germanico) are a wonderland of regional specialties, plus they offer the largest selection of imported foods in Rome, which they will pack for you but not ship. The prices are on the high side, but if you are having Skippy extra-chunk peanut butter withdrawal pangs or want tacos and refried beans for dinner, here is the place to satisfy your fix.

The second store sells an array of American brands of cake mixes, soups, cereals . . . even Pop Tarts. Also look for the small bottles of olive oil and different types of dried pastas that make great gifts to take home to lucky friends.

TELEPHONE 06-687-4383

CREDIT CARDS MC, V

HOURS Mon–Sat 7 A.M.–8 P.M.

ENGLISH Usually

(102) CATENA
Via Appia Nuova, 9 (at Piazzale Appio)

This luxury grocery store has one of the largest supplies of wrapped candy, purchased by the 100 grams. You'll also find vintage wines and liquors, coffees, hams, and cheeses, as well as regional specialties.

TELEPHONE 06-70-49-1664

HOURS Mon 3:30–7:30 P.M.; Tues–Sat 9:30 A.M.–1:30 P.M., 3:30–7:30 P.M.

CREDIT CARDS None, cash only

ENGLISH Yes

(103) ENOTECA COSTANTINI
Piazza Cavour, 16

If you are a serious wine lover and connoisseur, the Enoteca Cosantini should be on your A-list. The shop is on two levels, the first of which is devoted to an expensive restaurant and a wine bar where Cheap Eaters can happily munch their way through a variety of cheeses and bar snacks while drinking a glass or two of wines from the Italian wine-producing regions or from around the world. It also has shelf after shelf of distilled spirits, and bins of bargain—and not so bargain—wines. Downstairs is where the serious business of wine-tasting and wine selling takes place. Every Thursday and Saturday the family holds wine-tasting seminars here amid rows of bottles of magnificent wines they have been collecting for thirty years. These tastings, unfortunately, are not for the casual tourist, but for real aficionados who pay between L150,000 and 190,000 for six two-hour "wine-tasting lessons" where four wines are tasted and discussed. However, anyone can buy their wines, which range from L4,000 to Ll,000,000 a bottle, or stand at the bar upstairs and enjoy a glass or two of a fine vintage.

TELEPHONE 06-32-03-575, 06-32-11-502
FAX 06-32-13-210
CREDIT CARDS AE, DC, MC, V
HOURS Mon 4:40–8 P.M., Tues–Sat, 9 A.M.–1 P.M., 4:30–8 P.M.
ENGLISH Yes

(104) FRANCHI
Via Cola di Rienzo, 204

A rival to Castroni, Franchi has a deli of your dreams, with wonderful antipastis and roast meats to make up gourmet picnics, fresh coffee ground to order at their coffee bar, and an enormous selection of ham, cheeses, and wine from all over Italy.

TELEPHONE 06-686-4576
HOURS Mon–Sat 8:15 A.M.–9 P.M.
CREDIT CARDS AE, DC, MC, V
ENGLISH Yes

(105) VOLPETTI
Via Marmorata, 47 (Testaccio)

Volpetti is recognized as not only one of the best food shops in Rome, but in all of Italy. At first glance, you may wonder why, but if you speak with Claudio, who is responsible for the care of their products, you will see how it earned its deserved high reputation. Let's start with their cheeses, most of which come from Norica in Umbria and are stored in a climate-controlled cellar. Every day Claudio washes the rinds with whey and turns them, the way his mother did, to keep the cheeses clean and uniform. Claudio is passionate about his products, and works twelve hours a day. He says, "climate, terrain, and the hand of man make a cheese. The animal is the means to the cheese, but the land is the source." He can explain the cheeses, tell you what wine and foods to serve with them, offer samples, and put your choices in vacuum packs for the trip home. In addition to the fabulous cheeses, Volpetti sells a tremendous variety of meats, breads, aged vinegars, and interesting salsas. For a real taste of their foods and products, treat yourself to lunch at their cafeteria-style restaurant, Volpetti Piú, around the corner (see page 122 for details).

TELEPHONE 06-57-42-352

HOURS Mon–Sat 8 A.M.–2 P.M., 5–8:15 P.M.; closed Thur afternoon from June–Oct

CREDIT CARDS AE, MC, V

ENGLISH Yes, ask for Claudio

Health Food Stores

(106) ALBERO DEL PANE
Via S. Maria del Pianto, 19/20 (Jewish Quarter)

One of the better health food stores in Rome, with a good collection of food supplements, herbs, essential oils, olive oils, yogurt, cheese, breads, wines, and pastas, all sold by a helpful staff.

TELEPHONE 06-686-5016

CREDIT CARDS AE, MC, V

HOURS Winter: Mon–Wed, Fri–Sat 9 A.M.–7:30 P.M.,Thurs 9 A.M.–2 P.M.; summer: Mon–Sat 9 A.M.–1:30 P.M., 5–7:30 P.M.; closed Sat afternoon from July 5–Aug

ENGLISH Yes

Supermarkets

(107) STANDA
Viale Trastevere (Trastevere)

A supermarket and a dimestore-quality department store, Standa is good if you need a few things quick. Most of the produce is prepackaged, but the prices are fair and the grocery selections are outstanding.

Note: Two other branches of this supermarket are located near the Vatican (Via Cola di Rienzo) and at Viale Regina Margherita, on the outskirts of Rome.

HOURS Mon 3:30–7:30 P.M., Tues–Sat 9 A.M.–7:30 P.M.

CREDIT CARDS MC, V

ENGLISH Limited

VENICE

Venetians . . . know all too well that they are picturesque, in Venice one never loses the sense that life is being staged for the onlooker.

—*Jonathan Raban,*
Arabia through the Looking Glass, *1979*

When I went to Venice, my dream became my address.

—*Marcel Proust, 1906*

Founded over fifteen hundred years ago on a cluster of mudflats, Venice became Europe's trading post between the East and West, reaching the height of its power in the fifteenth century. Although it no longer enjoys the elite status, it remains a glorious reflection of its rich past, while depending for its income on the mass of visitors who arrive every year to marvel at its glorious relics.

In Venice, one always has the feeling of being suspended in time. Little has changed over the centuries to diminish the harmony of colors, lights, and sounds that float dreamlike over the canals and lagoons. Composed of more than 100 islets and 150 canals linked together by 400 bridges, it is little wonder that getting lost is so easy, even for a native. However, becoming hopelessly lost in the maze of *rios, campos,* and *campiellos* will be one of the most pleasurable experiences of your visit to this romantic city on the Adriatic.

Since you cannot drive a car, hop on a bus, or hail a cab, what you will do in Venice is walk, walk, and walk. To save yourself supreme confusion, it is necessary to become familiar with the six districts, or *sestieri,* that make up the city. They are San Marco, Castello, Cannaregio, San Polo, Dorsoduro, and Santa Croce. Addresses are usually given only by the district and number (i.e., Dorsoduro 3437), often omitting the name of the street. All of the listings in the Venice section of *Cheap Eats in Italy* include the name of the street and the number (i.e., Calle dell' Oro, 5678), with restaurants listed by district. This will help, but you may still get lost; street names may repeat in more than one district, some buildings have more than one set of numbers, and addresses close to one another mathematically may indicate buildings at opposite ends of the district, since within *each* district there are some six thousand numbers with no clear-cut sequence. It is just as bizarre as it sounds, and often leads to hair-tearing and extreme frustration, especially when you mistakenly try to use logic.

Though you may be lost . . . *do not panic.* Look for the yellow signs posted throughout the city to find the direction you want. For example:

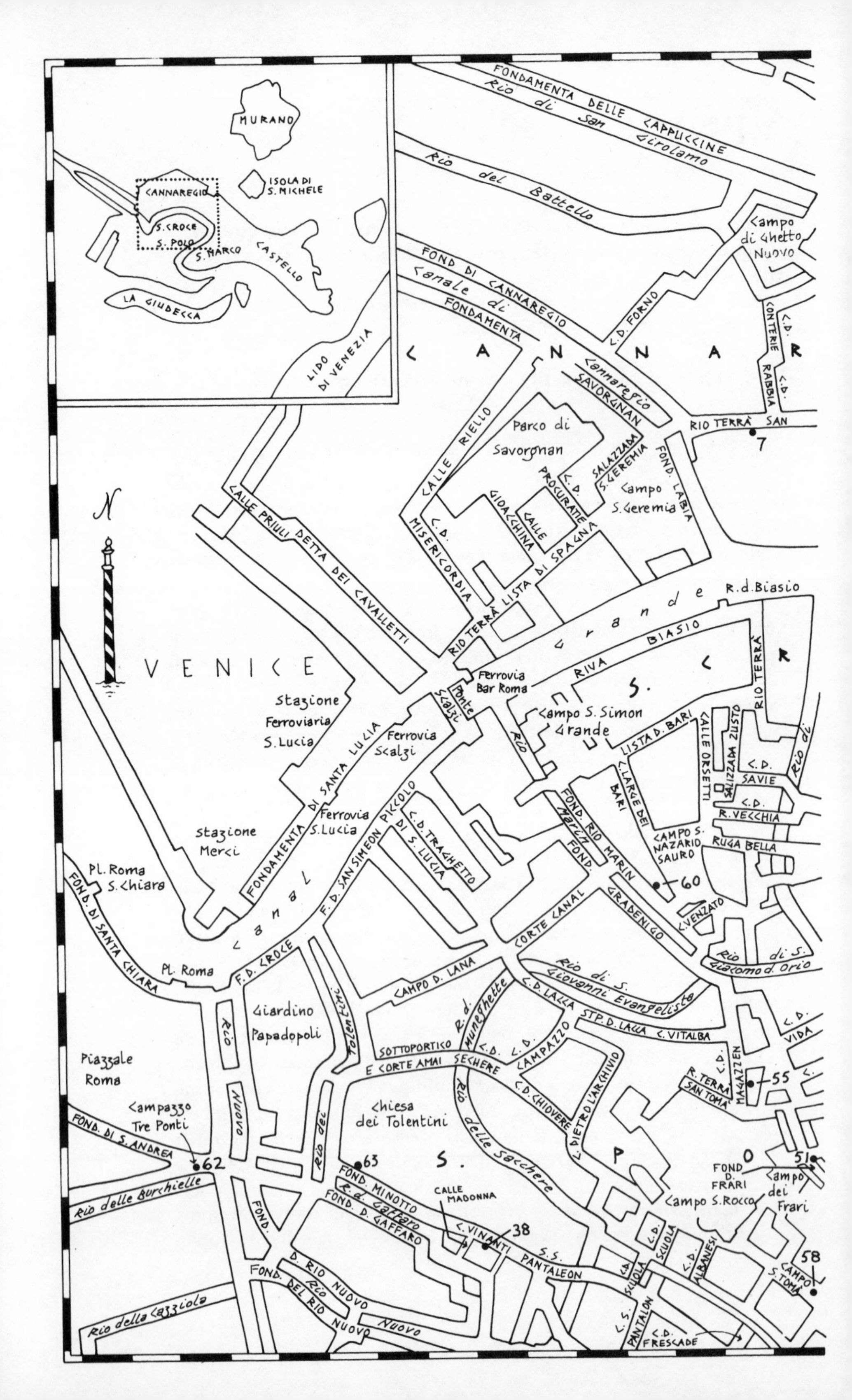

MURANO
ISOLA DI S. MICHELE
CANNAREGIO
S. CROCE
S. POLO
S. MARCO
CASTELLO
LA GIUDECCA
LIDO DI VENEZIA
FONDAMENTA DELLE CAPPUCCINE
Rio di San Girolamo
Rio del Battello
Campo di Ghetto Nuovo
FOND DI CANNAREGIO
Canale di Cannaregio
FONDAMENTA SAVORGNAN
C.D. FORNO
C.D. CONTERIE
C.D. RABBIA
C A N N A R
RIO TERRÀ SAN
7
CALLE RIELLO
Parco di Savorgnan
SALIZZADA S. GEREMIA
C.D. PROCURATIE
CALLE GIOACCHINA
Campo S. Geremia
FOND. LABIA
C.D. MISERICORDIA
LISTA DI SPAGNA
RIO TERRÀ
CALLE PRIULI DETTA DEI CAVALLETTI
N
VENICE
Canal Grande
R.d. Biasio
RIVA BIASIO
RIO TERRÀ
Rio di
S. C R
Ferrovia Bar Roma
Ponte Scalzi
Stazione Ferroviaria S. Lucia
Ferrovia Scalzi
Campo S. Simon Grande
Rio
LISTA D. BARI
CALLE ORSETTI
SALIZZADA ZUSTO
C.D. SAVIE
C.D. R. VECCHIA
RUGA BELLA
C. LARGE DEI BARI
FOND. RIO MARIN
FOND. Marin
CAMPO S. NAZARIO SAURO
60
FONDAMENTA DI SANTA LUCIA
Ferrovia S. Lucia
F. D. SAN SIMEON PICCOLO
C.D. TRAGHETTO DI S. LUCIA
Stazione Merci
Pl. Roma S. Chiara
FOND. DI SANTA CHIARA
Pl. Roma
F. D. CROCE
C. VENZATO
GRADENIGO
CORTE CANAL
Rio di S. Giacomo d. Orio
CAMPO D. LANA
Rio di S. Giovanni Evangelista
Rio
Giardino Papadopoli
Tolentini
R. d. Muneghette
C.D. LACCA
STP. D. LACCA
C. VITALBA
C.D. VIDA
SOTTOPORTICO E CORTE AMAI
C.D. SECHERE
C.D. CAMPAZZO
C.D. MAGAZZEN
Piazzale Roma
R. TERRÀ SAN TOMÀ
55
Rio delle Sacchere
C.D. CHIOVERE
C. DIETRO L'ARCHIVIO
Campazzo Tre Ponti
Nuovo
Rio del
chiesa dei Tolentini
FOND. DI S. ANDREA
62
63
S. P O
FOND D. FRARI
51
Campo dei Frari
Rio delle Burchielle
FOND. MINOTTO
R. d. Gaffaro
FOND. D. GAFFARO
CALLE MADONNA
Campo S. Rocco
FOND.
C. VINANTI
38
S.S. PANTALEON
C.D. SCUOLA
C.D. ALBANESI
58
CAMPO S. TOMÀ
D. RIO NUOVO
FOND. DEL RIO NUOVO
Rio Nuovo
Rio della Cazziola
C.S. PANTALON
C.D. FRESCADE

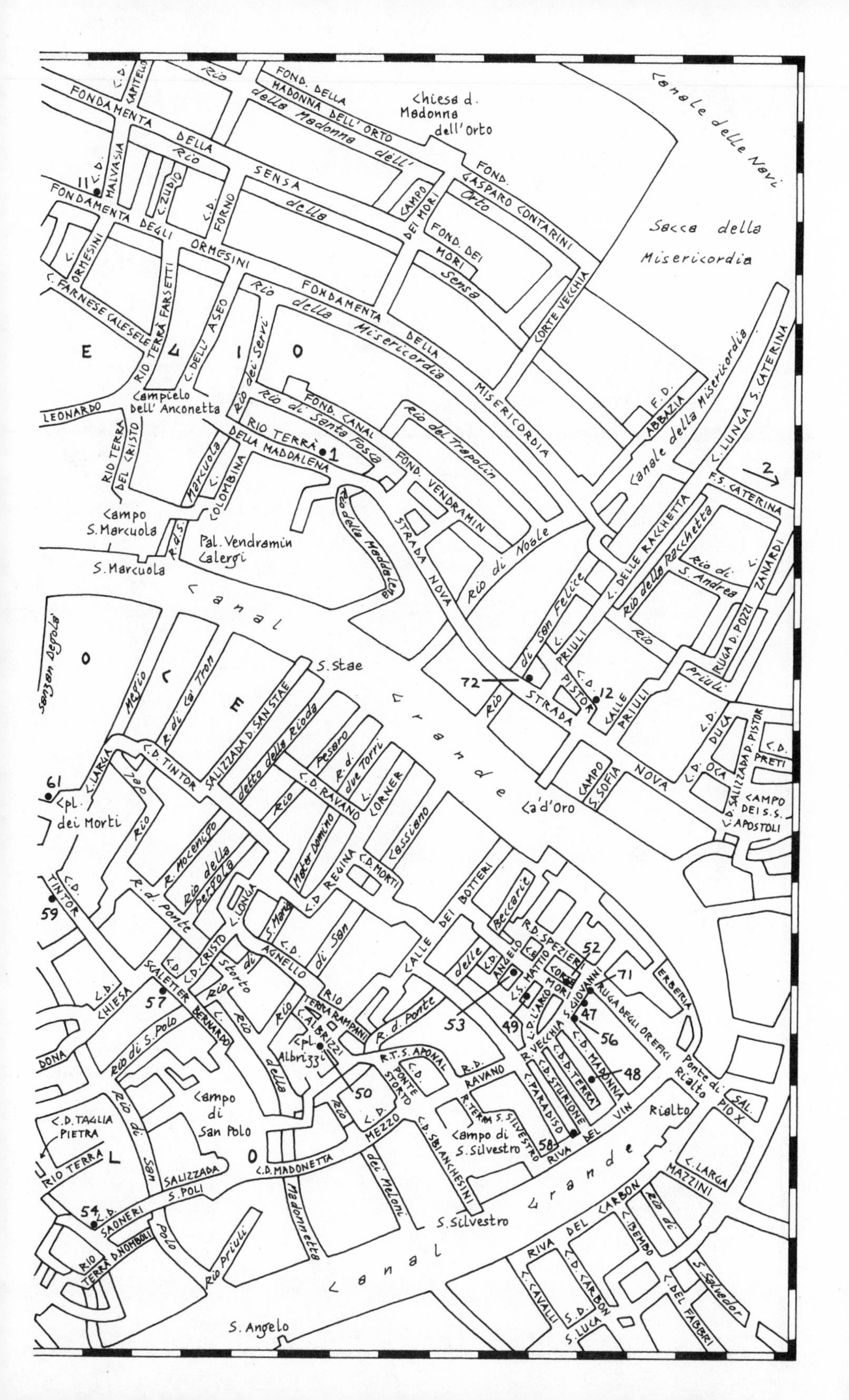

Chiesa d. Madonna dell'Orto
Canale delle Navi
Sacca della Misericordia
FOND. DELLA MADONNA DELL'ORTO
Rio della Madonna dell'Orto
FOND. GASPARO CONTARINI
FONDAMENTA DELLA SENSA
Rio della Sensa
FONDAMENTA DEGLI ORMESINI
C.D. MALVASIA
C. ZUDIO
C.D. FORNO
CAMPO DEI MORI
FOND. DEI MORI
Rio della Sensa
CORTE VECCHIA
FONDAMENTA DELLA MISERICORDIA
Rio della Misericordia
F.D. ABBAZIA
Canale della Misericordia
C. LUNGA S. CATERINA
F.S. CATERINA
C. FARNESE
CALESELE
RIO TERRÀ FARSETTI
C. DELL' ASEO
Rio dei Servi
E
G
I
O
Campielo Dell' Anconetta
LEONARDO
RIO TERRA DEL CRISTO
Rio di Santa Fosca
RIO TERRÀ DELLA MADDALENA
FOND. CANAL
Rio del Trapolin
FOND. VENDRAMIN
Marcuola
C. COLOMBINA
Campo S. Marcuola
R.d.S.
Pal. Vendramin Calergi
S. Marcuola
Rio della Maddalena
STRADA NOVA
Rio di Noale
Rio di San Felice
L. DELLE RACCHETTA
Rio della Racchetta
Rio di S. Andrea
ZANARDI
RUGA D. POZZI
Rio Priuli
C. PRIULI
CALLE PRIULI
C.D. PISTOR
STRADA NOVA
CAMPO S. SOFIA
Canal Grande
Ca' d'Oro
S. Stae
72
1
2
11
12
Rio di San Zan Degolà
O
C
M
Megio
R. di Ca' Tron
SALIZZADA D. SAN STAE
detto della Rioda
Rio Pesaro
R.d. due Torri
C.D. RAVANO
C. CORNER
Cassiano
C.D. TINTOR
C. LARGA
Rio Mocenigo
Rio della Pergola
Mater Domini
C.D. REGINA
C.D. MORTI
cpl. dei Morti
61
C.D. TINTOR
59
R. d. Ponte
CALLE DEI BOTTERI
Beccarie
R.D. SPEZIER
C.D. DUCA
SALIZZADA D. PISTOR
C.D. PRETI
C.D. OCA
CAMPO DEI S.S. APOSTOLI
C.D. CHIESA
57
SCALETTER
C.D. CRISTO
C. LONGA
S. Maria
Rio Storto
C.D. AGNELLO
Rio di San
C.S. MATTIO
C.D. ANGELO
CORTE
52
53
49
71
47
56
48
S. GIOVANNI
RUGA DEGLI OREFICI
ERBERIA
BERNARDO
Rio di S. Polo
Rio della
RIO TERRA RAMPANI
C. ALBRIZZI
cpl. Albrizzi
R. d. Ponte
R.T.S. APONAL
R.D. RAVANO
C.D. PONTE STORTO
50
R. VECCHIA
C.D. MADONNA
C.D.D. TERRA
C.D. STURIONE
C. PARADISO
R. TERRA S. SILVESTRO
Campo di S. Silvestro
58
RIVA DEL VIN
Ponte di Rialto
Rialto
SAL. PIO X
DONA
Campo di San Polo
C.D. TAGLIA PIETRA
RIO TERRA
L
O
C.D. MADONETTA
C.D. MEZZO
C.D. SBIANCHESINI
Rio dei Meloni
S. Silvestro
SALIZZADA S. POLI
54
C.D. SAONERI
RIO TERRÀ D. NOMBOLI
Rio di San Polo
Madonnetta
Rio Priuli
Canal Grande
C. LARGA MAZZINI
RIVA DEL CARBON
C. BEMBO
Rio di S. Salvador
C.D. CARBON
C. CAVALLI
S.D. S. LUCA
C. DEL FABBRI
S. Angelo

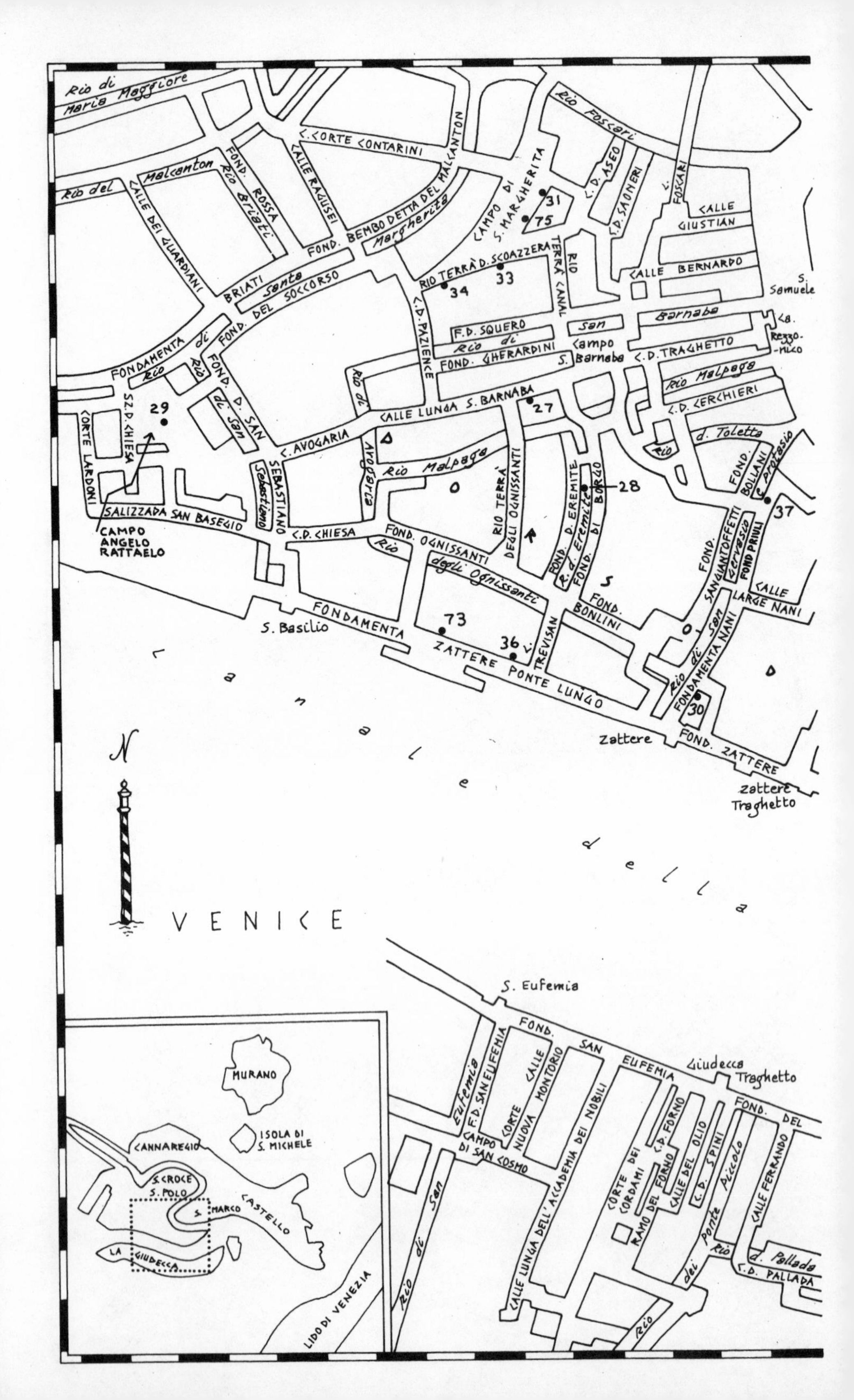

Rio di Maria Maggiore
C. CORTE CONTARINI
Rio Foscari
Rio del Malcanton
CALLE DEI GUARDIANI
FOND. ROSSA
Rio Briati
CALLE RAGUSEI
FOND. BEMBO DETTA DEL MALCANTON
Margherita
CAMPO DI S. MARGHERITA
C. D. ASEO
C. D. SAONERI
C. FOSCARI
CALLE GIUSTIAN
31
75
RIO TERRÀ D. SCOAZZERA
TERRÀ CANAL
RIO
33
34
CALLE BERNARDO
S. Samuele
BRIATI
Santa
FOND. DEL SOCCORSO
C. D. PAZIENCE
F. D. SQUERO
Rio di
FOND. GHERARDINI
San Barnaba
Campo S. Barnaba
C. D. TRAGHETTO
Ca. Rezzonico
FONDAMENTA di Rio
FOND. D. SAN
Rio di
Rio Malpaga
C. D. CERCHIERI
CALLE LUNGA S. BARNABA
27
29
S. Z. D. CHIESA
CORTE LARDONI
di San
C. AVOGARIA
Avogaria
Rio Malpaga
RIO TERRÀ DEGLI OGNISSANTI
FOND. D. EREMITE
R. d. Eremite
FOND. DI BORGO
28
d. Toletta
Rio
FOND. BOLLANI
e Protasio
37
SEBASTIANO
Sebastiano
SALIZZADA SAN BASEGIO
CAMPO ANGELO RAFFAELO
C. D. CHIESA
FOND. OGNISSANTI
Rio degli Ognissanti
FOND. SANGIANTOFFETTI
Gervasio
FOND PRIULI
CALLE LARGE NANI
FOND. BONLINI
S. Basilio
FONDAMENTA
73
36
TREVISAN
ZATTERE PONTE LUNGO
Rio di San
FONDAMENTA NANI
30
Zattere
FOND. ZATTERE
Zattere Traghetto
N
Canale della
VENICE
S. Eufemia
FOND. SAN EUFEMIA
Giudecca Traghetto
FOND. DEL
Eufemia
F. D. SANEUFEMIA
CORTE NUOVA
CALLE MONTORIO
CAMPO DI SAN COSMO
CALLE LUNGA DELL' ACCADEMIA DEI NOBILI
CORTE DEI CORDAMI
RAMO DEL FORNO
C. D. FORNO
CALLE DEL OLIO
C. D. SPINI
Rio dei ponte Piccolo
CALLE FERRANDO
Rio d. Pallada
C. D. PALLADA
Rio di San
Rio
MURANO
ISOLA DI S. MICHELE
CANNAREGIO
S. CROCE
S. POLO
S. MARCO
CASTELLO
LA GIUDECCA
LIDO DI VENEZIA

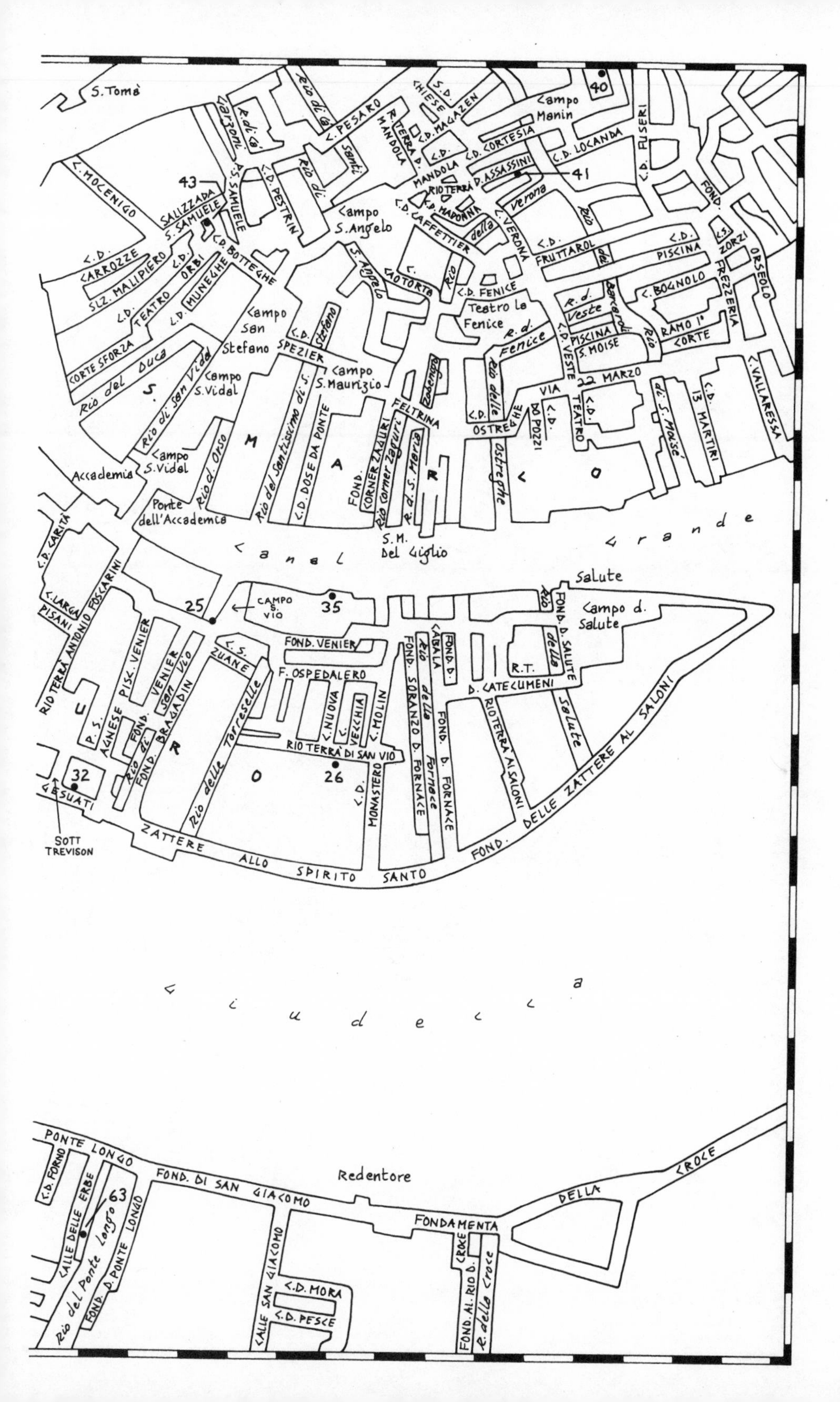

S. Tomà
Campo Manin
40
41
43
C. Pesaro
C.D. Locanda
C.D. Cortesia
C.D. Fuseri
C. Mocenigo
Salizzada S. Samuele
Campo S. Angelo
C.D. Caffettier
Rio Terrà D. Assassini
C.D. Fruttarol
C.D. Piscina
C.D. Carrozze
Slz. Malipiero
C.D. Botteghe
Campo San Stefano
C.D. Fenice
Teatro La Fenice
C. Bognolo
Orseolo
Frezzeria
Corte Sforza
Rio del Duca
Campo S. Vidal
Campo S. Maurizio
Spezier
Feltrina
Via 22 Marzo
C. Vallaressa
13 Martiri
Accademia
Ponte dell'Accademia
C.D. Dose da Ponte
Rio del Santissimo di S. Stefano
Fond. Corner Zaguri
S.M. Del Giglio
Canal Grande
Salute
Campo d. Salute
Campo S. Vio
35
25
C.D. Carità
C. Larga
Pisani
Rio Terrà Antonio Foscarini
Fond. Venier
F. Ospedalero
Rio Terrà di San Vio
26
32
Gesuati
Sott Trevison
Rio delle Torreselle
Zattere allo Spirito Santo
Fond. delle Zattere al Saloni
Rio Terrà ai Saloni
D. Catecumeni
Giudecca
Ponte Longo
Fond. di San Giacomo
Redentore
Fondamenta della Croce
63
C.D. Forno
Calle delle Erbe
Rio del Ponte Longo
Fond. D. Ponte Longo
Calle San Giacomo
C.D. Mora
C.D. Pesce
Fond. al Rio D. Croce
R. della Croce

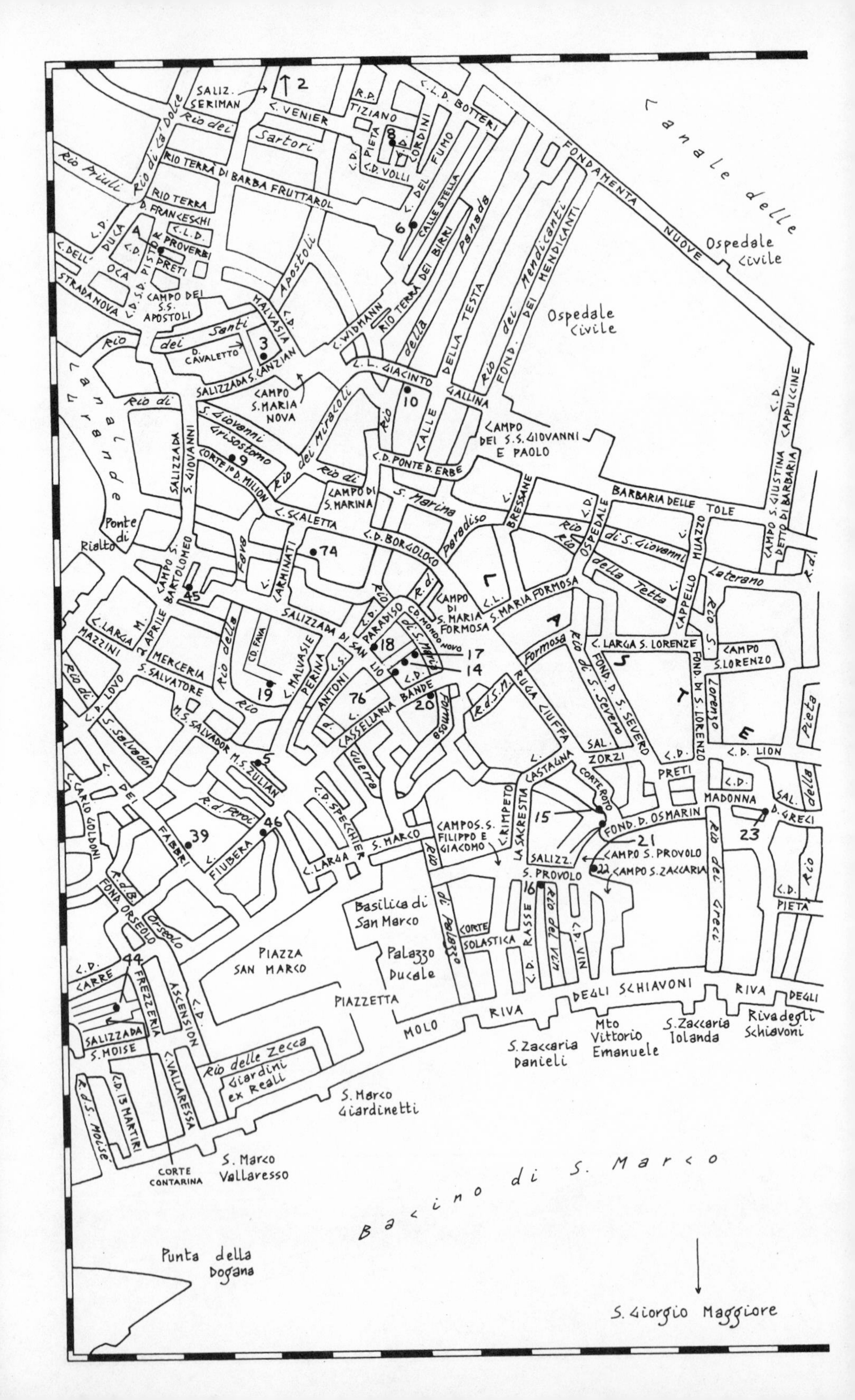
SALIZ. SERIMAN
2
Rio dei Sartori
C. VENIER
R.D. TIZIANO
C.L.D. BOTTERI
PIETA
8
CORDINI
C.D. VOLLI
Rio di Ca' Dolce
Rio Priuli
RIO TERRÀ DI BARBA FRUTTAROL
RIO TERRÀ D. FRANCESCHI
C.L.D.
C.D. DUCA
A
PISTOR
PROVERBI
C.D. PRETI
C. DELL' OCA
STRADA NOVA
CAMPO DEI S.S. APOSTOLI
Apostoli
C. DEL FUMO
CALLE STELLA
6
RIO TERRÀ DEI BIRRI
Rio della Panada
FONDAMENTA NUOVE
Canale delle
Ospedale Civile
Ospedale Civile
Rio dei Mendicanti
FOND. DEI MENDICANTI
MALVASIA
C.D.
Rio dei Santi
3
D. CAVALETTO
SALIZZADA S. CANZIAN
CAMPO S. MARIA NOVA
C. WIDMANN
C.L. GIACINTO
GALLINA
CALLE DELLA TESTA
10
Rio dei Miracoli
Canal Grande
Rio di S. Giovanni Grisostomo
SALIZZADA S. GIOVANNI
CORTE 1° D. MILION
9
Rio di S. Marina
CAMPO DI S. MARINA
C.D. PONTE D. ERBE
CAMPO DEI S.S. GIOVANNI E PAOLO
C.D. CAPPUCCINE
CAMPO S. GIUSTINA DETTO DI BARBARIA
BARBARIA DELLE TOLE
BRESSANE
C.D. OSPEDALE
Rio di S. Giovanni Laterano
Rio della Tetta
MUAZZO
CAPPELLO
C. SCALETTA
Paradiso
C.D. BORGOLOCO
Ponte di Rialto
CAMPO S. BARTOLOMEO
Fava
CARMINATI
74
45
L A S T E
S. MARIA FORMOSA
CAMPO DI S. MARIA FORMOSA
C.L.
Rio Paradiso
C.D. MONDO NOVO
SALIZZADA DI SAN LIO
C. LARGA MAZZINI
MERCERIA S. SALVATORE
Rio della Fava
CD. FAVA
C.L. MALVASIE
PERINA
18
17
14
76
19
ANTONI
CASSELLARIA BANDE
20
Formosa
Rio di S. Severo
FOND. D. S. SEVERO
C. LARGA S. LORENZE
CAMPO S. LORENZO
FOND. DI S. LORENZO
Rio S. Lorenzo
Rio della Pietà
C.D. LION
R.d.S.M.
RUGA GIUFFA
Rio di Lovo
M.S. SALVADOR
Rio di S. Salvador
M.S. ZULIAN
5
Guerra
C.D. SPECCHIER
C. LARGA S. MARCO
C. CARLO GOLDONI
FABBRI
R.d. Ferai
FIUBERA
46
39
R.d.B.
FOND. ORSEOLO
Rio Orseolo
SAL. ZORZI
PRETI
C.D. RIMPETO
LA SACRESTIA
CASTAGNA
CORTE ROTO
15
FOND. D. OSMARIN
21
CAMPO S. PROVOLO
SALIZZ. S. PROVOLO
22 CAMPO S. ZACCARIA
16
CAMPO S.S. FILIPPO E GIACOMO
Rio di Palazzo
Basilica di San Marco
Palazzo Ducale
CORTE SOLASTICA
C.D. RASSE
Rio del Vin
C.D. VIN
MADONNA
SAL. D. GRECI
23
Rio dei Greci
C.D. PIETA
PIAZZA SAN MARCO
PIAZZETTA
MOLO
RIVA DEGLI SCHIAVONI
RIVA DEGLI
C.D. CARRE
44
FREZZERIA
ASCENSION
SALIZZADA S. MOISE
Rio delle Zecca
Giardini ex Reali
C. VALLARESSA
C.D. 13 MARTIRI
R.d.S. Moisè
CORTE CONTARINA
S. Marco Vallaresso
S. Marco Giardinetti
S. Zaccaria Danieli
Mto Vittorio Emanuele
S. Zaccaria Iolanda
Riva degli Schiavoni
Bacino di S. Marco
Punta della Dogana
S. Giorgio Maggiore

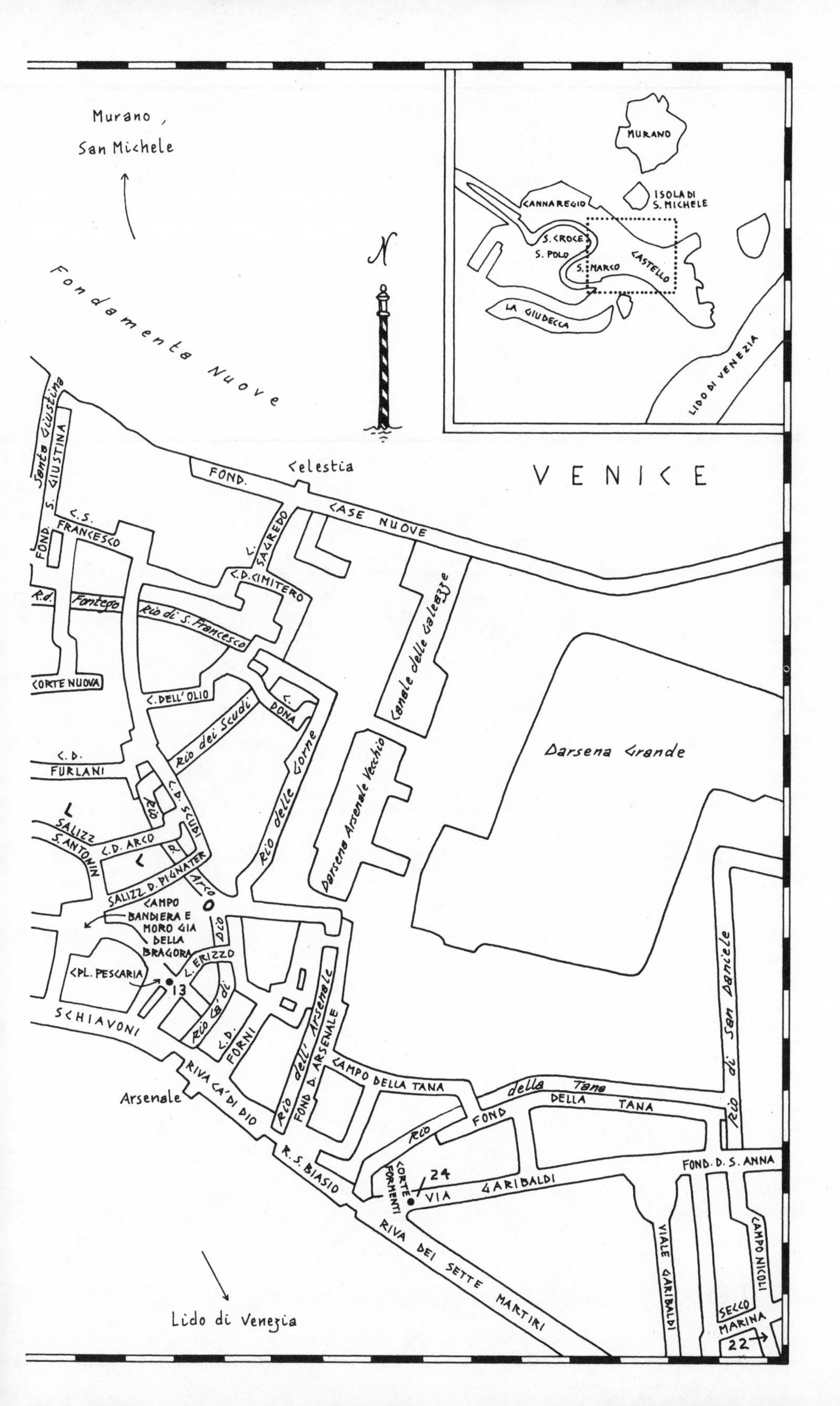
Murano, San Michele
Fondamenta Nuove
N
MURANO
ISOLA DI S. MICHELE
CANNAREGIO
S. CROCE
S. POLO
S. MARCO
CASTELLO
LA GIUDECCA
LIDO DI VENEZIA
VENICE
Celestia
FOND.
CASE NUOVE
Santa Giustina
FOND. S. GIUSTINA
C. S. FRANCESCO
L. SAGREDO
C. D. CIMITERO
R. d. Fontego
Rio di S. Francesco
Canale delle Galeazze
CORTE NUOVA
C. DELL' OLIO
C. DONA
Rio dei Scudi
Rio delle Gorne
Darsena Arsenale Vecchio
Darsena Grande
C. D. FURLANI
C. D. SCUDI
Rio
SALIZZ. S. ANTONIN
C. D. ARCO
R. d. Arco
SALIZZ. D. PIGNATER
CAMPO BANDIERA E MORO GIA DELLA BRAGORA
CPL. PESCARIA
L. ERIZZO
13
Rio Ca' di Dio
C. D. FORNI
SCHIAVONI
Rio dell' Arsenale
FOND. D. ARSENALE
CAMPO DELLA TANA
Rio della Tana
FOND. DELLA TANA
Rio di San Daniele
Arsenale
RIVA CA' DI DIO
Rio
R. S. BIASIO
CORTE FORMENTI
24
VIA GARIBALDI
FOND. D. S. ANNA
RIVA DEI SETTE MARTIRI
VIALE GARIBALDI
CAMPO NICOLI
SECCO MARINA
22
Lido di Venezia

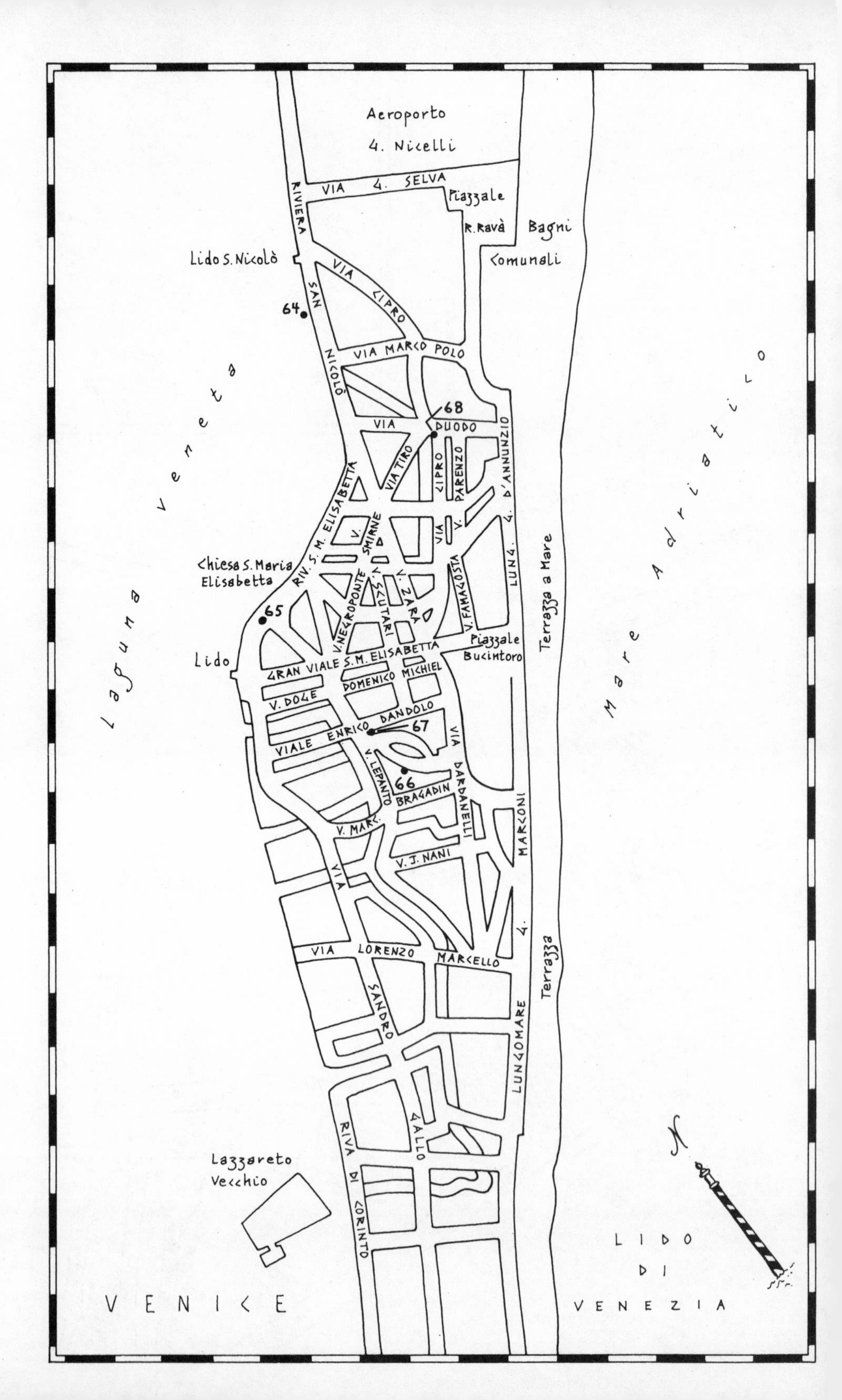
Aeroporto
G. Nicelli
VIA G. SELVA
Piazzale
R. Ravà
Bagni
Comunali
RIVIERA
Lido S. Nicolò
VIA CIPRO
SAN NICOLÒ
64
VIA MARCO POLO
68
VIA DUODO
VIA TIRO
CIPRO
PARENZO
LUNG. G. D'ANNUNZIO
V.
VIA
RIV. S. M. ELISABETTA
V. SMIRNE
Chiesa S. Maria Elisabetta
V. NEGROPONTE
V. SCUTARI
V. ZARA
V. FAMAGOSTA
Laguna Veneta
Mare Adriatico
Terrazza a Mare
65
Lido
Piazzale Bucintoro
GRAN VIALE S. M. ELISABETTA
DOMENICO MICHIEL
V. DOGE
VIALE ENRICO DANDOLO
67
66
V. LEPANTO
BRAGADIN
VIA DARDANELLI
V. MARC.
V. J. NANI
VIA
LUNGOMARE G. MARCONI
VIA LORENZO MARCELLO
SANDRO
Terrazza
GALLO
RIVA DI CORINTO
Lazzareto Vecchio
LIDO DI VENEZIA
VENICE

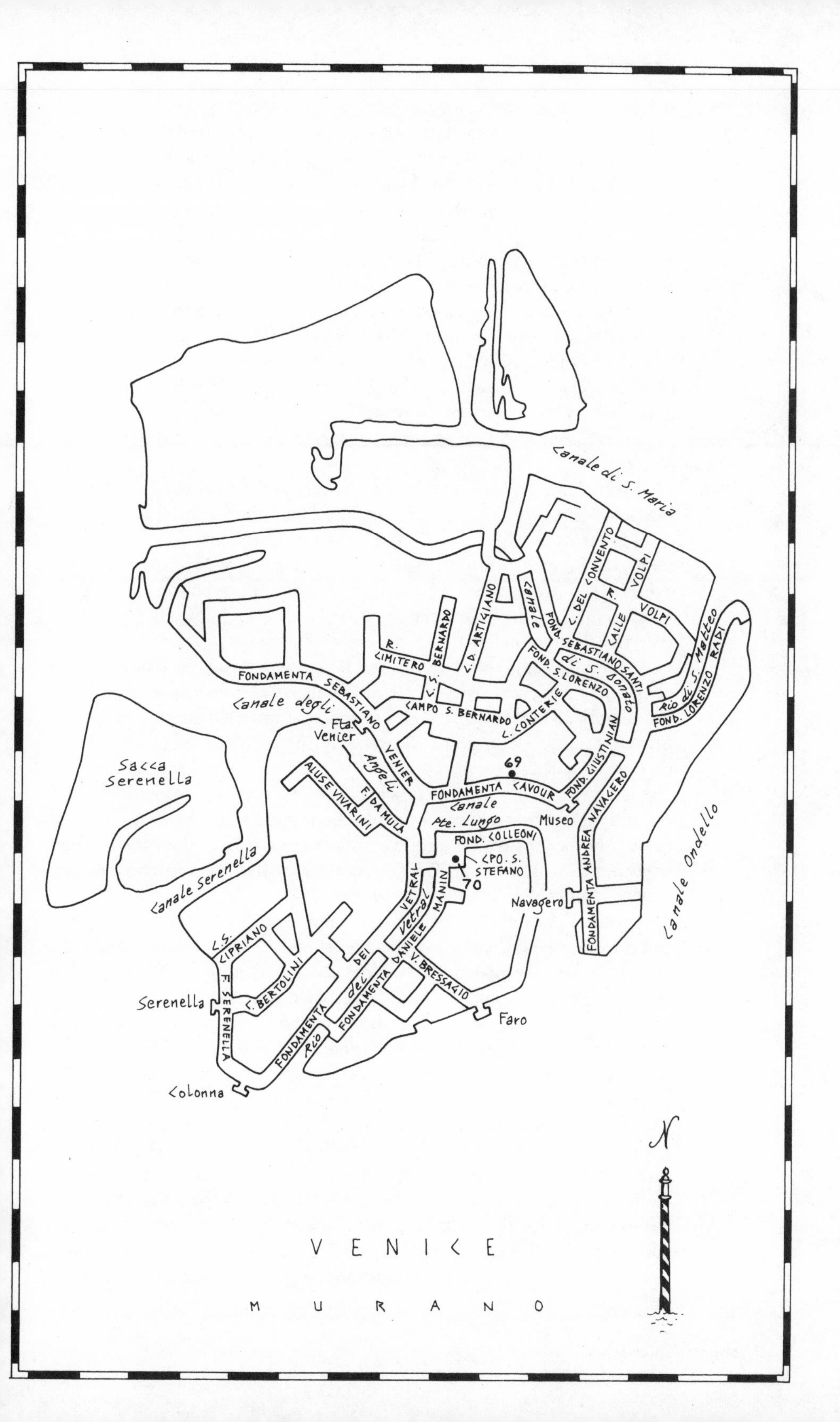

Canale di S. Maria
C. DEL CONVENTO
R. VOLPI
Canale
R. CIMITERO
BERNARDO
C.D. ARTIGIANO
FOND. SEBASTIANO SANTI
CALLE VOLPI
di S. Donato
Rio di S. Matteo
FOND. LORENZO RADI
FOND. S. LORENZO
FONDAMENTA SEBASTIANO
C.S.
CAMPO S. BERNARDO
L. CONTERIE
Canale degli
Fta Venier
Angeli
VENIER
FOND. GIUSTINIAN
Sacca Serenella
69
ALUSE VIVARINI
F. DA MULA
FONDAMENTA CAVOUR
Canale
Pte. Lungo
Museo
FONDAMENTA ANDREA NAVAGERO
Canale Ondello
FOND. COLLEONI
CPO. S. STEFANO
70
Canale Serenella
VETRAI
Vetrai
MANIN
Navagero
C.S. CIPRIANO
FONDAMENTA DANIELE
DEI
V. BRESSAGIO
dei
Serenella
F. SERENELLA
C. BERTOLINI
Faro
FONDAMENTA
Rio
Colonna
N
VENICE
MURANO

Look for the sign saying Rialto, the bridge that connects the San Marco district with San Polo, when you are going to shop at the Rialto Bridge. Accademia is your direction if you want to see the Guggenheim Collection. If you are going back to get to your parked car, watch for signs saying Piazzale Roma. If your destination is St. Mark's Square, look for signs pointing to San Marco. If you are leaving Venice on the train, go in the direction marked *ferrovia* (train station).

Venice celebrates a number of holidays (*feste*). The most important is Carnivale, held during the ten days before Lent and ending on Shrove Tuesday with a masked ball for the elite and dancing in St. Mark's Square for the rest of us. Crowds during this time defy description. Unless you enjoy elbow-to-elbow, pushing mob scenes and the-sky-is-the-limit prices in hotels and restaurants, it is best to avoid this time of year in Venice.

If you think food is expensive in Florence and Rome, you have not yet eaten in Venice, where even Italians used to runaway inflation consider dining out to be expensive. While Venice is a city of romantic enchantment, the high cost of living here and the endless flow of tourists keep the prices in the stratosphere. The best word-of-mouth recommendation for a Venetian restaurant is that the prices are not *too* high. My own feeling is that the short-term visitor to Venice should seriously consider casting aside thoughts of great economy and take the philosophical view that he or she may never pass this way again. This is not to say that good-value restaurants do not exist, because I have found many wonderful ones. I am just warning you that you will probably spend more for food in Venice than you want to.

One way to shave food costs is to lunch at a snack bar. Most Venetians do, and many order a plate of *cicchetti:* little appetizers similar to Spanish tapas. Another option is a plump *tremezzino,* a sandwich filled with almost anything you can think of. The Cheapest Eat will be a picnic you make up yourself from foods bought at a market or deli.

Venetian cuisine is known for its simplicity, and its best dishes often come from the sea, such as *granseole* (spider crabs), *molecche* (soft-shell crabs), *sarde in saor* (marinated sardines), and *seppie in nero* (squid cooked in its own black ink and usually served with pasta or polenta). When ordering at a restaurant, remember that on Sunday and Monday the Rialto Market is closed, so any fish served on these days will not be fresh that day. Risotto is the favored starch, sauced with delicate seafood or tender seasonal vegetables. Polenta appears not only with fish but with the famous *fegato alla veneziana,* calves' liver with onions. Pastries and sweets abound. Try the ring-shaped cookies called *bussolai,* which are the specialty of Burano, or the thin, oval cookies called *baicoli.* Particular foods are traditional to eat on certain feast days. During Carnivale you will see small doughnuts known as *frittelle,* which come plain, with fruit (*con frutta*), or with cream (*con crema*). When you buy a bagful, you have a marvelous excuse to eat them almost on the spot because they do not keep well. The most popular wines are from nearby Fruili and the neighboring Veneto, especially the white Soave or the red Valpolicella and Bardolino. *Prosecco* is a light, champagnelike wine that is a delicious aperitif. Grappa, strong and fiery enough to blow you away if you do not exercise caution, is made from plums, grapes, and juniper berries.

While most restaurants in other cities take their annual holidays in either July or August, the most popular months to close in Venice, in addition to July and August, are December, January, and February until the beginning of Carnivale, when the dampness and all-embracing cold of Venice subsides. However, the period between Christmas and New Year's is becoming an increasingly popular time to visit Venice, so to meet the tourist demand, many restaurants will open during this time, then close again until Carnivale.

Venice has a group of independent restaurateurs called Ristoranti della Buona Accoglienza. This organization pledges a proper price-to-quality ratio, the use of fine products, and exceptional service in an agreeable atmosphere. Most of these restaurants are Big Splurges, but you are virtually guaranteed a wonderful meal. If you have any complaints about the food or service in any of the member restaurants, please call 041-52-39-896, or write to them at Castella Postale No. 624, 30100 Venezia, Italy. The members listed in *Cheap Eats in Italy* are:

Ai Gondolieri, page 179
Al Covo, page 171
Alla Madonna, page 192
Fiaschetteria Toscana, page 166
Ignazio, page 195
Osteria da Fiore, page 197

Rolling Venice Card

If ever there was a discount-card deal for Cheap Eaters between the ages of fourteen and twenty-nine, the Rolling Venice Card is it. Not only receiving discounts in participating restaurants, cardholders are entitled to at least a 10 percent discount on hotels, admissions to various museums (except the Accademia), and some store purchases. The participating establishments are listed on a map you receive when you get your card. The cost of the card is L5,000, and you will need to show your passport and have a passport-size photo to affix to your card. You can purchase the card at the train station in the summer or at the following address any time of year.

Comune di Venezia
Assessorato alla Gioventù
Calle Contarina, 1529, San Marco
Tel: 041-27-47-651
Hours: Mon–Fri 9 A.M.–1 P.M., Tues, Thur 3–5 P.M.

Venetian Street Terms

Calle	main alleyway
Campiello	small square
Campo	square, usually with a church on it with the same name as the square
Corte	courtyard
Fondamenta	pavement along a section of water
Piscina	former pool
Ramo	small side street
Rio	canal
Riva	major stretch of pavement along water
Ruga	main shopping street
Salizzada	sometimes spelled *salizada,* the main street of a district
Sestiere	district
Sottoportico	small alley running beneath a building

Restaurants in Venice

The number in parentheses before each restaurant corresponds to a number that marks the restaurant's location on the Venice map (an entry with no number before it is located outside the parameters of the map); a dollar sign ($) indicates restaurants in the Big Splurge category.

RESTAURANTS

FOOD SHOPPING IN VENICE

Cannaregio

This is the northern, most populated *sestiere,* and the one most visitors first see if they arrive by train at Piazzale Roma or car across the bridge from Mestre. It is also one of the most authentic districts, because it does not have to rely solely on tourism. The area around the train station is the exception. It is very touristy, and if you don't know where to go, you can easily be overwhelmed by the assault of greasy spoons and questionable hotels. In the center of Cannaregio is the Jewish Quarter, sometimes referred to as the Jewish Ghetto, whose Italian name, *ghetto,* became the universal term for a poor, restricted group of people. Part of the *sestiere* along the Grand Canal is lined with aging *palazzos,* the most famous of which is Ca' d'Oro, which holds an impressive art collection. In the northern part of the *sestiere* is the Madonna dell'Orto, a Gothic church with Tintoretto's *Presentation of Mary at the Temple.*

(1) ALLA MADDALENA
Rio Terra della Maddalena, 2348

TELEPHONE
041-72-07-23
OPEN
Mon–Sat, bar and lunch only
CLOSED
Sun, Aug
HOURS
7:30 A.M.–9 P.M.; hot lunch 12:30–2 P.M.

Where to go when you find yourself stranded in the dining desert around the train station and do not want to settle for the unappetizing tourist food that is the rule rather than the exception here? One answer is Alla Maddalena, a fine place for a sandwich, a plate of rigatoni, *tagliatelle,* or the daily hot special. All the food is made

RESERVATIONS
Not accepted
CREDIT CARDS
None
À LA CARTE
Sandwiches from L2,200, main dishes from L6,800, beverage extra
MENÙ TURISTICO
None
COVER AND SERVICE CHARGES
No cover, service included
ENGLISH
Limited; as the barman said, "We don't speak English, only Venetian."

fresh daily and in some cases in limited supply, so when they run out of roast beef or the pasta of the day, you are out of luck. The desserts are brought in, so I recommend going to the *gelateria* across the street and having a scoop or two. At Alla Maddalena, you can enjoy your repast standing at the bar and kibitzing with the friendly bartenders or sitting on a tall stool by the window and watching the foot traffic hustle by.

(2) ANTICA TRATTORIA DA NINO
Salizada Seriman, 4858

TELEPHONE
041-52-85-266
OPEN
Mon–Fri; Sat, lunch only
CLOSED
Sun, Jan
HOURS
Bar 9 A.M.–9 P.M.; restaurant: 11 A.M.–2:30 P.M., 6:30–8:30 P.M.
RESERVATIONS
Not necessary
CREDIT CARDS
AE, MC, V
À LA CARTE
L30,000, beverage extra
MENÙ TURISTICO
There are two for L20,000, three courses; coffee, cover, and service included in one, no coffee in the other; L25,000, two courses (both fresh fish) and salad, cover and service included; L29,000, two courses (both fish, better quality) and salad; service and cover included
COVER AND SERVICE CHARGES
Cover L2,500, 12% service added
ENGLISH
Yes, and menu in English

Every once in a while we need a port in a storm, and this little trattoria is just that. It is certainly nothing to write home about or worth a special trip, but if you are en route to take the boat to Murano and need a little sustenance, this is an answer. The key is to remember where you are and not to expect gourmet renderings from a sophisticated chef. Order what can be prepared at the moment and you will do fine. The interior used to be cluttered with collections of soccer scarves, plastic plants, and assorted posters, but the walls have been repainted white, and now sport only framed sailor's knots and pictures of Venice. The only piece of true kitsch left is the big wristwatch clock hanging over the bar.

The best Cheap Eat is the simple *menù turistico.* Start with spaghetti in a tomato sauce, and order either the mixed fish fry, roast pork, or veal for the main course. The vegetables are usually truly awful . . . canned. Instead, have a mixed salad and fruit salad or gelato for dessert. The house wine will cost extra, but the coffee is included. When you have finished you will have had a filling meal and be on your way without having put a major hole in your budget.

NOTE: Please take a minute while you are in this area to look into Chiesa di S. Maria Assunta (Gesuiti) with works by Tintoretto. The church is located down the street from the restaurant and is open from 10 A.M. to noon and from 4 to 6 P.M. Mass is at 5:30 P.M.

(3) BOLDRIN
San Chianciano, 5550

In Venice you can spend the whole day getting lost inside the liquid maze of canals and narrow passageways that link one area to another. Adding to the fun of it all are the mystifying maps, which do not necessarily spell the names of the streets the same way you will see them spelled on corner street signs or on business cards, if, in fact, they are even listed in these places. A good case in point is this sensational lunch Cheap Eat, Boldrin, located on San Chianciano if you go by the map, or San Canciano if you go by the *enoteca*'s business card. Pick one. Both map and business card have the restaurant located in the same spot on the street, whichever way you want to spell it, so let's be happy with that.

What is the Cheap Eat news about another cafeteria-style lunch? First, it is a hot ticket for locals, from overalled workmen to ladies draped in designer duds and gold jewelry. Why? Because the food is always fresh and plentiful, beautifully prepared and displayed, and a quantum leap above the average deli-style dining that passes for lunch in Venice. There are at least a dozen first- and second-course choices, with an emphasis on fish, pastas (including risotto and lasagna), and colorful vegetables, but no desserts. Cheap Eating, even in a cafeteria, is always better with good wines, and there is no lack of these at this *enoteca,* which has two walls filled from ceiling to floor with more bottles than anyone cares to tally. In order to blend in, your m.o. is to get your food, pay, then hope you can snag a seat. Seating is along the walls next to the wine shelves, or at the wraparound bar where the dishes and *tramezzini* (sandwiches) are displayed.

TELEPHONE
041-52-37-859

OPEN
Mon–Sat, lunch only

CLOSED
Sun

HOURS
9 A.M.–9 P.M., hot lunch from noon–2:30 P.M., *tramezzini* anytime

RESERVATIONS
Not necessary

CREDIT CARDS
None

À LA CARTE
Sandwiches from L3,000, hot foods L8,000–12,000 per dish

MENÙ TURISTICO
None

COVER AND SERVICE CHARGES
None

ENGLISH
Limited

(4) DA BEPPI
Salizzada D. Pistor, 4550

One hundred years ago this was a rough-and-ready watering hole for the workers who cleaned the canals. Today, only the beamed ceiling remains as a reminder of those rowdy days. Inside this modest little trattoria near Ca' d'Oro are two wood-paneled rooms with the usual paintings of Venice hanging about. In front is a shaded patio that is perfect for combining warm-weather dining with people-watching. The food at Da Beppi is good because Loris, Delfina, and Bepe, who own it, do the cooking *and* the serving, which creates the type of

TELEPHONE
041-52-85-031

OPEN
Mon, Wed–Sun

CLOSED
Tues, Jan–Feb (until Carnivale)

HOURS
Noon–3 P.M., 7–10 P.M.

RESERVATIONS
Advised for weekends

CREDIT CARDS
MC, V

À LA CARTE
L45,000, beverage extra
MENÙ TURISTICO
None
COVER AND SERVICE CHARGES
Cover L3,000, service included
ENGLISH
Yes

Venetian homestyle atmosphere everyone hopes to find.

The daily specials depend on the season and whatever they find fresh at the market. No matter what time of year it is, you can expect to find *baccalà* (creamed salted cod), marinated sardines, liver and onions, and a wonderful homemade chocolate almond cake with creamy chocolate frosting. The pastas are served in generous portions with a basket of crusty bread on the side to lap up the last drops of sauce.

(5) FIASCHETTERIA TOSCANA ($)

Salizzada San Giovanni Grisostomo, 5719

TELEPHONE
041-52-85-281
OPEN
Mon, Wed–Sun
CLOSED
Tues, 1 week after Carnivale, part of July and Aug (dates vary)
HOURS
12:30–2:30 P.M., 7:30–10:30 P.M.
RESERVATIONS
Essential
CREDIT CARDS
AE, DC, MC, V
À LA CARTE
L55,000–80,000, beverage extra
MENÙ TURISTICO
None
COVER AND SERVICE CHARGES
Cover and service charges included
ENGLISH
Yes, and menu in English
MISCELLANEOUS
A member of Ristoranti della Buona Accoglienza; see page 159 for details.

Fiaschetteria Toscana is the top choice of many Venetians for a celebration meal. The trick is to be sure to reserve a table downstairs, where the Murano wall lights and candles cast a soft and romantic aura on the evening. Here the air is cooler, the tables farther apart, and the service better. The brightly lit, beamed upstairs room can get hot, smoky, and crowded, with tables so closely spaced that only models could wedge in between them.

No matter where you are seated, the seasonally prepared food will be memorable. The fish is always excellent, but the price tags on most of these could send the bill quickly into triple digits. Better to start with warm artichoke hearts or a plate of designer greens, and then order *tagliolini* with scampi and zucchini flowers, a creamy vegetable risotto, or maybe the gnocchi with bacon and radicchio. For the second course, the mixed grill is sufficient for any stevedore, the baked eel with bay leaves will please those who love something different, and the baked sea bass with potatoes will satisfy the cautious. Fish isn't the only wonderful possibility. There are grilled *fiorentina* steaks, Irish angus beef, and veal scallops with marsala wine. I think it is important to have dessert here, even if you have to share. The caramel apple cake with a scoop of vanilla ice cream is my favorite, but if there is a piece of the dense almond cake available, I am always torn, and reluctant to share either in the end.

(6) LA COLONNA

Calle del Fumo, 5329 (at Campiello Pestrin)

TELEPHONE
041-52-29-641
OPEN
Mon–Sat

"It's going to be good," I said to my dining pal, "just look at the locals filling every table." I was right, the neighborhood likes and respects the simple takes the chef has on succulent seafood, and loyal patrons probably run into him shopping on a daily basis at the Rialto Market. The small brick interior is correctly set with white linens, and the outdoor terrace is romantically lit at night. As you walk in, be sure to notice the beautiful window display of fresh fruits and produce that will be part of your meal. There is a two-course fixed-price Cheap Eat option, but I would suggest splashing out a bit and paying close attention to the easy-to-read handwritten menu, which reflects the chef's shopping safaris. You may sample crab with tiny asparagus tips, or a special risotto made to order for two, fresh sardines prepared with onions and pine nuts and served with polenta, a beautiful grilled or baked fish, and, for dessert, fat, juicy red strawberries. The satisfying food is cooked to order and served by one waiter, who manages to be gracious and accommodating despite his work overload. At home, he would be unionized and six people would be on the books to do his job!

CLOSED
Sun, Nov or maybe Jan

HOURS
Noon–2:30 P.M., 7:30–10 P.M.

RESERVATIONS
Advised, especially at night

CREDIT CARDS
AE, DC, MC, V

À LA CARTE
L40,000–50,000, beverage extra

MENÙ TURISTICO
L22,000, two courses plus salad or vegetable; cover and service included, beverage extra

COVER AND SERVICE CHARGES
Both included

ENGLISH
Yes

(7) L'ISOLA DEL GELATO

Rio Terra San Leonardo, 1525 (just before Campo San Leonardo)

The strip of real estate leading from the *ferrovia* (train station) on Rio Terra di Spagna, across Campo S. Geremia and along Rio Terra San Leonardo, is full of tourist traps. You really need to know what you are doing here to avoid getting your budget soaked by poor-quality restaurants and greedy shopkeepers selling mostly garish junk. As you may have already guessed, this is not my favorite Venice neighborhood. However, you may find yourself here, and if so, there are a few redeeming places worthy of a stop. L'Isola del Gelato is one of them. From 9 A.M. until midnight, 365 days a year, you can indulge in cones, cups, sundaes, banana splits, and other ice cream treats, including spaghetti ice cream made with vanilla and strawberry gelato and topped with coconut. Everything you eat is made with delicious gelato manufactured on the premises by Fabio, the hardworking and friendly owner. With a nod toward health-conscious customers, low-fat yogurt is also available and so are zero-fat and zero-sugar soya ices, including chocolate. While not worth a *vaporétto* trip from St. Mark's Square, this warrants a stop if you are in the neighborhood.

TELEPHONE
041-52-40-454

OPEN
Daily

CLOSED
Never

HOURS
9 A.M.–midnight

RESERVATIONS
Not accepted

CREDIT CARDS
None

À LA CARTE
Gelato from L1,500–7,000; L16,000 per kilo packed to go

MENÙ TURISTICO
None

COVER AND SERVICE CHARGES
None

ENGLISH
Limited

(8) OSTERIA ALLA FRASCA
Corte della Carità, 5176

TELEPHONE
041-52-85-433
OPEN
Mon–Wed, Fri–Sun
CLOSED
Thurs, 2–3 weeks in Jan, 1 week mid-Aug
HOURS
Winter 8 A.M.–9 P.M., lunch 12:30–2:30 P.M., dinner 7:30–9 P.M.; summer 8 A.M.–11 P.M., lunch 12:30–2:30 P.M., dinner 7:30–10 P.M.
RESERVATIONS
Advised
CREDIT CARDS
None
À LA CARTE
Cicchetti from L1,400, meals L25,000–30,000, beverage extra
MENÙ TURISTICO
None
COVER AND SERVICE CHARGES
Cover L3,000, no service charge
ENGLISH
Enough

No trip to Venice is complete without losing yourself in the sinking city's seductive byways, and the hunt for this hidden gem is a golden opportunity to do just that. Actually, you do not have to become an expert cartographer in the quest, just follow these directions. If you are coming from Fondamenta Nuove, walk down Calle del Fumo to Calle D. Volto, turn right and Corte della Carità is the second opening on your right; you will see the restaurant at the back of the little square. This is a real Venetian square, where people have lived all their lives and hung their weekly laundry to blow in the breeze and flap against the aging buildings. Bright flowers are lovingly tended in window boxes, dogs and children play after school, old ladies gossip, and the men talk politics and sports. For local color, it does not get much better.

The *osteria* itself isn't much to look at, but it does have an interesting past. It was the storeroom where Tiziano kept his art supplies. There is no evidence of this now in the tiny interior with four tables and a weekly menu taped to the refrigerator door. There are more tables outside, weather permitting. As you can imagine, the food here is comforting rather than trendy, and its mainstay is fish, served every day but Monday, when it is *bollito* (boiled meat) and tripe. On Tuesday it is fish and *pasta e fagoli,* Wednesday risotto of some sort, and the rest of the week, fish again. Dessert consists of hard cookies to dip in sweet wine. It sounds plain, but after a while, you will become addicted to this special Italian finale to your meal. If you aren't in the mood for fish, there will always be one or two choices, maybe a pasta with a simple tomato sauce or a steak, but frankly, all I can recommend here is the fish. *Cicchetti* are served at the bar, but if you sit down with yours, you will pay the cover charge.

(9) OSTERIA AL MILION ($)
Corte al Milion, 5841 (in back of San Giovanni Criostomo Church)

TELEPHONE
041-52-29-302
OPEN
Mon–Tues, Thur–Sun
CLOSED
Wed, Aug
HOURS
Noon–3 P.M., 6:30–11 P.M.

"We spoil our guests," says Raoul, the longtime manager and now owner of Osteria Al Milion, a rather hidden *osteria* and trattoria that is reliably good, always busy, and known and loved by almost everyone in Venice.

Fish, cooked with skill and restraint, is the backbone of the menu, starting with three antipasti selections, several soups and pastas, and continuing on to the main-course roster. Other dishes that earn high marks are the liver or kidneys, veal scaloppine in white wine, and the homemade desserts, especially the *torta della casa,* an apple tart, the *tiramisù*, or the light *sorbetto al limone.* On Saturday, you can't call for reservations because they do not take them, so to avoid a wait arrive early during the meal service and join old-timers and gondoliers at the bar and have a glass of wine before going to your table. Anytime you come, bring folding money; they don't take credit cards.

RESERVATIONS
Recommended; not accepted on Sat

CREDIT CARDS
None

À LA CARTE
L50,000–60,000, beverage extra

MENÙ TURISTICO
None

COVER AND SERVICE CHARGES
Cover L4,000, 10% service added

ENGLISH
Yes

(10) OSTERIA DA ALBERTO
Calle Largo Giacinto Gallina, 5401

The rustic two-room *osteria* sits alongside a canal, with several tables overlooking the waterway. You would think tables on the canal would be the place to sit. Late in the evening, maybe, but especially at lunch, you want to be up front near the bar, where all the action is taking place. You are here for fun, food, and Venetian-style camaraderie. The order of the day should be a sandwich, a plate with assorted *cicchetti,* or the daily hot dish washed down with ample glasses of the *vino della casa*.

TELEPHONE
041-52-38-153

OPEN
Mon–Sat

CLOSED
Sun, 15 days before or after Carnivale, 3 weeks in Aug

HOURS
9:30 A.M.–3 P.M., 5:30–11 P.M.

RESERVATIONS
Advised for dinner

CREDIT CARDS
None

À LA CARTE
From L2,500 for snacks, L35,000 full meal

MENÙ TURISTICO
None

COVER AND SERVICE CHARGES
Both included

ENGLISH
Yes

(11) TRATTORIA ALL'ANTICA MOLA
Fondamenta degli Ormesini, 2800

Venice exists today because of the huge influx of tourists who spend over $100 million a year here. A visitor to Venice can easily become a sitting duck for dining rip-offs. With a little extra effort and some ingenuity, venturing off the beaten tourist track can yield not only better food but a great increase in value. Sitting along a canal on the edge of the Jewish Quarter is Trattoria all'Antica Mola, where you will be assured a close encounter with the natives along with a decent meal at a fair price. It is an unassuming place, but you

TELEPHONE
041-72-74-92

OPEN
Daily

CLOSED
Never

HOURS
Noon–midnight, continuous service

RESERVATIONS
Advised

CREDIT CARDS
AE, DC, MC, V

À LA CARTE
L35,000–45,000, beverage extra

MENÙ TURISTICO
None

COVER AND SERVICE CHARGES
Cover L2,500, service included

ENGLISH
Yes

will be able to spot it as you approach: it is the one with the flags flying beside the canal-side tables. The easiest way to find it is to cross the Campo di Quarter Nuovo to Fondamenta degli Ormesini and turn right, or walk along Rio Terrà Farsetti, cross the bridge, and turn left.

Time and tradition stand behind the food and the dowdy atmosphere. The two rooms, hung with old copper, postcards from regulars, and signed drawings on napkins, are in need of redecorating, but no one is thinking of doing anything like that anytime soon. The most satisfying meal lire will be spent on the simple pastas and second courses based on fish. If dessert is part of your plan, look at the fruit-topped custard tarts or the orange cake. The house wines are good . . . and cheap. Another bonus: The food is served nonstop from noon to midnight every day.

(12) TRATTORIA CA' D'ORO, OSTERIA DALLA VEDOVA

Calle del Pistor and Ramo Ca' d'Oro, 3912–3952 (off Strada Nova)

TELEPHONE
041-52-85-324

OPEN
Mon–Wed, Fri–Sat; Sun, dinner only

CLOSED
Thur, 2 weeks after Carnivale, Aug–Sept (dates vary)

HOURS
11:30 A.M.–3 P.M., 6:30–11 P.M.

RESERVATIONS
Advised

CREDIT CARDS
None

À LA CARTE
L25,000–35,000, beverage extra

MENÙ TURISTICO
None

COVER AND SERVICE CHARGES
Cover L1,500, service included

ENGLISH
Most of the time

The name on the business card reads: Trattoria Ca' d'Oro—Ostaria dalla Vedova. But on the window it's simply La Vedova, which is how it's known by all of its patrons.

This spot has been in the same family for 130 years, and judging from the inside, little has changed in that time. The two rooms are filled with what looks like original furniture, a marvelous collection of copper pots hanging from the ceiling, and pretty antique lights. Anytime you go you find the owners, Lorenzo and Mirella, his sister, mixing and mingling with an interesting sampling of area regulars, who sit at the plain wooden tables sharing a bottle of *vino rosso* and arguing about Sunday's soccer scores or the latest Italian political scandal.

Even though there is no proper menu and they do not serve dessert, this is a good place to keep in mind for a light lunch and dinner. Find out what the chef has prepared for that day, maybe a pasta with fresh clams or a hearty soup, and pair that with the plate of antipasti, a few chunks of bread, and a sturdy wine, and you will be all set. The service has been known to be cool, but after a few glasses of wine, your Italian should improve, and you will feel more welcome.

Castello

Lying on the eastern half of Venice, Castello is the largest of the *sestieri,* and the only one without real estate along the Grand Canal. The central building is the huge Gothic church of Santi Giovanni e Paolo, with the equestrian monument of Bartholomeo Colleoni by Andrea del Verrocchio. In back of the church is the Ospedale Civile, where you can see the ambulance boats tied up at the dock alongside the canal ready to respond to emergencies. Campo Santa Maria Formosa serves as a major crossing point between Piazza San Marco and the Rialto Bridge, and an interesting place to sip a cool drink in the afternoon and watch the neighborhood children gather to play while their moms and nannies gossip or buy produce from one of the two stalls in the center of the square. Also in this district is the Arsenale—the shipyards of Venice—and the Riva degli Schiavoni—Venice's premier promenading ground, lined with grand hotels (the Danieli for one) and waves of tourists. To the east is Rio Terà Garibaldi, the lusty workingman's quarter.

(13) AL COVO ($)
Campiello della Pescaria, 3968

People often ask me, "If you had only one meal to eat in a city, where would it be?" In Venice the answer is simple: I would go to Al Covo for dinner. It was opened in 1987 by Diane and Cesare Benelli, a dynamic American/Italian couple who know and appreciate good food. The popularity of Al Covo is due to the excellence of its cuisine, prepared by Cesare, and the warm atmosphere created by Diane using their impressive collection of artwork. At night, fresh flowers and candles adorn the tables, which are formally set with floral-patterned china, heavy cutlery, and gleaming crystal.

While looking over the menu, a glass of complimentary champagne and some nibbles are brought to your table. The assorted breads are served with iced butter curls, a treat unknown in other Venetian restaurants. All of their dishes are prepared to order, using what the market offers each day and what products are in season. No frozen or canned foods are used, and neither do they use glutamates in making sauces. Cesare is justly well-known for his imaginative and delicate preparations of fresh seafood, prepared without the use of butter or other

TELEPHONE
041-52-23-812

OPEN
Mon–Tues, Fri–Sun

CLOSED
Wed, Thur, Jan, Aug (2 weeks)

HOURS
12:45–2:15 P.M., 7:45–10:15 P.M.

RESERVATIONS
Essential

CREDIT CARDS
None, but they will accept U.S. dollars

À LA CARTE
Lunch from L35,000; dinner L70,000–80,000; beverage extra

MENÙ TURISTICO
Lunch only, L45,000, three courses; cover included, beverage and service extra

COVER AND SERVICE CHARGES
Cover L6,000, service not included

ENGLISH
Yes, and menu in English

MISCELLANEOUS
Al Covo is a member of the Ristoranti della Buona Accoglienza; see page 159 for details.

animal fats. All the pastas are made daily in-house, as is the tomato sauce made from a recipe Cesare inherited from his grandmother. In winter, roasted wild local duck served with fresh mixed vegetables is an anticipated specialty of the house. At dinner, fish and seafood dominate the menu, but other tastes are graciously accommodated if you call ahead.

Their lunch offer has taken off like wildfire. In the tradition of trattorias, they have developed a midday menu consisting of a choice of appetizer or pasta dish of the day, main dish, and dessert. If you do not want this large of a meal, platters of mixed cheeses or vegetables, appetizers, soups, or just a bowl of pasta will be available. The atmosphere is casual, with bare tables, cloth napkins, and quick service geared to a repeat crowd of locals who have a limited time for lunch.

Whenever you eat at Al Covo (and I know readers who have found it and eaten *all* of their meals here while in Venice), you absolutely must promise me to try at least one or two of Diane's homemade desserts. If the pear and prune cake with grappa sauce is available, have it for sure. It is so good it was featured in *Gourmet* magazine. The other choices are endless: chocolate chip or oatmeal cookies to dip in sweet wine, a bitter chocolate cake, a walnut cake with caramel sauce spiked with aged rum, or *panna cotta* with dark chocolate sauce.

Service by the English-speaking staff is attentive and helpful. While the lunch prices will fit into most budgets, the dinner prices are definitely not for budgeteers, so reserve this special occasion for a last night in Venice with someone you love.

(14) ALLE TESTIERE ($)
Calle del Mondo Novo, 5801 (off Salizzada San Lio)

TELEPHONE
041-52-27-220

OPEN
Mon–Sat

CLOSED
Sun, 2 weeks at Christmas, 1 week in March, end of July for 3 weeks

HOURS
Noon–2 P.M., 7:30–11 P.M.

RESERVATIONS
Essential

CREDIT CARDS
None

À LA CARTE
L50,000–55,000, beverage extra

Where do the Venetians go for fish? When a place is "found," it is coveted and traded like insider stock market tips to a select few. Such was the case when Alle Testiere opened. Everything about the spot is modest, except the quality of the fish and the potential size of your check if you are not careful. Each of the six or so otherwise bare tables has a Murano vase with fresh flowers. Seating is on hard bistro chairs, and service is quick . . . they have to turn those tables several times during a meal to keep out of the red. Fish plays a central role in every dish on the small menu. It is, however, fresh, well-prepared, and a delight to eat. From a very meager beginning, the restaurant is now the talk of the town, and an insider favorite you should consider a solid investment.

MENÙ TURISTICO
None
COVER AND SERVICE CHARGES
Cover L3,000, 10% service added
ENGLISH
Yes

(15) AL VECIO CANTON
Corte Rotta, 4738/a

Yes, another shrine to pizza, but this one is hidden (off Ruga Guiffa), the natives pack the place, and few tourists other than you and I know about it. Other points in its favor include its close proximity to St. Mark's Square, the swift and sure service, the staggering list of pizzas available for both lunch and dinner (forget all the other stuff on the second page of the menu, this is a pizza joint . . . period), the fresh ingredients, and the high quality. The pizzas are, in a word, great, especially their specialty—starring tomatoes, buffalo mozzarella, and anchovies—which is deceptively rich and delicious down to the last crumb of crispy crust.

Finally, the prices will keep any Cheap Eater happy and in high spirits.

TELEPHONE
041-52-85-176
OPEN
Mon, Wed–Sun
CLOSED
Tues, Aug
HOURS
Noon–3:30 P.M., 7:30 P.M.–midnight
RESERVATIONS
Essential, especially for dinner and on the weekends
CREDIT CARDS
AE, DC, MC, V
À LA CARTE
Pizza L9,000–15,000, beverage extra
MENÙ TURISTICO
L19,000, two courses and vegetables; cover and service included, beverage extra
COVER AND SERVICE CHARGES
Cover L2,000, service included
ENGLISH
Yes, and menu in English

(16) ANTICA SACRESTIA
SS. Filippo e Giacomo, 4442

Your two teenagers are demanding pizza, your wife wants a vegetarian meal break, your mother-in-law thinks pasta and a salad would hit the spot, and you are yearning for ham and eggs (and some relief from this meal grief). No problem, simply head for Antica Sacrestia, about a ten-minute meander from San Marco. As you probably have guessed, this all-purpose Cheap Eat offers something for everyone . . . including a chocolate or banana pizza, some stiff cocktails, and, best of all, prices that are easy on your travel budget. The thirty-one pizzas are enhanced by a dozen specialties, four more feature white cheese and creamy vegetable toppings. For dessert, there's kiwi and liqueur-infused pizzas and those topped with chocolate and banana. The five *menù turisticos* cover all the bases, from a basic three-course Cheap Eat to two dominated by fish, one for vegetarians, and one described as having *porzioni enormi* (enormous portions) of all the house specialties. If this is not enough of a selection, there are two pages of à la carte menu items

TELEPHONE
041-52-30-749
OPEN
Tues–Sun
CLOSED
Mon, a few days at Christmas
HOURS
11:30 A.M.–3 P.M., 6:30–10:30 P.M.
RESERVATIONS
Advised
CREDIT CARDS
V
À LA CARTE
Pizza from L8,000, full meals L30,000–40,000
MENÙ TURISTICO
(all include cover and service, beverage is extra) L22,000, three courses. "Vegetariano": L30,000, three courses and salad. "Venetian": L35,000, three courses, all fish except liver as one main-course option. "Pesce": L45,000, three courses,

all fish. "Antiaca Sacrestia": L80,000, house specialties from appetizer to dessert

COVER AND SERVICE CHARGES
Cover L2,000, 12% service added

ENGLISH
Yes

ranging from seventeen pasta combinations (including macaroni and cheese, crepes, and a vegetable torte) to fifteen fish dishes and as many with meat, twenty-one desserts, and, of course, the above-mentioned ham and eggs. If you can't find something to eat at Antica Sacresita, I give up.

(17) CIP CIAP

Calle del Mondo Novo, 5799

TELEPHONE
041-52-36-621

OPEN
Mon, Wed–Sun

CLOSED
Tues, 2–3 weeks in Dec or Jan (dates vary)

HOURS
9 A.M.–9 P.M., continuous service

RESERVATIONS
Not accepted

CREDIT CARDS
None

À LA CARTE
Pizza slices, calzones, and tortas sold by weight starting from L3,500; whole pizzas from L10,000

MENÙ TURISTICO
None

COVER AND SERVICE CHARGES
No cover, service included

ENGLISH
Sometimes

If you want a slice of good pizza, a bulging calzone, or an assortment of minipizzas to munch on for a quick snack, do not miss this busy little corner establishment off the Campo Santa Maria Formosa. This is Italian fast food and I love it. It was located close to my Venetian flat, and I will admit, I was a regular customer.

You can eat here if you want to stand along the Calle del Mondo Novo, or better, have your slices packaged to go. Dole out a worthwhile L3,500 or so per slice and a little more for the calzone, take your feast over to the Campo Santa Maria Formosa, and sit on a bench and watch the neighborhood at work and at play. It is a great way to feel Italian and have a satisfying Cheap Eat in the bargain.

(18) LA BOUTIQUE DEL GELATO

Salizzada San Lio, 5727

TELEPHONE
041-52-23-283

OPEN
Daily

CLOSED
Jan

HOURS
10 A.M.–8:30 P.M.

RESERVATIONS
Not accepted

CREDIT CARDS
None

À LA CARTE
Gelato from L2,000

MENÙ TURISTICO
None

COVER AND SERVICE CHARGES
None

ENGLISH
Yes

Italians know good *gelato* when they taste it, and nowhere is it much better than here. It's easy to find: just look for the line that weaves down the narrow Salizzada San Lio, which begins when they open around 10 A.M. and lasts until closing at 8:30 P.M. Run by an energetic trio—Sandra and Silvio Calvaldoro and her brother, Paolo—this tiny operation does an amazing business. They are smart: they offer a few knockout flavors sold by the cone or cup, or packaged to go. There is no seating at all and no beverages available. I passed the shop coming and going to my flat each day, and every time it was all I could do not to stop in for a scoop of *nocciolosa* (a creamy chocolate gelato laced with nuts) or their specialty (and secret recipe) the *millefoglie.* Sandra and Silvio both speak English and have friends in San Francisco whom they often visit. If you are anywhere near their Venice *gelateria,* please have a scoop or two for me.

(19) OSTERIA AL PORTICO

Calle della Fava, near Salizzada San Lio

It is picturesque, with copper pots, low beams, barflies, and wine barrels crowding the small room. Luigi, the affable owner, speaks English and welcomes everyone to his really great Venetian hangout. Here you eat *cicchetti,* or the hot specials of the day, neatly written on a piece of olive-brown construction paper. Your wine will be from the Veneto and your check from heaven.

TELEPHONE
Not available

OPEN
Mon–Sat

CLOSED
Sun, 1 week in June and 1 week in Nov

HOURS
9–10 A.M., continuous bar and *cicchetti,* hot food noon–2 P.M., 7–9 P.M.

RESERVATIONS
Not necessary

CREDIT CARDS
None

À LA CARTE
Cicchetti from L2,500, two-course meal L25,000

MENÙ TURISTICO
None

COVER AND SERVICE CHARGES
None

ENGLISH
Yes

(20) RISTORANTE "DA CARLETTO"

Calle delle Bande, 5272

To get almost anyplace during my recent three-month stay in Venice to do the research for the *Cheap Sleeps* and *Cheap Eats in Italy* series, I walked by the Ristorante "da Carletto." I always liked what I saw . . . a pretty dining room with decorative plates hanging between beams, pink tablecloths, fresh flowers, candles at night, and an owner on duty to oversee the properly clad waiters. When I tried it, I was not disappointed. My fellow diners were an attractive blend of visitors and neighborhood regulars who obviously appreciate the intimate atmosphere and the honest cooking, which is a blend of Venetian standards with fish as the highlight. During the several times I ate here, the service by the accommodating waiters was always excellent and everyone was treated with equal dignity and respect.

To begin, I suggest the *insalata caprese,* made with fresh tomatoes, *bufala* mozzarella, and leafy basil. When I commented to my waiter about the pretty presentation, he said, "I think it looks like the Italian flag." It did—and it certainly reminded me I was having dinner in my favorite Italian city. The pastas are all delicious, and served in just the right portions to allow you to go on to a second course of fish or meat. To add to the enticement, there is a very well priced lunchtime *menù turistico.*

TELEPHONE
041-52-27-944

OPEN
Daily

CLOSED
Mon in winter

HOURS
Noon–3 P.M., 7 P.M.–midnight

RESERVATIONS
Advised

CREDIT CARDS
AE, DC, MC, V

À LA CARTE
L40,000–45,000, beverage extra

MENÙ TURISTICO
Lunch only, L27,000, two courses and vegetable or salad; cover and service included, beverage extra

COVER AND SERVICE
No cover, 12% service added

ENGLISH
Yes, and menu in English

(21) TRATTORIA ALLA RIVETTA
Ponte San Provolo, 4625

TELEPHONE
041-52-87-302
OPEN
Tues–Sun
CLOSED
Mon, Aug (dates vary)
HOURS
10 A.M.–10 P.M., continuous service
RESERVATIONS
Not necessary
CREDIT CARDS
AE, MC, V
À LA CARTE
L35,000–40,000, beverage extra
MENÙ TURISTICO
None
COVER AND SERVICE CHARGES
Cover L2,000, 12% service added
ENGLISH
Some, and menu in English

Trattoria alla Rivetta, squeezed in on the right just before the Ponte San Provolo and off Campo S.S. Filipino e Giancomo, is a genuine and reasonable alternative to the many touristy alternatives that plague this area of Venice. A good sign, as always, is that the locals know about it and eat here in droves, filling every seat in the house almost as soon as it is open. You will see everyone from gondoliers on their breaks grabbing a snack at the bar and a glass of *vino della casa* to women out for a gossipy afternoon with their friends and other savvy *Cheap Eats in Italy* readers. True, it has been discovered, but that fact has not diminished its authenticity one bit. The menu is printed in English, and the restaurant serves full meals from 10 A.M. to 10 P.M., two distinct advantages for the Venetian visitors.

The portions are not for the light eater. In fact, the bowl of mussels ordered as a first course will be plenty if you add a salad and the fresh bread that comes with every Italian meal. Growing boys and other hungry diners can start with the *tagliolini ai granchio,* pasta with fresh crab, or a time-honored spaghetti with meat sauce. The squid cooked in its own black ink served with polenta and the grilled jumbo shrimp are delicious entrées. There is also a full line of meats, including Venetian liver and onions, veal chops, and boiled beef with pesto sauce. Desserts are run-of-the-mill except for the house *tiramisù,* that heavenly rum-spiked cake layered with triple-cream cheese and dusted with chocolate.

(22) TRATTORIA DAI TOSI
Secco Marina, 738

TELEPHONE
041-52-37-102
OPEN
Mon–Tues, Thur–Sun
CLOSED
Wed, Aug 15-22, Christmas (1 week)
HOURS
Noon–3 P.M., 6:30–11 P.M.
RESERVATIONS
Suggested for Sat and Sun
CREDIT CARDS
MC, V

Trattoria dai Tosi, which used to be called Alla Lampara, occupies small but vibrant quarters that are further in spirit from tourist central than they are in kilometers. Located off Via Garibaldi (take Calle Correra until you get to Secco Marina and it will be on your left), about a twenty-minute walk east of Piazza San Marco, this neighborhood gathering place is owned and run by two former waiters at Harry's Bar: Fabio and his wife, Lorena, and Paolo and his English wife, Jackie, who shares the cooking responsibilities with Lorena. Jackie did not start out to be a chef. On a lark, she left her native Cornwall at age seventeen and came to the Lido, where she taught pony riding to children. She worked her way up, finally becoming well-known as a trainer for the top Italian show jumpers. Along the way she met Paolo, and the rest is history: they married, had two children, and became partners in this restaurant. Pictures of their children hang on the left wall in the room beyond the bar.

At noon, blue-collar workers troop in for Jackie's specials and her *pasta della casa,* an imaginative mix of vegetables, scampi, shrimp, calamari, pepperoni, zucchini, and carrots all tossed with spaghetti and a spoonful of cream. This makes a nice meal, accompanied by one or two of her homemade crusty rolls, an *insalata mista,* and a glass of the house red wine. In the evening, almost fifty pizzas, ten of which are vegetarian, are featured, and the diners are a sampling of the area's younger residents.

NOTE: If you go for lunch, be sure to take the time to see the oldest church in Venice, which is quite close by. The San Pietro di Castello is open daily from 8 A.M. to noon and 3 to 6 P.M., and on holidays from 8 A.M. to noon and 4:30 to 7:30 P.M.

Whenever you go, if you mention *Cheap Eats in Italy* you will be offered a *sgroppino,* a lemon and vodka digestif made from a secret recipe.

À LA CARTE
L25,000–30,000, beverage extra; pizza from L9,000

MENÙ TURISTICO
None

COVER AND SERVICE CHARGES
Cover L3,000, service included

ENGLISH
Yes, and menu in English

(23) TRATTORIA DA REMIGIO ($)
Salizzada dei Greci, 3416

At Trattoria da Remigio, any choice of appetizer, pasta, and fish or meat course will be a happy one. For a new twist on an old dish, try the *gnocchi alla pescatora,* potato-based pasta puffs with fish. For best results, always pay close attention to the handwritten daily specials, especially the seafood catch. The desserts will have you doing penance on a Thighmaster when you get home. Arrive late and you will need a shoehorn to get in. The restaurant enjoys the fiercely devout patronage of Venetians, and they virtually pack it out back day and night, so get your name in for a reservation and be on time.

TELEPHONE
041-52-30-089

OPEN
Wed–Sun; Mon, lunch only

CLOSED
Tues, Jan, Aug

HOURS
12:30–2:30 P.M., 7:30–10:30 P.M.

RESERVATIONS
Essential

CREDIT CARDS
AE, MC, V

À LA CARTE
L40,000–50,000, beverage extra

MENÙ TURISTICO
None

COVER AND SERVICE CHARGES
Cover L2,500, 12% service added

ENGLISH
Limited

(24) TRATTORIA TOFANELLI
Via Giuseppe Garibaldi, 1650

TELEPHONE
041-52-35-722
OPEN
Mon–Tues, Thur–Sun
CLOSED
Wed, Jan 4–Feb 15 (until Carnivale)
HOURS
Noon–3 P.M., 6–9 P.M.
RESERVATIONS
Not accepted
CREDIT CARDS
None
À LA CARTE
L24,000, beverage extra
MENÙ TURISTICO
L20,000, three courses; cover and service included, beverage extra
COVER AND SERVICE CHARGES
Cover L1,000, service included
ENGLISH
None

"I was born right here and that makes me older than the street," said Micole Tofanelli when I asked how long she and her sister, Nella, had been serving homespun food at their corner location, a twenty-minute stroll east of St. Mark's Square. As you can imagine, the trattoria is as old as the hills, and nothing has been done to bring it up to the moment, and won't be. But it is tidy and very appealing in its own way. Inside are eight tables with brown-and-white tablecloths, an old-fashioned icebox in the corner, and green plants sitting everywhere, all in need of various amounts of TLC.

The small handwritten menu hanging in the window features meat and pasta, with fresh fish making only a cameo appearance. The sisters are best known for their *bigoli*—fresh egg pasta with anchovies and salsa—and veal scaloppine in marsala sauce. None of the food hits the high notes of gourmet cuisine, but it is filling and the portions are ample. The best part is that the prices are about as old-fashioned as the setting, a real plus for any Cheap Eater in Venice.

NOTE: No smoking is allowed. The sisters also operate a small hotel in connection with the restaurant. See *Cheap Sleeps in Italy* for details.

Dorsoduro

Dorsoduro is in the southern part of Venice, and is known for its beautiful churches, the magnificent artworks hung in the Accademia, the contemporary counterpart of the Peggy Guggenheim Collection housed in her *palazzo* along the Grand Canal, its university student population, and Campo Santa Margherita, one of the city's largest squares and a center of local activity with a daily food market.

(25) AI CUGNAI
Campo San Vio, 857

TELEPHONE
041-52-89-238
OPEN
Tues–Sun
CLOSED
Mon, Aug 1–25
HOURS
Noon–2:30 P.M., 7–9:30 P.M.

Those in search of a Cheap Eat near the Peggy Guggenheim Museum will do well to eat at Ai Cugnai. This cheapie, not too far from the Accademia *vaporétto* stop, has been run for almost fifty years by two sisters, their brother, and their combined families. Elegant it is not, but the down-home atmosphere makes for an authentic Venetian experience. As you enter, you will find a cluster of neighbors standing at the bar, comparing notes on their day. Eventually, they will go on their way or sit at one of the tables in back to have a meal.

The food is far from fancy, but it is surprisingly good, especially the daily specials and their renditions of fresh crab, when it is in season. If you want to keep your check in the Cheap Eat department, you will unfortunately have to forgo the fresh fish and go for the *menù turistico,* which allows you to select from certain dishes on the à la carte menu and includes not only the wine and coffee but cover and service charges. Be sure to ask which of the vegetables are fresh; you don't want canned spinach. For dessert, I would not miss another piece of their velvety chocolate cake for anything. But if it is all gone, the almond cake is special, too.

RESERVATIONS
Not necessary

CREDIT CARDS
None

À LA CARTE
L35,000, beverage extra

MENÙ TURISTICO
L30,000, two courses; beverage, cover, and service included

COVER AND SERVICE CHARGES
Cover L2,000, 10% service added

ENGLISH
Limited, but menu in English

(26) AI GONDOLIERI ($)
Rio Terra San Vio, 366

When reserving your table at Ai Gondolieri, ask to be in the main dining room, where you will sit at blue linen–covered tables set with smart china and crystal, fresh flowers, and glowing candles in the evening. The other narrow room, off the bar, has the same pretty place settings but has uncomfortable wooden benches along the wall and serves as a corridor for restaurant patrons coming and going.

The food at Ai Gondolieri is more expensive than some, which is why it should be saved for a Big Splurge. The restaurant is well-known for *not* serving fish, for its superb cheese list, for truffles from November to January, for its homemade pastas and especially for *risotto de secoe,* an ancient Venetian specialty made with pieces of meat from the vertebrae of a cow, cooked for hours with onions and vegetables and served in a hollowed-out loaf of bread. The best buy is definitely the *menù degustazione,* since it includes all of chef Giovanni Trevisan's monthly changing, seasonally inspired dishes, from appetizer to dessert. Wine is extra. You will start with three or four antipasti choices, including snails in Burgundy wine sauce, an unusual treatment of polenta cooked with smoky bacon, or a baby artichoke torte. Next will be homemade pasta, perhaps early spring asparagus tossed with buttery egg noodles, or tiny ravioli with truffles. The main course might be a tender guinea hen garnished with seasonal vegetables, steak with mushrooms, perfectly cooked liver with polenta, or the chef's daily

TELEPHONE
041-52-86-396

FAX
041-52-28-688

OPEN
Mon, Wed–Sun

CLOSED
Tues, Christmas Day

HOURS
Noon–2:30 P.M., 7:15–10 P.M.

RESERVATIONS
Advised, especially for dinner and Sun

CREDIT CARDS
AE, DC, MC, V

À LA CARTE
L90,000–100,000, beverage extra

MENÙ DEGUSTAZIONE
L90,000, six courses; cover and service included, beverage extra, minimum two persons

COVER AND SERVICE CHARGES
Cover L7,000, 10% service added

ENGLISH
Yes

special. Wrapping it all up is a choice of such luscious homemade desserts as ricotta cheesecake with fresh strawberry sauce, or a slice of warm apple pie lightly dusted with cinnamon.

NOTE: Under the same management is the Museum Cafe at the Peggy Guggenheim Collection; see page 184 for more details.

(27) AL PROFETA
Calle Lunga San Barnaba, 2671

TELEPHONE AND FAX
041-52-37-466
OPEN
Mon–Tues, Thur–Sun
CLOSED
Wed, Jan
HOURS
Noon–3 P.M., 7–10:30 P.M.
RESERVATIONS
Advised on weekends for garden tables
CREDIT CARDS
AE, DC, MC, V
À LA CARTE
Pizza and a salad, L25,000, beverage extra
MENÙ TURISTICO
None
COVER AND SERVICE CHARGES
Cover L2,000 for pizza, 3,000 otherwise, 12% service added
ENGLISH
Yes

Compared to many of its soggy cousins across the Atlantic, pizza in Italy has been raised to an art form. Ask Italians who know and love their pizza and they will tell you that thin, crisp crusts are in, thick crusts are out. Regulars at Al Profeta know to ignore most of the regular menu and order one of the chef's eighty varieties of pizza. The most popular choices are the *capriociosa*—tomatoes, mozzarella cheese, ham, mushrooms, and artichokes—or Pizza Profeta, with everything. For groups who can agree, there are king-size pizzas to fill four hungry souls. To go with your pizza, there are five large salads, all perfect candidates for sharing, and a very good wine selection. Of course, the menu lists the usual dishes, but frankly, you should come here only if you are in the mood for pizza. In addition to a two-room indoor eating area, this popular neighborhood dining choice boasts a large back garden that is tented in winter and open in summer. There is also a nonsmoking section.

(28) ANTICA LOCANDA MONTIN ($)
Fondamenta delle Eremite, 1147

TELEPHONE
041-52-27-151
OPEN
Mon, Thur–Sun; Tues, lunch only
CLOSED
Wed, Jan 6–25, Aug 1–10
HOURS
12:30–2:30 P.M., 7:30–10 P.M.
RESERVATIONS
Essential, especially in summer
CREDIT CARDS
AE, DC, MC, V
À LA CARTE
L50,000–55,000, beverage extra
MENÙ TURISTICO
None

Reservations are essential at this seventeenth-century inn, where the large dining room looks as if it has been the recipient of every piece of furniture and painting accumulated during the past forty years. The paintings were donated by or purchased from many renowned patrons, including Modigliani, Mark Rothko, Jackson Pollock, and virtually every other artistic figure who has passed through Venice since the end of World War II. The arbor-covered garden in back is a popular warm-weather place to dine and to experience the real Venice.

Although the quality of the food and service can be erratic, the chef's versions of Venetian standards are all good, especially the marinated sardines, *spaghetti alle seppie* (with squid), *rigatoni ai quattro formaggi* (with four cheeses), liver scaloppine with butter and sage, and

Adriatic fish either deep-fried or grilled. The desserts, so loaded with butter, cream, and sugar that they should carry health warnings, include a summer treat, *semifreddo* with strawberries, and a rich chocolate torte slathered in whipped cream.

NOTE: The Locanda also has hotel rooms. See *Cheap Sleeps in Italy* for details.

COVER AND SERVICE CHARGES
Cover L4,000, 12% service added

ENGLISH
Yes

(29) ANZOLO RAFFAEL

Campo Angelo Raffaele, 1722

In tourist terms, Anzolo Raffael is located a block beyond Mars, and it certainly should not be thought of as destination dining. But for Cheap Eaters *no-matter-what* who are looking for fresh fish at a price that will not reduce them to a diet of beans and bread for the next few meals, this is one answer. Tucked on a *campo* across from a church, it boasts true local color: the waitress, wearing a porch-dress and slippers, serves an aging clientele who show up every day, sporting the same suits and probably telling the same stories.

There is no proper menu; they will tell you what's cooking. Generally speaking, the menu consists of fish. All the favorites are here, it just depends on what is in season at the Rialto Market and the mood of the chef. Veggies, salads, and desserts are afterthoughts. The house wine is not, and is enthusiastically consumed by all who eat here.

TELEPHONE
041-52-37-456

OPEN
Wed–Sun

CLOSED
Mon, Tues, Aug (dates vary)

HOURS
12:30–2:30 P.M., 7:30–9 P.M.

RESERVATIONS
Not necessary

CREDIT CARDS
None

À LA CARTE
L30,000–40,000, beverage extra

MENÙ TURISTICO
None

COVER AND SERVICE CHARGES
Cover L2,500, 10% service added

ENGLISH
None

(30) CANTINA GIÀ SCHIAVI

Fondamenta Nani, 992

Beginning with Giaccomo, three generations of the Schiavi family have kept up a 110-year-old tradition of selling fine wines worldwide from this canal-side location. Every family member has a specific role to play, right down to the black house mascot, Lupo, a dog who proudly rides with her master in the motorboat when he delivers wine orders, and snoozes on the bow in between. In addition to selling wines by the bottle and case, it has become a favorite local wine bar selling sandwiches and *cicchetti* at lunch. In fact, Alessandra, the wife of the owner, makes over three hundred sandwiches *per day,* which sell out by 2 P.M. When you multiply that by the week, month, and year, you know they have a hit. If you are looking for something unusual to give as a gift, try a bottle of their *Fagolina Bianco* (strawberry wine), which you can sample by the glass and buy by the half-liter.

TELEPHONE
041-52-30-034

OPEN
Mon–Sat

CLOSED
Sun, Aug–Sept (2 weeks)

HOURS
Bar 8:30 A.M.–2:30 P.M., 3:30–8:30 P.M.; sandwiches noon–2:30 P.M.

RESERVATIONS
Not accepted

CREDIT CARDS
None

À LA CARTE
Sandwiches from L4,500, *cicchetti* from L1,500

MENÙ TURISTICO
None

COVER AND SERVICE CHARGES
No cover, service included

ENGLISH
Yes

When you arrive, don't be confused by the sign outside that reads "Vin: Al Bottegon"—you're at the right place.

(31) DUE TORRI
Campo Santa Margherita, 3408

TELEPHONE
041-52-38-126
OPEN
Mon–Sat, bar and lunch only
CLOSED
Sun, Christmas to New Year's, 3 weeks in Aug
HOURS
Bar 7 A.M.–9 P.M.; lunch noon–2:30 P.M.
RESERVATIONS
Not accepted
CREDIT CARDS
None
À LA CARTE
L18,000–25,000, beverage extra
MENÙ TURISTICO
None
COVER AND SERVICE CHARGES
No cover, service included
ENGLISH
None

No one has thumbed through fat-free cookbooks, called an interior decorator, or ever considered changing a thing in this local pit stop, where English is not tolerated and the cooking is as rough-hewn as the characters eating it. It is basically a no-frills lunchtime gathering place for ruddy workers, who sit around plastic-covered tables telling the same old war stories and polishing off a few glasses of red before digging into their pasta and fresh fish lunch. Those in a hurry stand at the bar and indulge in the selection of *cicchetti.* There is no menu, no dessert served, and no rules about smoking. Even the waiters may smoke on the job, but no one notices or minds because they are busy puffing their brains out, too. I recommend this place because the plain food is honest, filling, and cheap, and above all the restaurant provides a visitor with a look into the real lives of everyday Venetians.

(32) GELATI NICO
Fondamenta Zattere ai Gesuiti, 922

TELEPHONE
041-52-25-293
OPEN
Daily
CLOSED
Thurs from Oct–Jan, Dec 15–Jan 15
HOURS
Feb–Sept 6:30 A.M.–midnight, Oct–Jan 7 A.M.–10 P.M., continuous service
RESERVATIONS
Not accepted
CREDIT CARDS
None
À LA CARTE
Gianduiotto to go, L4,000; at a table, L7,000; other ice cream from L6,000
MENÙ TURISTICO
None
COVER AND SERVICE CHARGES
None
ENGLISH
Yes

The Zattere, the southernmost promenade in Venice, is especially popular with families who spend their Sunday afternoons strolling along the walkway that borders the Giudecca Canal. Along the way, there are several *gelaterie,* but Nico is far and away the best and most popular. I was first here on a freezing April afternoon during a driving rainstorm, and there were ten people ahead of me in line waiting to dig into their specialty, a *gianduiotto:* a large slice of dense chocolate hazelnut ice cream buried in whipped cream and served in a cup. You can eat here, but Cheap Eaters will certainly order theirs *passeggio,* to go, because then it will cost only L4,000. To have it served at a tiny table inside, or on the deck overlooking the canal, will set you back L7,000. The same man has been dipping out *gianduiottos* for almost four decades; others have tried to imitate him, but none have ever equaled his version. There are other ice cream treats available, from sundaes to frappés, but about the only thing anyone orders here is the famous *gianduiotto.*

(33) IL DOGE GELATERIE

Campo Santa Margherita, 3058A

I must confess, I adore Italian gelato. Nowhere in Venice is it any better than at Il Doge Gelaterie, a shrine to this scrumptious treat. All the ice cream is made here, and there are more than forty-seven superb flavors in the repertoire, including black-and-white coffee, rum, amaretto, *marron glace, tiramisù,* and English trifle. He also makes countless fruit *sorbettos* in summer and, to keep insistent dieters happy, soya gelato made with no sugar and several low-fat yogurts. The best of these is the coffee yogurt, which slips down like silk. However, this is the place to put your diet on hold, because there is one flavor you positively cannot miss, and that is his special *panna cotta del Doge,* a custard-based ice cream swirled with ribbons of caramel. It sounds rather pedestrian, but let me assure you, after one taste you will agree that it is anything but. Just thinking about it makes me wish I was there right now eating another scoop or two of this celestial gelato.

TELEPHONE
041-52-34-607

OPEN
Daily

CLOSED
Mon in winter (Nov–Jan)

HOURS
Summer 10 A.M.–2 A.M.; winter 10:30 A.M.–8 P.M.

RESERVATIONS
Not accepted

CREDIT CARDS
None

À LA CARTE
Gelato from L2,500

MENÙ TURISTICO
None

COVER AND SERVICE CHARGES
None

ENGLISH
Limited

(34) L'INCONTRO ($)

Campo Santa Margherita, 3062A

L'Incontro (near Ponte dei Pugni across Rio Terra Canal) is the kind of place you always hope will be just around the corner, and it was for me. The first time I researched Venice for *Cheap Eats in Italy,* I lived on Campo Squellini, near the Campo Santa Margherita in Dorsoduro. Naturally, I tried every Cheap Eat candidate in the vicinity, and L'Incontro topped my list of favorites. I liked it because it was local and extremely popular; it served dependable, well-priced food; and it was, until now, totally undiscovered. During my last stay in Venice, while working on the third edition, I ate here several times, and I am happy to say I still love this restaurant.

The small establishment is composed of two rooms divided by a bar, and a sidewalk terrace. The low-beamed ceilings, lacy window curtains, flowered tablecloths, baskets on the walls, and strawflower arrangements create a cozy, old-world atmosphere. If you go for dinner, arrive about 8:30 or 9 P.M. to give it a chance to fill up with other diners. When planning your meal, forget the long printed menu and stay strictly with the handwritten daily one, which changes for lunch and dinner. The owner, Luciano, is Sardinian, so the dishes reflect his

TELEPHONE
041-52-22-404

OPEN
Tues–Sun

CLOSED
Mon, July

HOURS
12:30–3 P.M., 7:30–11 P.M.

RESERVATIONS
Advised

CREDIT CARDS
AE, MC, V

À LA CARTE
L45,000–50,000, beverage extra

MENÙ TURISTICO
None

COVER AND SERVICE CHARGES
Cover L3,000, service included

ENGLISH
Yes

love for the cooking of this region. The specials include generous servings of homemade pastas, including wonderful versions of gnocchi dressed in pecorino cheese sauce or with artichokes. The chef does not prepare any fish, concentrating instead on wild game in season, Chianti beef, and grilled, roasted, or stewed veal and pork. The desserts are adequate but not thrilling, so I always pass on the sweet course and walk over to Il Doge Gelaterie (see above) for a scoop of my favorite gelato. The house wine is light and refreshing.

NOTE: When I first discovered L'Incontro, there was no sign. Now there is, but that does not mean it is going to be a snap to locate. It's toward the lower left end of the Campo Santa Margherita as you head toward Campo Santa Barnaba and the floating vegetable market. At lunch and dinner you will see the daily menu taped to a small window to the left of the door. The restaurant is next to a mask shop. When all else fails, ask a shopkeeper. Everyone knows it.

(35) MUSEUM CAFE, PEGGY GUGGENHEIM COLLECTION

Dorsoduro, 707 (follow signs after Ponte Accademia)

TELEPHONE AND FAX
041-52-28-688

OPEN
Wed–Sun

CLOSED
Tues, and whenever the museum is closed

HOURS
Cafe hours 11 A.M.–5 P.M.

RESERVATIONS
Not necessary

CREDIT CARDS
AE, DC, MC, V

À LA CARTE
L25,000–35,000, sandwiches and desserts L10,000–20,000

MENÙ TURISTICO
None

COVER AND SERVICE CHARGES
None

ENGLISH
Yes, and menu in English

The Museum Cafe is as contemporary and inviting as its coolly elegant surroundings. Peggy Guggenheim was an extraordinary woman who amassed a brilliant collection of surreal and abstract art of the twentieth century. This museum, which was her home on the Grand Canal in Venice until her death in 1979, showcases her private collection of avant-garde paintings and sculpture.

The modern cafe wraps itself around a bar, an outside terrace, and several rooms displaying black-and-white photographs of the life of this remarkable and often controversial patron of the arts. The cafe is run by Giovanni Trevisan, the talented chef of Ai Gondolieri (see page 179), so you know it will not only be imaginative and delicious but slightly on the high side for some Cheap Eaters. The menu follows the seasons and offers large salads, pastas, main courses, sandwiches, and desserts. Many of the daily specials and first courses are the same as you would have at Ai Gondolieri, but for much less investment. You also have the option of ordering a full-scale meal or only a coffee. The cafe is open whenever the museum is, but to eat here you must buy a ticket for the museum, which in my opinion is certainly worth it.

(36) RISTORANTE RIVERA ($)
Zattere, Ponte Lungo, 1473

Everyone is known and greeted accordingly at Ristorante Rivera, a more comforting than trendy selection on the Zattere facing the Giudecca Canal. The small inside is formally set with rose-colored cloths on tables centered by a bouquet of fresh flowers. Over the bar are model ships, and beyond, a peek into the kitchen. During warm weather, patrons sit at tables along the canal. I recommend starting with either the fish or the vegetable risotto, then selecting whatever seasonal fish is being prepared and ordering a mixed vegetable salad to accompany it. Be sure to order a nice bottle of wine and come prepared to relax and enjoy your meal, because even though the service is gracious and correct, it can lag, especially during dinner.

TELEPHONE
041-52-27-621

OPEN
Tues–Sun

CLOSED
Mon; winter Tues–Thurs, Sun, dinner; 1 week in Nov, 1 week in Dec before Christmas, last 3 weeks in Jan

HOURS
12:30–2 P.M., 7:30–10 P.M.

RESERVATIONS
Strongly advised

CREDIT CARDS
AE, DC, MC, V

À LA CARTE
L50,000–60,000

MENÙ TURISTICO
None

COVER AND SERVICE CHARGES
Cover L2,400, 15% service added

ENGLISH
Yes

(37) TAVERNA SAN TROVASO
Fondamenta Priuli, 1016

The small and very popular Taverna San Trovaso is a family-run effort of six brothers, their one sister, and assorted spouses and offspring. You *must* call ahead for reservations and arrive on time if you expect to get a table. Readers of *Cheap Eats in Italy* as well as smart Venetians know and recommend it as a restaurant where a delicious, uncomplicated meal can be had for a moderate price. Restful and relaxing it is not, but full of happy locals having a good time and raising the noise level by the minute it is.

The *menù turistico* is a good value and offers enough choices to keep it interesting. The à la carte menu is varied and includes pizza noon and night, so it should appeal to everyone. The servings are tremendous, thus it is imperative to arrive hungry in order to do justice to it all.

TELEPHONE
041-52-03-703

OPEN
Tues–Sun

CLOSED
Mon, Dec 31–Jan 1, second week of July

HOURS
Noon–2:30 P.M., 7–9:30 P.M.

RESERVATIONS
Essential (and don't be late)

CREDIT CARDS
AE, MC, V

À LA CARTE
L40,000, beverage extra; pizzas from L8,000

MENÙ TURISTICO
L27,000, three courses; cover added, beverage included

COVER AND SERVICE CHARGES
Cover L2,500, service not included

ENGLISH
Yes, and menu in English

MISCELLANEOUS
There is a nonsmoking section.

(38) TONOLO
Salizzada San Pantalon, 3764

TELEPHONE
041-53-37-209
OPEN
Tues–Sun
CLOSED
Mon, 2 days after Carnivale, Aug
HOURS
8 A.M.–9 P.M., continuous service
RESERVATIONS
Not accepted
CREDIT CARDS
None
À LA CARTE
Pastries from L1,400
MENÙ TURISTICO
None
COVER AND SERVICE CHARGES
None
ENGLISH
Very limited

You will undoubtedly be the only tourist when you join the students, the blue-haired dowagers, the well-dressed businessfolk, and the shopkeepers at Tonolo, the most popular spot to have a cappuccino and pastry in the San Pantalon area of Venice. Before arriving, sharpen your elbows and your determination to better edge your way to the counter, where the young women somehow miraculously keep straight all the early morning orders as they are shouted. Open from 8 A.M. until 9 P.M., this constantly crowded bakery makes some of the best high-calorie treats in Venice, and everyone knows it. There are no tables, so you must eat standing or have your order packaged to go. In the morning, indulge in a fresh cream-filled doughnut, a plain or almond-topped *cornetto* (croissant), raisin pound cake, or buttery brioche. At lunch, try two or three little pizzas. In the late afternoon, any one of their indulgent pastries or cakes will make you even happier that you are in Venice.

San Marco

Piazza San Marco is the heart and soul of Venice, and has been since the first rulers built the Doge Palace and St. Mark's Basilica. Often flooded, ringed with outrageously expensive shops and *caffès,* and populated by people and pigeons, it is the place every tourist visits and usually spends money. It is also the focus of the Carnivale season leading up to Lent, when crossing the square is a virtual impossibility due to the throngs of costumed posers and revelers. San Marco is where most of the essential sights are centered as well as the posh hotels, shopping streets, and most overpriced restaurants. The don't-miss sights include the Correr Museum, a lovely untouched archaeological museum; the Bridge of Sighs; the Gothic San Stefano Church; the Palazzo Grassi, the city's most important venue for art shows; and La Fenice Opera, which tragically burned a few years ago but is being reconstructed amid great controversy.

(39) LE BISTROT DE VENISE
Calle dei Fabbri, 4685

TELEPHONE
041-52-36-651
FAX
041-52-02-224

Le Bistrot de Venise tries to cover too much ground to give it a rousing two thumbs up. However, it does have its virtues and if you are selective, you will like it.

Not only does the kitchen promote *antiche ricette della cucina popolare veneziana-populare*—old Venetian recipes—it touts pizza, crepes, and *cicchetti,* plus pastas and large salads. If you go early in the evening (any time before 9 P.M.), the back room is full of families with children and international tourists. I was seated between a family with two screaming children and a Japanese man videotaping his companion eating her dinner. Criticisms aside, I could not fault the food (a pizza), the presentation, or the service. On my next visit I went late, stayed up front, and ordered a bowl of pasta—big improvement in atmosphere. My advice is to either go for lunch or a plate of *cicchetti* at the bar, or go late. Whenever you go, stick to something simple that has to be prepared to order, say a pasta or perhaps a pizza, and in the evening, plan to hang out around the bar and enjoy the weekly poetry readings or live music performances. At these events, patrons are encouraged to mix with the artists, and this often turns out to be a pleasant way to feel more a part of Venice.

NOTE: Poetry and music performances start anywhere between 5–8 P.M. Call or fax for the schedule.

OPEN
Daily

CLOSED
Tues from Nov–Jan, Christmas Day

HOURS
Noon–1 A.M., continuous service

RESERVATIONS
Advised

CREDIT CARDS
MC, V

À LA CARTE
L35,000–45,000, pizza from L13,000, *cicchetti* L2,000

MENÙ TURISTICO
None

COVER AND SERVICE CHARGES
No cover, 15% service added

ENGLISH
Yes

(40) LEON BIANCO
Salizzada San Luca, 4153

When you want a snack or light meal and cannot face another slice of street pizza, try Leon Bianco (between Campo San Luca and Campo Manin), the type of place Venetians patronize day after day. Terrific *cicchetti* (finger-food snacks) and *tramezzini* (sandwiches) are served throughout the day, but hot food is offered only between noon and 3:30 P.M.

Rice or cheese croquettes, grilled shrimp, and roasted vegetables are only a few of the *cicchetti* you can pluck with a toothpick and pop into your mouth. There are always two or three hot dishes, and if you want to sample more than one, they will serve half portions. The *tramezzini*—toasted or plain bread filled with prosciutto, *funghi* (mushrooms), tomatoes, tuna, egg, shrimp, roast beef, or pork—are always some of the best I try each time I am in Venice. You can rub shoulders standing at the marble counters and bar or, if you want to take a more relaxed approach to your meal, you can sit on small benches around long tables and still not have any cover or service added to your bill. When you are finished eating, be local and take your dishes back up to the bar.

TELEPHONE
041-52-21-180

OPEN
Mon–Sat

CLOSED
Sun

HOURS
Snacks 8 A.M.–8 P.M., hot food noon–3:30 P.M.

RESERVATIONS
Not accepted

CREDIT CARDS
None

À LA CARTE
Cicchetti from L1,600, sandwiches from L2,000, hot dishes from L6,000

MENÙ TURISTICO
None

COVER AND SERVICE CHARGES
No cover, service included

ENGLISH
Limited

(41) OSTERIA AI ASSASSINI
Rio Terra dei Assassini, 3695

TELEPHONE
041-52-87-986

OPEN
Mon–Fri; Sat, dinner only

CLOSED
Sun, Aug (2 weeks)

HOURS
11:30 A.M.–3 P.M., 6:30 P.M.–midnight

RESERVATIONS
Advised

CREDIT CARDS
None

À LA CARTE
Cicchetti from L3,500; meals from L25,000, beverage extra

MENÙ TURISTICO
None

COVER AND SERVICE CHARGES
Cover L2,000, service included

ENGLISH
Yes

For years this was only a place to buy wine by the bottle or case. Then Giuseppe Galardi turned it into an *enoteca* (wine bar), and it has enjoyed popularity with the locals, probably because they are the only ones who can find it.

Actually, you can find it . . . if you have an abundance of determination and patience and are armed with the best street map of Venice that money can buy. To add to the fun of the hunt, there is no name outside. Just look for the yellow light over the door, which is turned on when the place is open.

Every day the long wooden tables and benches are filled with people having lunch or *cicchetti* while sipping a glass or two of the eighty to ninety varieties of Italian wines available. *Cicchetti* are little snacks similar to Spanish tapas, ranging from a piece of bread with a slice of prosciutto to meatballs, deep-fried veggies, and whipped salt cod. For many, a few *cicchetti* with a glass of nice wine to go with it can easily substitute for lunch or a light supper. The hot special changes daily, featuring a certain dish on each day of the week: Monday you will have soup, Tuesday stew, Wednesday *pasta e fagioli,* Thursday boiled meat or *baccalà,* Friday fish, and Saturday whatever the chef feels like cooking. Of course, pasta is served every day. The only dessert is a plate of *biscotti* to dip in sweet wine.

(42) OSTERIA A LA CAMPANA
Calle dei Fabbri, 4720

TELEPHONE
041-58-85-170

OPEN
Mon–Sat

CLOSED
Sun

HOURS
10 A.M.–3 P.M., 6:30–11 P.M.

RESERVATIONS
Not necessary

CREDIT CARDS
AE, MC, V

À LA CARTE
Cicchetti from L2,000, two- to three-course meal for L22,000–32,000, beverage extra

"Where do you go for a good, cheap lunch in this neighborhood?" I asked Nellie, the friendly owner of one of my favorite Cheap Sleeps in Venice (see Locanda Casa Petrarca in *Cheap Sleeps in Italy*). "I go to La Campana on Calle dei Fabbri," she said. Once you find it, you, too, will go back to this small, homey place with a dark wood interior that can charitably be called rustic. For the best selection at lunch, get there early, when the *cicchetti* are at their picture-perfect best. You can always find rice balls with a mozzarella cheese pocket inside, tuna or potato puffs, braised vegetables, frittatas, and chunks of cheese all displayed along a counter. For an even Cheaper Eat, have your *cicchetti* standing at the bar and you can deduct about L500 per item.

If you want something more substantial, ask what the chef prepared that morning. There is a posted menu, but no one bothers looking at it. Fish is the Friday special, and on other days look for bean soup, hearty stews, and assorted risottos and pastas.

MENÙ TURISTICO
None

COVER AND SERVICE CHARGES
Cover L2,000, service included

ENGLISH
Yes

(43) OSTERIA AL BACARETO
Salizzada S. Samuele, 3447

Emilio and his son Adriano told me, "You eat in this restaurant as a family." The house wine is good, the welcome always warm, the other diners interesting, and the prices fair. In short, this is a winner. Everyone seems to know each other at their comfortable family *osteria,* where you may see the neighborhood dogs sitting patiently by the door waiting for their masters to finish eating. At lunch, in order to feel part of the action, order a plate of *cicchetti* or a sandwich and a glass of the featured wine. Remember, if you stand at the bar to eat, you will save both the cover and the service charges. For dinner, reserve one or more of the sixteen places at any of the outside tables for a ringside seat on the evening *passeggiata.* If you stay with the chef's versions of Venetian dishes, the food will not disappoint. For example, *sarde in saor* (marinated sardines), the *risotti vari* (rice mixed with peas, squid, vegetables, or seafood), or the *bigoli in salsa* (wholemeal pasta with anchovy and onion sauce) are surefire first courses. Move on to the excellent seafood offerings, or liver and onions served with polenta, and close with your choice of the three house desserts: *Buranelli biscotti* (Venetian cookies from Burano dipped in dessert wine), *tiramisù*, or amaretto mousse.

TELEPHONE
041-52-89-336

OPEN
Mon–Fri; Sat, lunch only

CLOSED
Sun, Christmas Day, Easter Day, sometimes in Aug

HOURS
Noon–3 P.M., 7–10 P.M.

RESERVATIONS
Advised

CREDIT CARDS
AE, MC, V

À LA CARTE
Cicchetti from L2,500, full meals L40,000–60,000, beverage extra

MENÙ TURISTICO
None

COVER AND SERVICE CHARGES
Cover L3,000, 12% service added

ENGLISH
Yes, and menu in English

(44) OSTERIA DA CARLA
Corte Contarina, 1535 (off Frezzaria)

Hidden? You bet. Discovered? Yes again, but by the *cognessetti* in Venice who say, "Let's go to the Carla," and everyone knows exactly what they mean and where it is, even though the sign over the doorway reads Pietro Panizzolo and if you don't know about it you will never find it.

I was introduced to the Carla by a great Cheap Eating pal from Florence who said he had been eating here for years, and that I simply had to try it. We arrived late on a Saturday afternoon when the place was almost empty and the crew was preparing to close. Nevermind, we were welcomed as if we were regulars. We settled in

TELEPHONE
041-52-37-855

OPEN
Mon–Sat

CLOSED
Sun, holidays

HOURS
7:30 A.M.–11 A.M., noon–2:30 P.M., 7:30–9 P.M.

RESERVATIONS
Not necessary

CREDIT CARDS
None

À LA CARTE
Sandwiches from L2,000, lunch or dinner L20,000–30,000

MENÙ TURISTICO
None

COVER AND SERVICE CHARGES
None

ENGLISH
Yes

with a plate of assorted sandwiches and shared a bottle of beer. It was a great late lunch and I knew I would come back when it was operating in full force. I did, several times, and was always amazed. This place is a super Cheap Eat and the food is terrific. Every morning the menu is pinned to a barrel out front. There will be two or three pastas, including a risotto, a meat and a fish dish, fresh vegetables, and homemade tarts. Not ready for a big meal? Then order a sandwich from the bar and sit at one of the tables inside or, on a warm day, snag one of the tables placed in the walkway of the small court in front.

NOTE: Here's how to find Osteria da Carla coming from Piazza San Marco: walk out the south exit from the piazza along Salizzada San Moisè and turn right on Frezzeria, and the first archway on your left will be Sotoportego e Corte Contarina. This is it . . . you will see the barrel at the end of the court with a bouquet of fresh flowers on top and the menu of the day pinned on it. *Buon appetito,* and *tante grazie,* Frank.

(45) ROSTICCERIA S. BARTOLOMEO

Calle de la Bissa, 5424/A (on Campo S. Bartolomeo, near the Rialto Bridge)

TELEPHONE
041-52-23-569

OPEN
Daily

CLOSED
Mon in winter

HOURS
9 A.M.–9 P.M., continuous service

RESERVATIONS
Not accepted

CREDIT CARDS
AE, MC, V

À LA CARTE
L30,000–35,000, beverage extra

MENÙ TURISTICO
L16,000–27,000, choice of several two-course meals; beverage, cover, and service included

COVER AND SERVICE CHARGES
No cover, service included

ENGLISH
Some

Cheap Eaters do not go to the upstairs restaurant here. Instead they stay downstairs, go through the self-service line, and take their food to one of the long bar tables by the window, thus avoiding the cover, service, and higher prices for almost the same food served upstairs.

The ground-floor cafeteria is a popular refueling stop for those who want a proper meal anytime between 9 A.M. and 9:30 P.M. Featured each day are salads, pastas, and hot dishes that include the Venetian specialties of *baccalà alla Vicentina* (salt cod simmered in milk and herbs), deep-fried mozzarella, *seppie con polenta* (squid in its own black ink sauce), and all the usual desserts. For around L16,000, you will get a two-course meal and a glass of house wine, and in Venice, this is definitely a Cheap Eat. Everything you see can be packaged to go.

NOTE: Prices quoted are for cafeteria dining.

(46) SEMPIONE ($)
Ponte Bareteri, 578

The beautiful canal-side setting, attentive service, and tempting Venetian cuisine draws me back to this restaurant time after time. Its privileged location near St. Mark's Square and some of the city's most luxurious shops makes it an ideal stop for a leisurely lunch or dinner. The best tables, naturally, are by the leaded windows overlooking the canal and the gondolas quietly floating by. The food is simple, with unfussy preparations and a lavish use of olive oil. *Pennette* (small penne) tossed with a well-flavored *amatriciana* sauce of tomatoes and sweet red peppers is a hit. So is the pasta with spider crab and the *spaghetti Sempione* with prawns, mussels, and octopus. Finish every drop, but save room for the heaping platter of scampi and squid, the calamari, or the fillet of *S. Pietro* cooked in butter. Meat lovers will be pleased to find liver and onions served with polenta, steaks, veal dishes, and roast chicken. For a pleasant ending, I like to have a bowl of fresh strawberries or a slice of pineapple.

TELEPHONE
041-52-26-022
OPEN
Mon, Wed–Sun
CLOSED
Tues, Dec–Jan
HOURS
11:30 A.M.–3 P.M., 6:30–10 P.M.
RESERVATIONS
Advised for dinner
CREDIT CARDS
AE, MC, V
À LA CARTE
L55,000–65,000, beverage extra
MENÙ TURISTICO
None
COVER AND SERVICE CHARGES
Cover L3,000, 12% service added
ENGLISH
Yes, and menu in English

San Polo

San Polo occupies a middle section of the Grand Canal and is the smallest of the six *sestieri*. It is named after the ancient church of San Polo, which stands on Campo San Polo, the largest square in Venice after St. Mark's. The Rialto area, once the center of the city's bargaining, buying, and selling, is still famous for its colorful market and tourist stalls lining the bridge. No one should miss the enormous Gothic church of the Frari, with three of Venice's best altarpieces (one of these Titian's *Assumption*), and the Scuola Grande di San Rocco, with its paintings by Tintoretto.

(47) ALIANI GASTRONOMIA
Ruga Vecchia S. Giovanni, 654-655 (main street leading to Rialto Bridge)

For fast, flavorful, and fabulous deli-style takeout, one of the best and most central spots is Aliani Gastronomia near the Rialto Bridge. The shop, owned and operated by Bruno Aliani, his charming wife, Lucia, and their son, Davida, has been doing business in this location for almost thirty years and only gets better with time. Fresh daily pastas, roast meats, fish on Friday,

TELEPHONE
041-52-24-913
OPEN
Tues–Sat; Mon, morning only
CLOSED
Sun 2–3 weeks in Aug
HOURS
8 A.M.–1 P.M., 5–7 P.M., continual service
RESERVATIONS
Not accepted

CREDIT CARDS
None
À LA CARTE
L10,000–20,000, beverage extra
MENÙ TURISTICO
None
COVER AND SERVICE CHARGES
None
ENGLISH
Yes

seasonal vegetables, a wide variety of Italian hams and cheeses, and bottles of wine from the Veneto keep customers returning. There are no tables or bar areas for dining here, and no beverages sold by the glass, so it is best to purchase drinks somewhere along this busy street and take your gourmet picnic elsewhere to enjoy.

Though the deli section is open for business on Monday, hot food is available only from Tuesday to Saturday. On Wednesday afternoon the meat and cheese section is closed.

(48) ALLA MADONNA

Calle della Madonna, 594

TELEPHONE
041-52-23-824
FAX
041-52-10-167
OPEN
Mon–Tues, Thur–Sun
CLOSED
Wed, Aug 1–15, Dec 20–Jan 31
HOURS
Noon–3 P.M., 7–10:30 P.M.
RESERVATIONS
Absolutely essential
CREDIT CARDS
AE, MC, V
À LA CARTE
L45,000, beverage extra
MENÙ TURISTICO
None
COVER AND SERVICE CHARGES
Cover L2,500, 12% service added
ENGLISH
Yes, and menu in English
MISCELLANEOUS
A member of Ristoranti della Buona Accoglienza; see page 159 for details.

Alla Madonna is in a pivotal location on a narrow street on the San Polo side of the Rialto Bridge. Almost every guidebook to Venice lists it as one of the restaurants you *must* visit, and for good reason. The fresh fish is always delicious and reasonable, and the atmosphere is authentic and pleasing. The unadorned tables are filled every day with a mix of chattering Venetians and visitors. If you arrive without reservations after about 12:15 for lunch or 7:30 for dinner, you can expect to wait up to an hour for a table, so beware. Service by white-coated waiters, some of whom have been on the job since time began, can be brusque, but given the number of tables they have to serve, it is easy to see why patience can run thin during the crunch.

From appetizer to pasta and main course, the star of the show is always fresh fish. As you enter, you will pass an iced display of only some of the many delicacies awaiting you. The specialties are seafood rice, spaghetti with black squid, squid with polenta, fried cuttlefish, mixed fish fry, and grilled sole. Add a salad or fresh vegetable and a slice of Madonna cake (cream-filled sponge cake), and you will be in seventh heaven, or close to it.

(49) ALL' ANTICO PIZZO'

Calle San Mattio, 814

TELEPHONE
041-52-31-575
OPEN
Tues–Sat; Sun, lunch only
CLOSED
Mon, 2 weeks in Jan, Aug (dates for both vary)
HOURS
12:30–2:30 P.M., 7:30–10 P.M.

The Rialto Market is one of the top tourist attractions in Venice, and I recommend it highly. Today the old commercial meeting place along the quay is a lively and colorful outdoor market crowded with countless stalls and shouting hawkers selling everything that is seasonally fresh. Housewives and chefs come early each morning for the best food available, and visitors wander through eager to soak up the local color and take advantage of the many interesting photo opportunities.

Whenever you are in this area, a good target for lunch is Antico Pizzo'. The two rooms with simply laid tables are filled every day with regulars, who come for the fine fish offered by Vittorio Marcolin and his two brothers, Mario and Fabio. As you enter, the fresh fish and antipasti display will tempt you. Fish is number one here, prepared without fanfare. Start with the fish risotto or the lasagna layered with fish. For the main course, I suggest the *fritto misto dell' Adriatico* (assorted fried Adriatic fish) or the *coda di rospo ai ferri* (grilled angler fish). Always ask what the daily specials are because they are bound to be winning choices. Landlubbers can settle for an omelette, liver with onions, or veal scaloppine, but frankly, the order of the day here should be fish. Desserts are not a high priority with the chef.

RESERVATIONS
Not necessary

CREDIT CARDS
MC, V

À LA CARTE
L45,000–55,000, beverage extra

MENÙ TURISTICO
None

COVER AND SERVICE CHARGES
Cover L3,000, service included

ENGLISH
Yes, and menu in English

(50) ANTICHE CARAMPANE ($)
Rio Terra de le Carampane, 1911 (near Campiello Albrizzi)

Almost everything, from the formal atmosphere to the reliably tasty food, remains unchanged at Antiche Carampane, reported to be one of the oldest taverns in Venice. For a dress-up meal designed to impress your boss, difficult mother-in-law, or important date, this should do very well, provided everyone likes fish, since that is all they serve. To help casual guests not "in the know," a sign posted outside states that they do not serve pizza, lasagna, or pasta with *ragù* sauce, and there is no fixed-price menu. They should add that there is no printed à la carte menu. The food you eat depends on what looked best that day at the Rialto Market. This is a Big Splurge designed for the old-school person who avoids life in the fast lane.

TELEPHONE
041-52-40-165

OPEN
Tues–Sat; Sun, lunch only

CLOSED
Mon, Aug

HOURS
Noon–3:30 P.M., 7–11 P.M.

RESERVATIONS
Advised

CREDIT CARDS
AE, DC, MC, V

À LA CARTE
L60,000–75,000, beverage extra

MENÙ TURISTICO
None

COVER AND SERVICE CHARGES
Cover L3,500, service included

ENGLISH
Yes

(51) CAFFÈ DEI FRARI
Fondamenta dei Frari, 2564

At this rambunctious *caffè* near the Campo dei Frari (at the foot of Ponte dei Frari), you will find yourself sitting with Venetian students, men quaffing a third glass of Chianti far too early in the day, and elderly women jump-starting their trip to the market with a latte or cappuccino. There is always neighborly service and made-to-order savory sandwiches served from dawn to dusk by owners Giorgio and Dodo and their casual

TELEPHONE
041-52-41-877

OPEN
Mon–Sat

CLOSED
Sun, first or last week of Aug (dates vary)

HOURS
7:30 A.M.–9 P.M., continuous service

RESERVATIONS
Not accepted

CREDIT CARDS
None
À LA CARTE
Sandwiches from L3,500
MENÙ TURISTICO
None
COVER AND SERVICE CHARGES
None, but prices higher for table service than at the bar
ENGLISH
Some

backup crew. I like to go around noon and order a pocket-bread sandwich filled with slices of *prosciutto crudo* (air-dried salt-cured ham) and thin slices of provolone or *mozzarella di bufala* cheese. For the best people-watching, sit downstairs at one of the six round tables along the padded banquette, or in summer, at one of the tables outside facing the canal. If you sit upstairs, you will pay an additional L1,000 to have the waiter negotiate the narrow stairs with your order.

(52) CANTINA DO MORI
Calle do Mori, 429

TELEPHONE
041-52-25-401
OPEN
Mon–Sat, bar and lunch only
CLOSED
Sun, July 15–Aug 15
HOURS
Bar 8:30 A.M.–9 P.M.
RESERVATIONS
Not accepted
CREDIT CARDS
None
À LA CARTE
Cicchetti from L2,500, sandwiches from L4,000
MENÙ TURISTICO
None
COVER AND SERVICE CHARGES
None
ENGLISH
Limited

For a glimpse of where the Rialto Market traders, delivery boys, and local officer workers go for wine and camaraderie in a decidedly male-dominated atmosphere, look no further than Cantina do Mori, off Ruga Vecchia S. Giovanni. Inside it is long, narrow, and dark, with hanging copper pots and a stand-up bar (there are no tables at all). You will eat great *cicchetti,* platters of local salami and prosciutto, enormous sandwiches, and drink wines sold by the glass. In existence since 1462, this time-worn *enoteca* is run by Rudi and Guinni, who will be happy to advise you on which wines you should drink with whatever you are eating. For instance, if it is salt cod, it should be a glass of *prosecco.* With winter sausage and beans, you will need a robust Cabernet.

(53) CANTINA DO SPADE DA GIORGIO
Calle do Spade, 860

TELEPHONE
041-52-10-574
OPEN
Mon–Sat; Sun, lunch only
CLOSED
Sun from Nov–April, Aug
HOURS
Bar and sandwiches 9 A.M.–3 P.M., hot lunch noon–2:30 P.M., dinner 5-11 P.M., Sun bar and lunch May–Oct 10 A.M.–3 P.M.
RESERVATIONS
Not necessary
CREDIT CARDS
AE, DC, MC, V
À LA CARTE
Sandwiches from L2,000, daily specials from L9,000

Cantina do Spade is almost lost in the Venetian labyrinth under the archways of the Do Spade Bridge, not far from the Rialto Market. Don't look for a sign, because there isn't one. Look for lanterns and wine barrels flanking the entrance and a blackboard with the day's specials handwritten on it hanging to the right—these will be the only indications that this is the place you are looking for.

For more than two decades, Giorgio Lanza and his family have been pouring wine while dispensing good cheer, wonderful snacks and sandwiches, and a lineup of hot dishes at noon to their multitude of dedicated returnees, many of whom consider this to be their semiprivate club. Over 220 wines are available by the glass.

And you will never run out of sandwich choices—try wild boar ham, salted cod, rabbit, elk, deer and the Do Spade Sandwich, spicy ham covered with fresh herbs and piled onto crusty bread. Arrive early to sample their hot dishes, such as *baccalà* with polenta, risotto with pumpkin, spaghetti with shrimp, and their "he-man" dish, *salsicca alla Veneziana con polenta e fagioli* (sausage with beans and polenta)—probably not for the Jenny Craig followers in your group, but good for those brave enough to withstand the calorie overload. For dessert, order the *biscotti* served with strawberry wine for dipping.

MENÙ TURISTICO
L25,000, two courses; includes wine

COVER AND SERVICE CHARGES
None

ENGLISH
Limited

MISCELLANEOUS
No coffee served

(54) IGNAZIO ($)

Calle Saoneri, 2749

Ignazio is named after Florenzo Scroccaro's father, who began this fine family-run restaurant in 1951. Then, as now, it served some of the best food in Venice. Just ask anyone who has ever eaten there and they will agree . . . I know I do.

Everything is impressive, from the host's warm greeting to the last forkful of dessert. Great pains are taken to lay a handsome table using delicate china and attractive glass and silverware. Beautiful fresh flowers add color. In summer, there is an added bonus of a leafy green outdoor garden for alfresco dining. The English-speaking waiters carry out their duties with professionalism.

One taste of the food prepared by the three hardworking chefs, including Ignazio's wife, and you will know you are in the hands of talented women. It is clear that they are all an important part of this extended family. When I was last there for lunch, one of the owner's daughters ran through the restaurant, heavy book bag in tow, and headed straight for the kitchen, where all work came to a halt and the girl was warmly greeted with kisses and hugs from everyone.

The meal begins with an assortment of antipasti, perhaps huge prawns bathed in lemon oil dressing or the mixed seafood plate. For the first course, I recommend their special *spaghetti alla trapanese con melanzane e zucchine* (egg pasta tossed with a mixture of eggplant, peppers, tomatoes, zucchini, and garlic in a light cream sauce). Although fish is king here, with grilled sole lobster or sea crab heading the list, meat eaters can order the Venetian-style sautéed liver and polenta or the veal scallop prepared "as you wish." Desserts, so often the least distinguished part of an Italian meal, are excellent,

TELEPHONE
041-52-34-852

OPEN
Mon–Fri, Sun

CLOSED
Sat, 2 weeks before Carnivale, last 2 weeks of July–first 2 weeks of Aug

HOURS
Noon–3 P.M., 7–10 P.M.

RESERVATIONS
Essential

CREDIT CARDS
AE, DC, MC, V

À LA CARTE
L55,000–70,000, beverage extra

MENÙ TURISTICO
None

COVER AND SERVICE CHARGES
Cover L3,000, 12% service added

ENGLISH
Yes, and menu in English

MISCELLANEOUS
A member of Ristoranti della Buona Accoglienza; see page 159 for details.

especially the homemade *tiramisù,* that rich favorite made with mascarpone, a sweet triple-cream cheese. Prices at Ignazio tend to run a little high, so if cost is a factor, select this one for a special occasion.

(55) MENSA UNIVERSITA CANTEEN
Calle Magazen, 2480

TELEPHONE
041-71-80-96, 72-10-25
OPEN
Mon–Sat; Sun, lunch only
CLOSED
School holidays, Aug
HOURS
11:45 A.M.–2:30 P.M., 6:30–8:30 P.M.
RESERVATIONS
None
CREDIT CARDS
None
À LA CARTE
None
MENÙ TURISTICO
Students studying in Venice: L6,000, three courses; beverage, cover, and service included; students with ID card or Rolling Venice Card and students with International Teacher Card, L11,000, beverage, cover, and service included. Half-meals are available from L4,500 for Venetian students to L9,500 for everyone else.
COVER AND SERVICE CHARGES
Both included
ENGLISH
Yes, usually
MISCELLANEOUS
Open only to university students and teachers with proper IDs.

The Mensa Universita Canteen is open to any student who can show a current ID card from his or her university, or has a Rolling Venice Card (see page 159 for details about this student discount deal available only in Venice). When I commented on what a Cheap Eat I thought this is, I was sternly told that this is expensive by some students' standards. In the south of Italy (they didn't say where), the same food goes for between L500 and L1,000 less. Nevermind, this is Venice, and for this expensive city, this must be the Cheapest Eat in any quarter of the city.

Here is what you get: a three-course meal starting with soup, rice, or pasta, followed by a meat course garnished with seasonal vegetables or a salad, bread, and dessert, cheese, or fruit. Included is a bottle of either plain or carbonated mineral water, a soft drink, wine, or beer. Almost any place else, food dished out at these giveaway prices would cause a stampede. But it is all quite civil here, with seating at long communal tables where you can brush up on your Italian with your fellow students.

NOTE: There is a second university canteen with the same charitable prices in Dorsoduro at Rio Novo, 3647, near Campo Santa Margarita (tel: 041-52-41-268, Mon–Fri, noon–2:15 P.M., 6:30–8:30 P.M., Sun noon–2 P.M.).

(56) OSTERIA ANTICO DOLO
Ruga Vecchia San Giovanni, 778

TELEPHONE
041-52-26-546
OPEN
Mon–Sat
CLOSED
Sun, Aug (middle 10 days), Dec 23–Jan 6 (sometimes)
HOURS
10:30 A.M.–3 P.M., 6:30–10:30 P.M.
RESERVATIONS
Advised

For good wine and food near the Rialto Bridge, stop by Antico Dolo, a picture-postcard version of a typical wine bar frequented by neighborhood residents. The front half is the wine bar, and seven tables are squeezed into the restaurant section in back, which is decorated with pots hanging on beams and a lazy ceiling fan slowly moving the air. The size does not seem to deter the faithful, including gondoliers, who swear by the chef's dishes of country sausages, hearty seafood pastas, locally caught fish, and tripe with Parmesan cheese. The wine selections are better than the dessert options, of which there are two: *biscotti* or gelato.

CREDIT CARDS
None
À LA CARTE
L25,000–40,000, beverage extra
MENÙ TURISTICO
None
COVER AND SERVICE CHARGES
None
ENGLISH
Yes

(57) OSTERIA DA FIORE ($)
Calle del Scaleter, 2202

Everyone has a favorite fish restaurant in Venice, and this is mine. Run by the charming Maurizio Martin, who works in front, and his wife, Mara, who is the capable chef, it has been in operation since 1978. Since that time they have built an enviable reputation for having the most sought after tables in Venice for the best and freshest seasonal seafood available. The well-designed interior is beautiful in its simple elegance. A vase of flowers graces each well-spaced table, set with soft yellow linen, large wineglasses, and shining cutlery. The formally dressed waiters are well-versed in explaining the menu and suggesting appropriate wines. Please note that meat is not served and only one pasta does not contain fish.

For delicious openers, you can always count on a seafood salad or a delicate fish soup. According to the time of year, you might see imaginative dishes featuring octopus, scallops, or razor clams. The first courses include a very light consommé with scampi and ravioli filled with a light whitefish. Be sure to save adequate room to do justice to the main courses, which also vary with the season. Look for grilled eel, fillet of striped bass splashed with balsamic vinegar, turbot baked in a potato crust, and soft-shell crab served with polenta. For dessert, the lemon *sorbetto* or the vanilla ice cream with a red wine–soaked pear are light finishes to this lovely meal. Yes, this is definitely a Big Splurge, but one I hope you will agree is worth it.

TELEPHONE
041-72-13-08
FAX
041-72-13-43
OPEN
Tues–Sat
CLOSED
Sun, Mon, Dec 15–Jan 6, Aug (dates vary)
HOURS
12:30–2:30 P.M., 7:30–10:30 P.M.
RESERVATIONS
Essential as far in advance as possible
CREDIT CARDS
AE, DC, MC, V
À LA CARTE
L75,000–95,000, beverage extra
MENÙ TURISTICO
None
COVER AND SERVICE CHARGES
Cover L5,000, service included
ENGLISH
Yes
MISCELLANEOUS
A member of Ristorante della Buona Accoglienza; see page 159 for details.

(58) TRATTORIA PIZZERIA SAN TOMÀ
Campo San Tomà, 2864A

Tasty pizza (with regular or whole-wheat crusts), delicious homemade pastas and bread, friendly waiters offering attentive service, a beautiful lighted garden, and an outside dining terrace perfect for people-watching all work together to create a memorable dining

TELEPHONE
041-52-38-819
OPEN
Daily

CLOSED
Closings can vary. Closed Tues from the 2nd week of Nov–Mar 15 (except Carnivale); Aug 4–13 (and some Tues in summer if the owner feels like it).
HOURS
Noon–3 P.M., 7:30–10:30 P.M. (until 11 P.M. for pizza)
RESERVATIONS
Advised for weekends and holidays
CREDIT CARDS
AE, DC, MC, V
À LA CARTE
Pizza: L9,000–15,000, one-plate meals from L18,000, full meals from L40,000, beverage extra
MENÙ TURISTICO
L24,000, three courses; cover and service included, beverage extra (L45,000 for Venetian specialties)
COVER AND SERVICE CHARGES
Cover L2,000, 12% service added
ENGLISH
Yes, and menu in English

experience at Bernardo Di-Zio's trattoria. If you don't order a pizza or plate of pasta, consider his very special paella, which you must order ahead when you make your table reservation. When you order this, you get to keep the bib that protects your clothing from this juicy dish. Also on the menu are the usual Venetian standards of marinated sardines, fried fish, and liver with polenta. In a nod to Bernardo's French wife, they serve a wonderful homemade beef *tartare.*

An advantage for many Cheap Eaters is that a full three-course meal is *not* necessary. You can order one of the meal-size salads or a *piatto unico*—a one-plate dish of goulash with pasta, lasagna, and salad or chicken and fries—and still be treated as though you were ordering the works. Because all the food servings are so big, dessert is kept to a minimum, with the emphasis on *sorbetto, tartufo,* or fruit.

Santa Croce

In the 1930s the Fascists built the Piazzale Roma, the gigantic car park just over the bridge from Mestre. Toward the eastern part of the district are weaving walkways that are relatively tourist-free. To the west, the area is mainly industrial and geared to dock and freight operations around the Stazione Marittima. Also here is the Manifattura Tabacci, the oldest industrial building in Venice still used for its original purpose: cigar and cigarette production. Flanking the Grand Canal are fading yet still imposing *palazzos.*

(59) AE OCHE
Calle del Tintor, 1552A-B

TELEPHONE
041-52-41-161
OPEN
Daily
CLOSED
Mon in winter
HOURS
Winter noon–3 P.M., 7–midnight; summer noon–midnight, continuous service

Ae Oche is young, fun, cheap, and good. This popular gathering ground for the Italian fast-food generation is *never* empty. I have yet to find a way to beat the Sunday crowd of families who arrive for one of the eighty-five varieties of crisp pizza and calzones. You can dine outside on a little deck, in a tented garden in the back, or at one of the inside booths with bench seats crafted from bed headboards.

Fire-eaters will love pizza No. 15, the *mangiafuoco* featuring spicy salami, pepperoni, paprika, and tabasco sauce. Tamer taste buds will appreciate No. 18, the *capricciosa* topped with prosciutto, mushrooms, and hearts of artichokes. The *disco volante* (flying saucer), two pizzas put together sandwich style, is not a stellar choice, and neither is the house wine. You are better off with something from their long international beer list, which offers brews from Australia and Mexico to the United States and Spain. There is also a regular trattoria menu with all the familiar antipasti, pastas, meats, and side dishes. A word of caution if you order from this part of the menu: The list is too long to all be fresh . . . order with extreme caution.

NOTE: There are two streets named Calle del Tentor, and it can be spelled Tentor or Tintor. On the map it is Tintor, on the street, Tentor, and in *Cheap Eats,* Tintor. You want the one that leads into Campo S. Giacomo dell' Orio.

RESERVATIONS
Advised, especially on weekends and holidays

CREDIT CARDS
MC, V

À LA CARTE
Pizza from L8,600, full meal from L28,000, beverage extra

MENÙ TURISTICO
Lunch only, no pizza, L20,000, two courses; beverage, cover, and service included

COVER AND SERVICE CHARGES
Cover L2,500, 12% service added

ENGLISH
Yes

(60) LA BOUTIQUE DEL DOLCE
Rio Marin, 890

On my long early morning walks I often passed by the large picture window of a bakery kitchen where a corps of hardworking women were busy pulling trays of pastries from the ovens, putting the finishing touches on decorated cakes, and filling individual tarts with fresh fruit. It was an impressive operation. After asking around, I found that this was the kitchen for a well-known Venetian pastry shop just across the canal. Of course, I rushed right over, and I can tell you I liked what I found.

La Boutique del Dolce is owned by Gino and Gilda Viviani. Gilda makes all the divinely sinful pastries, and is justifiably proud of the world acclaim her talents have brought her. To assuage a degree or two of guilt on your part, all of her products are made using only pure ingredients without coloring or additives. Gino worked for twenty years as an artisan glassblower on Murano. He also lived in Montreal, Canada, but does not admit to speaking English. His welcome is brusque and rather sharp. Maybe it is because his feet hurt and he feels overworked . . . who knows. It doesn't matter because, despite this, people beat a daily path to their shop, which sells some of the best pastries in Venice, and let me assure you the competition is stiff. Whenever you go,

TELEPHONE
041-71-85-23

OPEN
Mon–Tues, Thur–Sun

CLOSED
Wed, Aug

HOURS
6:30 A.M.–8 P.M., continuous service

RESERVATIONS
Not accepted

CREDIT CARDS
None

À LA CARTE
Pastries from L1,400, individual pizzas and sandwiches from L2,500

MENÙ TURISTICO
None

COVER AND SERVICE CHARGES
None

ENGLISH
None, but Gilda speaks French

expect a crowd, especially on Sundays around noon, when handsome fathers with several young children in tow walk here to purchase dessert for their midday meal. In the morning, order several fruit-filled croissants. Later on, vegetable-based puff pastries, individual pizzas, and sandwiches made on their own breads go like hot cakes. In the afternoon, stop in for coffee and an airy rum meringue dusted with chocolate, or pick up a bag of their cookies or a box of hand-dipped chocolates for a special treat. Even if you don't buy a thing (a guaranteed impossibility), do go by to admire . . . and to smell.

(61) LA ZUCCA

Campo San Giacomo dell' Orio, 1762 (by the Ponte del Megio)

TELEPHONE
041-52-41-570

OPEN
Mon–Sat

CLOSED
Sun

HOURS
Noon–3 P.M., 7–10:30 P.M.

RESERVATIONS
Advised for dinner and holidays

CREDIT CARDS
AE, MC, V

À LA CARTE
L40,000, beverage extra

MENÙ TURISTICO
None

COVER AND SERVICE CHARGES
Cover L2,500, service included

ENGLISH
Yes

Collectors of unusual cuisine twists take note: this may be your only chance to sample pumpkin pasta or pumpkin soup, two tasty treats from which this appealing little trattoria takes its name. Unfortunately, you will have to time your visit in the fall or winter, since these dishes are only available seasonally. The rest of the food shows a degree of originality, and while not everything works all the time, most of it does. The menu changes almost daily, and the young and enthusiastic owners strive to please a snappy group of youthful habitués, many of whom are vegetarians and appreciate the interesting ways the chef has with fresh vegetables.

Aside from the pumpkin creations, pasta tossed several ways—including with tomato and fresh ricotta cheese—are the first-course front-runners. The beer-marinated pork served with rice or the boiled veal tongue vinaigrette would seem more appropriately found in a *gasthaus* in central Europe, but the herb-roasted lamb looks right at home on the menu. Veggie admirers will want to try the carrots cooked with lemon and seasoned with curry, small onions simmered in *prosecco* wine, or the potato-provolone gratinée. For dessert, the *panna cotta* with honey and nuts on top and the chocolate cream torte are first class in their simplicity.

I think the best seating is toward the back at a window table on the Rio delle Megio canal rather than up front in the bar and kitchen area, where the shoulder-to-shoulder crowd can get a little loud at times. When you go, be sure to take a look at the modern paintings of pumpkins in every guise imaginable lining the oak-paneled walls.

(62) TRATTORIA ALLE BURCHIELLE
Fondamenta Burchielle, 393

Trattoria alle Burchielle was founded on this site in 1503 and is considered one of the oldest in continuous operation in Venice. Eighty-five years ago, Bruno Pagin's uncle took charge, and now, under Bruno and his niece Serena's direction, it is still going strong as a local favorite best known for its treatment of fresh fish. The restaurant is along a pretty canal in a picturesque corner of Venice, not too far from Piazzale Roma. On a summer evening, it is wonderful to sit outside and watch the boats drifting by while enjoying textbook examples of traditional Venetian preparations of fish.

Noteworthy among the first courses are the seafood lasagna and the spaghetti with whole clams. The most popular main courses are the *soglicla ai ferri* (grilled sole) and the giant prawns in a lemon, garlic, and olive oil marinade. There are a few meat dishes, but they are not the reason to eat here. And the sweets that adorn the pastry cart are not made in-house. A nice change of pace for dessert is a selection of Italian cheeses. The menu is translated into English, but if you can understand restaurant Italian at all, ask for the Italian version and the list of daily specials. There is also a "hidden" *menù turistico*—you have to know to ask for it because it is not automatically handed out.

TELEPHONE
041-71-03-42

OPEN
Tues–Sun

CLOSED
Mon, Jan

HOURS
Noon–3 P.M., 7–10 P.M.

RESERVATIONS
Advised

CREDIT CARDS
AE, DC, MC, V

À LA CARTE
L38,000–45,000, beverage extra

MENÙ TURISTICO
L27,000, three courses; cover and service included, beverage extra

COVER AND SERVICE CHARGES
Cover L1,700, 10% service added

ENGLISH
Yes, and menu in English

Burano Island

Burano is synonymous with lace. The best place to see the real thing is at the school in Piazza Galuppi and in its museum and shop. Shops selling more lace than you could ever wash and iron in three lifetimes line the main street that extends from the exit ramp from the boat dock clear across the island. Buyers along this stretch should beware, because most of the work comes straight from Hong Kong or the Philippines. Despite this, the island is a photographer's dream, with colorful houses nestled along narrow alleys and walkways. Burano is still a fishing community, and as you walk around the island you will see the boats and nets lining the quays.

TRATTORIA AL GATTO NERO
Via Giudecca, 88

TELEPHONE
041-73-01-20
OPEN
Tues–Sun
CLOSED
Mon, 7–10 days in Jan, Nov (last 10 days)
HOURS
Noon–3 P.M., 7:30–9 P.M.
RESERVATIONS
Advised
CREDIT CARDS
AE, DC, MC, V
À LA CARTE
L40,000–50,000, beverage extra
MENÙ TURISTICO
L35,000, two courses; beverage, cover, and service included
COVER AND SERVICE CHARGES
Cover L3,000, service extra
ENGLISH
Yes, and menu in English

Most visitors come to Burano from Venice for two reasons: to buy the handmade lace and to eat fish. Tourists rarely stray from the Via Baldessare Galuppi, which is lined with shops selling linen and lace and a selection of overpriced eating places featuring greasy fried fish guaranteed to induce acute heartburn. Just beyond all of this is the most attractive part of Burano, one blissfully free of fellow travelers. It is here that you will find Al Gatto Nero. For the last four decades it has been owned by Ruggero, the chef; his son, Massimiliano; and the house cat, Ciccio, a contented, gray, fat cat who chooses his customers and indicates his favoritism by sleeping on an empty chair near their table.

Al Gatto Nero is widely recognized as one of the best trattorias on the island, thanks to its charm and character, not to mention good food at moderate prices. In addition to two large rooms inside, there is a covered canal-side terrace for warm-weather dining. One of the more impressive aspects of the service is the unique china, made especially for the restaurant. The large white dishes are ringed with an artist's conception of Burano buildings, and if you look very carefully, you will see Al Gatto Nero and Ciccio portrayed in the design. It is the most crowded at lunchtime, when local residents order the *menù turistico,* which includes two courses, wine, and *biscotti* and coffee for dessert. You may want to skip the broiled eel, but not the fresh prawns, broiled sardines, or fresh sole. Desserts do not play a starring role, so you can concentrate fully on the rest of the meal. Of course, you will skip the meat dishes; they are real understudies.

Giudecca Island

Giudecca Island was where the wealthy Renaissance aristocrats built their summer palaces. Michelangelo stayed here when he left Florence in 1529. Today the wealthy hide out at the famed Cipriani Hotel and eat and drink in Harry's Dolce (a slightly less expensive spin-off of Harry's Bar in Venice). There is also a private garden, the Garden of Eden, named after the English gardener who began it, and Andrea Palladio's Church of La Zitelle. The panorama from the *fondamente* along the water offers a magnificent view of Doge's Palace and the island of San Giorgio Maggiore.

(63) ALTANELLA ($)
Calle delle Erbe, 268–270

Altanella has what Italians call a *buona forchetta* ("a good fork") and a *buon bicchiere* ("a good glass"). Buried halfway down a narrow street on Giudecca Island, at Rio de Ponte Lungo, the Stradella family restaurant has been in business since the turn of the century preparing *only* fish. It looks undiscovered because there is no sign, only a light outside, but it is firmly on the map. Hemingway was a customer in his day, as was François Mitterand. However, fame has not gone to anyone's head . . . the food is still marvelous.

During warm weather, reserve a table on the irresistibly romantic terrace overlooking the island's central canal. Otherwise, you can sit at one of the tables inside, where there are pictures of the restaurant in its early days and a photo of the founder over the kitchen door. Dishes I look forward to having again are the risotto with fish, the freshly made gnocchi with squid ink, sauced with cuttlefish (a prized recipe of one of the grandmothers in the family), mussels and sweet peppers, the grilled sea bream, and the flavorful tuna. The desserts are made here, so be sure to plan on a piece of the lush chocolate cake, the unusual pumpkin cake, or, if you are here at Easter, their special almond cake.

TELEPHONE
041-52-27-780

OPEN
Wed–Sun

CLOSED
Mon, Tues, Jan–Carnivale, Aug 10–20

HOURS
12:30–2 P.M., 7:30–9 P.M.

RESERVATIONS
Essential in summer, advised rest of the year

CREDIT CARDS
None

À LA CARTE
L50,000–60,000, beverage extra

MENÙ TURISTICO
None

COVER AND SERVICE CHARGES
Cover L2,500, 10% service added

ENGLISH
Yes, and menu in English

Lido Island

Early in the 1900s, Lido, which is Italian for "shore," was developed as a Belle Epoque resort. Today it is a playground with something for everyone's pocketbook and taste. It is known for its stretches of well-kept private beaches, and dismal public ones, a gambling casino and film festival, and hotels—both dowager and flashy. One of the best ways to appreciate Lido is to rent a bike for the day and pedal. Lido is the only lagoon island with roads. It comes alive around Easter and closes down by the end of the year.

(64) PIZZERIA DA MASSIMO
Riviera San Nicolò, 11/A

Pizza and pizzerias are a dime a dozen on Lido, and almost all are touristy in the worst sense. This pizzeria is more local than most. Just a few minutes from all the tourist hype on the main street, it offers decent pizza in a clean, informal setting. In summer it is always nice to sit

TELEPHONE AND FAX
041-52-60-859

OPEN
Wed–Mon, dinner only

CLOSED
Tues, annual closing varies

HOURS
5 P.M.–midnight
RESERVATIONS
Not necessary
CREDIT CARDS
AE, DC
À LA CARTE
Pizza L7,000–16,000, beverage extra
MENÙ TURISTICA
None
COVER AND SERVICE CHARGES
Cover L2,000, service included
ENGLISH
Yes

on the outside terrace and enjoy your meal while soaking up the view across the canal or gazing at all the people strolling by in various forms of dress, or undress, depending on the temperature. The pizzas run the gamut from A to Y, starting with *al funghi porcini*—covered with tomato, mozzarella, porcini mushrooms, and a dash of oregano—to *yoghi e bubu*—with tomatoes, mozzarella, capers, and black olives. In between are all the cornerstones of a pizza joint with few surprises. The desserts are not worth worrying about, but after a big pizza, you won't have much room left over anyway. There is also an à la carte menu, but the choices are boring. Best to think *only* pizza here.

(65) RISTORANTE BELVEDERE ($) E TAVOLA CALDA

Piazzale la Santa Maria Elisabetta, 4

TELEPHONE
041-52-60-115, 52-60-164
OPEN
Tues–Sun
CLOSED
Mon; Ristorante Belvedere: Nov–April; Tavola Calda: 2 weeks in Nov
HOURS
Noon–2:30 P.M., 7–9:30 P.M.
RESERVATIONS
Advised for Ristorante, not accepted at Tavola Calda
CREDIT CARDS
AE, DC, MC, V
À LA CARTE
Ristorante, L75,000, beverage extra; Tavola Calda, L10,000–22,000, beverage included
MENÙ TURISTICO
L35,000, three courses; beverage, cover, and service included
COVER AND SERVICE CHARGES
Ristorante, cover L4,000, service included; Tavola Calda, none
ENGLISH
Yes, and menu in English at Ristorante

If you are visiting Lido for the day, chances are you will want to eat. Unless you know where to go, most of the food is overpriced tourist pizza or deadly dull and ludicrously expensive hotel dining; there does not seem to be much middle ground. Enter the Ristorante Belvedere and its Tavola Calda snack bar next door, which are part of the Hotel Belvedere (see *Cheap Sleeps in Italy*).

Everyone agrees that some of the best food to be had in this tourist mecca is at the Belvedere, right across the street from the Venice *vaporétto* stop. At the restaurant, Cheap Eaters will order the *menù turistico,* a L35,000 value that includes three courses, cover and service charges, and the beverage. The food, which features marvelous fresh fish, is served on a pretty streetside terrace or in the formal hotel dining room with big picture windows.

Confirmed card-carrying Cheap Eaters will skip the *ristorante* side completely and head straight for the Tavola Calda, which adjoins it. This is just the answer for the visitor with lots on the agenda and no time or desire for a fancy meal. The same kitchen is used for both places, but the prices here are much lower. Every day there are pastas, roast chicken, fish, and an excellent selection of vegetables, salads, and made-to-order sandwiches. Another benefit is that it is open year-round Tuesday through Sunday, while the hotel restaurant is closed from November to Easter.

(66) TRATTORIA AFRICA
Via L. Mocenigo, 9

The Cannizzaro family runs their trattoria like a private kingdom immune from modernity. Everyone gets into the act. Grandmother cleans the shrimps, Mama runs the restaurant, and her sons prepare the food. This is a place where the workers come for lunch, bring their families on Sunday, and the rest of us hope to get a table. As you walk in through the sidewalk terrace area set off from the street by shrubs and blooming plants, you are faced with the kitchen and knotty-pine bar that has a few tables, and another room filled with a huge collection of old-time Lido photographs. The specialty of the house is fish, fried, grilled, or stewed. If you see *granseola*—spider crabs—as an appetizer, order it. Otherwise, begin with their popular seafood antipasti, or *sarde in saor,* sardines in a sweet/sour dressing topped with onions. If there are four of you, the *risotto di pesce* is another house favorite. *Seppie in umido,* stewed cuttlefish in black sauce, grilled sole, or the ever-present *frittura mista,* a plate of mixed fried fish, are reliable main courses. If you can still think about dessert, there is a fruit tart, *panna cotta,* or *biscotti* to dip in sweet strawberry wine. The house red or white wine from the Veneto should round out your meal at this Lido institution.

TELEPHONE
041-52-60-186

OPEN
Wed–Mon

CLOSED
Tues, Jan

HOURS
Noon–2:30 P.M., 7–10 P.M., 10:30 P.M. in summer

RESERVATIONS
Suggested, especially in summer

CREDIT CARDS
AE, MC, V

À LA CARTE
L35,000–45,000, beverage extra

MENÙ TURISTICO
None

COVER AND SERVICE CHARGES
Cover L3,000, service included

ENGLISH
Yes

(67) TRATTORIA ANDRI ($)
Via Lepanto, 21

Trattoria Andri is in a pretty neighborhood only a five- or ten-minute stroll from the usual tourist track on the island of Lido. There are ninety places outside on a covered terrace and maybe fifty more inside this lovely old villa. The interior is open and airy, featuring white walls hung with modern abstract paintings and brass platters. Silk flowers adorn each table, and a fresh bouquet brightens up the bar. The same family has been serving Lido residents for more than thirty years.

The best first course is the house specialty: *spaghetti Andri,* featuring fat shrimp. Grilled turbot or filet of sole sautéed in butter make winning main-course selections. Dessert calls for something light, and the best choice, in my opinion, is not listed on the menu and does not have a name. Ask for the *limone digestif*—a frothy, refreshing mix of lemon, ice, sparkling wine, and vodka blended together like a milkshake and served in a champagne flute.

TELEPHONE
041-52-65-482

OPEN
Wed–Sun

CLOSED
Mon–Tues, Jan, Feb

HOURS
Noon–3 P.M., 7:30 P.M.–midnight

RESERVATIONS
Advised

CREDIT CARDS
MC, V

À LA CARTE
L50,000, beverage extra

MENÙ TURISTICO
None

COVER AND SERVICE CHARGES
Cover L2,500, 12% service added

ENGLISH
Yes, and menu in English

(68) TRATTORIA FAVORITA ($)
Via Francesco Duodo, 33

TELEPHONE
041-52-61-626
OPEN
Tues–Sun
CLOSED
Mon, Jan
HOURS
12:30–2:30 P.M., 7:30–10:30 P.M.
RESERVATIONS
Essential
CREDIT CARDS
AE, DC, MC, V
À LA CARTE
L50,000–65,000, beverage extra
MENÙ TURISTICO
None
COVER AND SERVICE CHARGES
Cover L3,500, service included
ENGLISH
Yes, and menu in English

The regulars at Trattoria Favorita come for the wine and the dependable fish preparations turned out by a hardworking squad of chefs. I like it because of its location: hidden in a pretty residential district about a twenty-minute walk from the *vaporétto* stop.

Summer seating on the vine-covered terrace is always in demand, but the seats are hard plastic without cushions, and thus not many deals are made or romances begun while sitting here. The inside is more comfortable, and it is air-conditioned, a real bonus during the sizzling Venetian summers. The two large rooms have great atmosphere, with heavy beams, a nice collection of country furniture, liberal use of green plants and fresh flowers, and soft pink table linens.

The kitchen does not feature daily specials; instead, it concentrates on doing a superb job with everything listed on the sensible menu. The emphasis is on fish. In fact, if you are not a fish eater you have two entrée choices: steak, either plain or with peppers. The gnocchi with crab is perfect, and so is the spaghetti with fresh clams. Grilled filet of sole, bass, a mixed grilled fish platter, and turbot make up the bulk of the main courses. The wine list is exceptional, listing only regional wines in all price categories. If something sweet is called for at the end of your meal, sip the vodka-lemon-*prosecco* smoothie.

Murano Island

Visitors to Venice make the trip to Murano for two purposes: to buy glass and to eat fish.

(69) ANTICA TRATTORIA MURANESE
Fondamenta Cavour, 20

TELEPHONE
041-73-96-10
OPEN
Daily, lunch only
CLOSED
Never
HOURS
Noon–3 P.M., hot lunches
RESERVATIONS
Not necessary
CREDIT CARDS
AE, MC, V

Situated on the canal about halfway down from the Venice *vaporétto* stop is the Antica Trattoria Muranese, a reliable bet for an unassuming seafood lunch in Murano. Thanks to the tourists who arrive by the boatload from Venice, Murano stays in business selling its famous glass. There are no real "local" spots, but at least here the food is honest and cheap . . . for Murano. There is a summer garden in back with tables and umbrellas. In the cooler months, seating is inside two steamy rooms with little in the way of interior decoration.

Cheap Eaters are going to want the *menù turistico.* Haute cuisine is not one of the kitchen's strengths, so for maximum results, think simple. Rely on what has to be prepared to order, such as grilled fish or whatever they are pushing as the special. There are two *menù turisticos,* one offering a fish risotto as a first course, and the second, grilled cuttlefish for the main dish. The uninteresting bakery desserts make it easy to bypass this course, and besides, you have to pay extra for it if you are doing the *menù turistico.* The house wine is okay, but a beer is probably better.

À LA CARTE
L35,000–40,000, beverage extra

MENÙ TURISTICO
L25,000, three courses; cover and service included, beverage extra

COVER AND SERVICE CHARGES
Cover L2,000, 12% service added

ENGLISH
Some

(70) TRATTORIA BUSA ALLA TORRE DA LELE ($)
Campo S. Stefano, 3

Welcome to Lele and Christina's trattoria, where knowledgeable Venetians eat when they visit the island of Murano. More expensive, yes, but certainly worth the extra cost. Lele, a big man with red hair and a twinkle in his eye, is a Murano fixture who meets and greets his guests with gusto. His wife, Christina, keeps things moving from behind the bar. The waiters offer casual service, but time should not be a top priority on your visit here. There are two rooms inside the thirteenth-century building, but if weather permits, sit outside. Settle in at one of the terrace tables on the *campo* by the clock tower and enjoy a romantic, leisurely lunch, accompanied by a nice bottle of Venetian wine and someone very special . . . and be glad you are not home having to mow the lawn or grappling with bill paying.

The food probably will not sweep you off your feet with exotic or nouvelle interpretations, but the kitchen does know how to turn out classic fish dishes with finesse and just the right amount of dash. You will have the best success if you stick to any of the fresh fish offerings, paying close heed to whatever the chef offers for the daily special. The pasta with fresh clams, a brimming fish soup, and *tagliolini* with crab are only a few of the regular first courses. Sixteen main courses feature local fish, or you can order omelettes, beef, or veal. But what for? Here you eat fish.

TELEPHONE
041-73-96-62

OPEN
Daily, lunch only

CLOSED
Jan 10–30

HOURS
Noon–3:30 P.M.

RESERVATIONS
Advised

CREDIT CARDS
AE, DC, MC, V

À LA CARTE
L50,000–65,000, beverage extra

MENÙ TURISTICO
L20,000, two courses with vegetable or salad; cover and service included, beverage extra

COVER AND SERVICE CHARGES
Cover L2,000, 12% service added

ENGLISH
Yes, and menu in English

Food Shopping in Venice

Outdoor Markets

Open-air markets selling fruits, vegetables, and flowers are set up in various squares every day but Sunday. They are all open in the mornings and sometimes in the afternoon. You will find them at Santa Maria Formosa (Castello), Santa Margherita (Dorsoduro), Campiello dell'Anconetta (Cannaregio), Rio Terrà San Leonardo (Cannaregio), and on a barge off Campo Santa Barnaba (Dorsoduro). Generally speaking, the hours are from Monday to Saturday 8:30 A.M. to 12:30 P.M., and afternoons, except Wednesday, from 3:30 to 7:30 P.M.

The market to end all markets, however, is the famous Rialto Market (San Polo), next to the Rialto Bridge. The hawker stalls lining the bridge sell everything from T-shirts, masks, jewelry, and glassware to fake and real lace. These sellers are open from around 9 A.M. until 6 P.M. in winter and later in summer. The vegetable market (*erberia*) is the best, least expensive, and most colorful in Venice. It is open *only* in the morning from Monday to Saturday, 8 A.M. to 1 P.M. The fish market (*pescheria*) is one of the finest in Europe. Here you will see every known variety of fresh fish, and some you never knew existed. This is worth a trip, and don't forget your camera. Open Tuesday to Saturday from 8 A.M. to 1 P.M.

Specialty Shops

(71) GIACOMO RIZZO
San Giovanni Grisostomo, 5778 (San Polo)

One of the best gourmet food shops in Venice is Giacomo Rizzo, which has been dispensing its handmade pastas, balsamic vinegars, truffles, extra-virgin first-pressed olive oils, honeys, and dried mushrooms since 1905. The dried pastas are made without preservatives or colors, and range from a simple spinach *tagliatelle* to others flavored with radicchio, smoked salmon, cuttlefish, and beetroot.

TELEPHONE AND FAX 041-52-22-824
OPEN Mon–Sat
CLOSED Wed afternoon, Sun, a few days in Aug
HOURS 7:30 A.M.–1 P.M., 3:30–7:30 P.M.
CREDIT CARDS None

Supermarkets

Big supermarkets do not exist in Venice, and most of the so-called supermarkets are well-hidden. Hours are usually from 8:30 A.M. to 12:30 or 1 P.M. and 3:30 to 7:30 P.M. from Monday through Saturday, except Wednesdays, when they are closed in the afternoon. Sunday, of course, is a full day of rest.

(72) STANDA
Strada Nova, 3660 (Cannaregio)

There is a second location on Lido at Via Corfù.

Smaller markets include:

(73) BILLA
Zattere al Ponte Lungo, 1491 (Dorsoduro)

(74) DOGAL
Calle del Pistor, 3989 (Castello)

(75) MINIMARKET
Campo Santa Margherita 3019/3112 (Dorsoduro)

(76) SUVE
Calle Mondo Nuovo, 5812 (Castello)

This is the most central market, and it has a good meat and cheese selection.

Glossary

This glossary is broken down into two sections: the first half gives Italian equivalents for some general words and phrases you might need to use while ordering in a restaurant. The second half give English translations of Italian words you might find as you read a menu. Many restaurants have menus in English, but invariably they do not include the daily specials, which most often are the best items to order. This glossary is designed to help you make sure there will not be a difference between what you eat and what you actually order.

Hello (telephone)	*pronto*
Hello/goodbye (familiar)	*ciao*
Good morning	*buon giorno*
Good afternoon	*buon pomeriggio*
Good evening	*buona sera*
Goodnight	*buona notte*
Goodbye	*arrivederci*
Please	*per favore*
Thank you	*grazie*
You are welcome	*prego*
Yes/No	*si/no*
Excuse me	*mi scusi*
I am sorry	*mi dispiace*
I want/I would like	*desidero, vorrei*
Do you speak English?	*parla inglese?*
I don't speak Italian	*non parlo italiano*
I understand	*capisco*
I don't understand	*non capisco*
Where are the restrooms?	*dov'è la toilette* [*per signore* (women), *per signori* (men)]
How much is it?	*quanto costa?*
A little/A lot	*poco/tanto*
More/Less	*più/meno*
Enough/Too much	*abbastanza/troppo*
Open/Closed	*aperto/chiuso*
Please telephone for a taxi	*per favore, telefoni per un tassi*
No smoking	*vietato fumare*
I am hungry	*ho fame*
I am diabetic	*ho il diabete*
I am on a diet	*sono a dieta*
I am vegetarian	*sono vegetariano (a)*
I cannot eat	*non posso mangiare*
It is hot/cold	*è caldo/freddo*
Please give me	*per favore, mi dia*
Today/Tonight/Tomorrow/Yesterday	*oggi/stastera/domani/ieri*

Days of the week

Monday	*lunedì*
Tuesday	*martedì*
Wednesday	*mercoledì*
Thursday	*giovedì*
Friday	*venerdì*

Saturday	*sabato*
Sunday	*domenica*

Numbers

1	*uno*
2	*due*
3	*tre*
4	*quattro*
5	*cinque*
6	*sei*
7	*sette*
8	*otto*
9	*nove*
10	*dieci*
11	*undici*
12	*dodici*
13	*tredici*
14	*quattrodici*
15	*quindici*
16	*sedici*
17	*diciasette*
18	*diciotto*
19	*diciannove*
20	*vente*
21	*ventuno*
30	*trenta*
40	*quaranta*
50	*cinquanta*
60	*sessanta*
70	*settanta*
80	*ottanta*
90	*novanto*
100	*cento*

Restaurant Basics

A table for ___, please	*un tavolo per___persone, per favore*
Waiter/Waitress	*cameriere/cameriera*
Breakfast	*prima colazione*
Lunch	*pranza/colazione*
Dinner	*cena*
The menu, please	*la lista, per favore*
The wine list, please	*la lista dei vini, per favore*
May I have this?	*vorrei questo?*
The bill, please	*il conto, per favore*
The bill is not correct	*il conto non è giusto*
Service Charge	*servizio*
Cover charge	*pane e coperto*
Is the service included?	*il servizio è incluso?*
Service is included	*il servizio è compreso/incluso*
Antipasti	*appetizers*
First courses	*primi piatti*
Second courses	*secondi piatti*
Side dishes	*contorn*
Dessert	*dolce*
Fixed-price menu	*menù turistico/prezzo fisso*
Dish of the day	*piatto del giorno*
Specialty of the house	*specialità della casa*
In season	*di stagione*

I need a:	*ho bisogno di*
knife	*un cotello*
fork	*una forchetta*
spoon	*un cucchiaio*
cup	*tazza*
plate	*piatto*
side dishes	*contorni*
dessert	*dolce*
ashtray	*portacenere*
hair	*sedia*
table	*tavola*
napkin	*il tovagliolo*
I would like:	*vorrei*
a cup of	*una tazza di*
a glass of	*un bicchiere di*
a bottle of	*una bottiglia di*
a half-bottle of	*una mezza bottiglia di*
a carafe of	*una caraffa di*
a liter of	*uno litro di*

Places

Alimentari	*grocery store*
Caffè	*café*
Enoteca	*wine shop/bar*
Gastronomic	*grocery store*
Gelateria	*ice cream shop*
Il forno	*bread shop, bakery*
Latteria	*cheese and dairy store*
Osteria	*blue-collar wine bar*
Paninoteca	*sandwich bar*
Pasticceria	*pastry shop*
Salumeria	*grocery store*
Tabaccheria	*tobaccanist, a place to get newspapers, bus tickets, lottery tickets, pens, etc.*

Reading the Menu

Cooking Methods

baked	*al forno*
barbecued	*alla brace*
boiled	*bollito/lesso*
cooked (not raw)	*cotto*
cooked in tomato sauce	*pizzaiola*
cooked in wine	*brasato*
firm, not overcooked (as in pasta)	*al dente*
fried	*fritto*
fried in egg and breadcrumbs	*milanese*
frozen	*surgelato*
grilled	*alla griglia/ferri*
grilled with olive oil	*al ferro*
on the spit	*allo spiedo*
poached	*in umido*
rare	*al sangue/poco cotto*
raw	*crudo*
roast	*arrosto*
smoked	*affumicato*
steamed/stewed	*al vapore/in úmido*
stuffed	*ripieno*

well-done	*ben cotto*
wrapped or rolled	*involitini*

Types of Pasta

agnolotti	filled pasta
bigoli	round, solid pasta (Venice)
bucatini	hollow spaghetti
cannelloni	stuffed pasta tubes
capelli d'angelo	angel hair pasta
conchiglie	pasta shells
crespelle	crepes
farfalle	butterfly-shaped pasta
fettuccine	long, thin flat pasta
fusilli	spiral-shaped pasta
gnocchi	small potato dumplings
lasagne	large, flat noodles layered with ingredients and baked
maccheroni	macaroni
orecchiette	ear-shaped pasta
paglia e fieno	green and yellow tagliatelle
pappardelle	wide noodles
pasta verde	spinach noodles
pasticcio	baked pasta pie with cheese, vegetables, and meat
penne	narrow, diagonally cut macaroni
ravioli	filled pasta squares
rigatoni	large macaroni
risotto (ai funghi, alla Milanese)	rice (with mushrooms, saffron)
rotelle	spiral-shaped pasta
tagliatelle	thin, flat egg pasta ribbons
taglierini	thin pasta ribbons
tagliolini	thin, flat noodles
tonnarelli	square-shaped spaghetti
tortelli	ravioli with a filling of potato or spinach and ricotta cheese
tortellini	small meat or cheese-filled pasta dumplings
tortellone	large tortellini
vermicelli	thin spaghetti
zite/ziti	short, wide, tube-shaped pasta

Pasta Sauces

aglio e olio (e peperoncino)	tossed in garlic, olive oil (hot peppers)
al burro (e salvia)	with butter (and sage)
al sugo	with puréed tomatoes
amatriciana	bacon, tomatoes, onion, hot pepper
arrabbiata	spicy tomato sauce with chilies
bolognese	meat sauce
bucaniera	seafood, tomato, garlic, parsley, oil
cacciatora	tomato, onion, peppers, mushrooms, garlic, herbs, wine sauce
cacio e pepe	cheese and ground pepper
carbonara	cream, ham or bacon, egg, Parmesan cheese
frutta di mare	seafood
funghi	mushroom
matriciana	pork and tomato sauce
panna	cream
parmigiano	Parmesan cheese
pesto	ground pine nuts, basil, garlic, pecorino cheese
pomodoro	fresh tomato sauce

putanesca	tomatoes, capers, red peppers, anchovies, garlic, oil
quattro formaggi	with four cheeses
ragù	tomato-based meat sauce
vongole	clams or mussels, tomatoes, garlic

Pizza

Most pizzerias have dozens of variations on the following basics.

calzone	stuffed pizza
capricciosa	ham, hard-boiled or fried egg, artichokes, olives
frutta di mare	seafood, usually mussels, prawns, squid, clams
funghi	mushrooms (from a can unless specifies *funghi freschi*)
margherita	tomato, mozzarella, basil
marinara	plain tomato sauce, oregano and sometimes anchovies, never cheese
napoli or *napoletana,* sometimes called *romana*	tomato, mozzarella, anchovy
pizza bianca	without tomato
quattro formaggi	four cheeses
quattro stagioni	literally means four seasons; winter—mozzarella, spring—artichoke or arugula, summer—fried egg, and fall—mushrooms
salsiccia	sausage, tomato, mozzarella

Drinks

acqua	water
acqua minerale	mineral water
acqua di selz	soda water
aranciata, il succo d'arancia	orange drink, orange juice
aperitivo	before-dinner drink
bicchiere	glass
birra	beer
caffè	coffee
cioccolata calda	hot chocolate
ghiaccio (con ghiaccio)	ice (on the rocks)
granita	iced drink
latte	milk
limonata	lemonade
liquore	liqueur
spremuta	fresh fruit juice
succo (di frutta)	juice (fruit)
tè	tea
vino (locale, bianco, rosso)	wine (local, white, red)
secco	dry
dolce	sweet
litro	liter
mezzo	half-liter
quatro	quarter-liter
whiskey scozzese, lo scotch	scotch

Other Menu and Food Terms

A	*abbacchio*	milk-fed spring lamb
	acciughe	anchovies
	aceto	vinegar
	acqua cotta	thick vegetable soup poured over bread
	acqua minerale (gassata, naturale)	mineral water (sparkling, still)
	affettai misti	assorted cold cuts
	affettato	sliced
	affumicato	smoked

	aglio	garlic
	agnello	lamb
	agrume	citrus fruit
	albicocca	apricot
	al carbone	charcoal grilled
	al forno	baked
	alici	fresh anchovies
	alla/all'	in the style of/with
	alla brace/alla griglia	charcoal grilled/grilled
	ananas	pineapple
	anatra	duck
	aneto	dill
	anguilla (Veneziana)	eel (cooked with lemon and tuna)
	antipasti misto	assorted appetizers
	antipasto	appetizer
	aperitivo	apéritif
	a piacere	as you like it
	aragosta	lobster, crayfish
	arancia	orange
	aringa	herring
	arista	roast pork
	arrosto	roast
	asciutto	dry
	asparagi	asparagus
	assaggio	a taste
	assagi	a series of small portions
	astaco (astice)	lobster
B	*baccalà filetto di*	dried salt cod, sometimes simmered in milk or fried in batter
	bacelli	fava beans (Tuscan)
	barbabietola	beet
	basilico	basil
	Bel Paese	soft, mild cheese
	bieta, bietola	Swiss chard
	bigoli in salsa	spaghetti with butter, onion, sardines (Venetian specialty)
	birra	beer
	biscotti	cookies
	bistecca	beef steak
	bistecca alla fiorentina	T-bone steak, grilled over coals, served very rare
	bollito misto	mixed boiled meats
	braciola	steak, chop, slice of meat
	branzino	sea bass
	bresaola	air-cured beef, thinly sliced
	briosca	croissant (also called *cornetto)*
	brodetto	fish soup
	brodo (pastina in brodo)	broth (with pasta pieces)
	bruschetta	toasted bread rubbed with raw garlic topped with tomatoes, olive oil, or olive paste
	budino di cioccolato	chocolate mousse
	bue	beef, ox
	burro	butter
	bussolài buranèli	"s" or doughnut-shaped cookies made on Burano
C	*cacciagione*	game
	caffè	coffee, café
	calamaro (calamaretto)	squid (baby squid)
	caldo	hot/warm

	calzone	stuffed pizza
	camomilla	chamomile tea
	cannellini	white beans
	cannoli (Siciliana)	custard-filled pastry with pieces of candied fruit (pastry shells filled with ricotta cheese and dusted with sugar)
	caponata	eggplant salad
	cappa santa	scallops
	capperi	capers
	capra (capretto)	goat (baby goat)
	caprese	fresh tomato, mozzarella, and basil salad
	capriolo	venison
	carbonade	beef stewed with red wine
	carciofo (alla giudia)	artichoke (deep-fried)
	carne	meat
	carpaccio	thinly sliced raw beef
	casalinga	homestyle
	cassata	ice cream with candied fruit
	castagne	chestnuts
	cavolfiore	cauliflower
	cavolo (nero)	cabbage (dark)
	ceci	chickpeas
	cernia	grouper
	cervella	brains
	cetriolo	cucumber
	cicchetti	snacks (Venice)
	cicorie	endives
	ciliegia	cherry
	cinghiale	wild boar
	cioccolato	chocolate
	cioccolato caldo	hot chocolate
	cipolla	onion
	cocomero	watermelon
	coda di bue alla vaccinara	oxtail stew
	coda di roposso	monkfish
	congelato	frozen
	coniglio	rabbit
	contorni	side dishes (vegetables, salads, potatoes)
	coperto	cover charge added per person to bill
	cornetto	croissant (also called *briosca*)
	cotoletta	chop or cutlet
	cozze	mussels
	crema	custard
	crespelle	crepes
	crostata	open-faced fruit tart
	crostini	toasted bread, topped with grilled cheese spread with pâté
	crudo	raw (as in *prosciutto crudo,* raw ham)
	cucina	kitchen, cooking
	cuore	heart
D	*da portare Via*	to take out
	degustazione	tasting
	di stagione	of the season
	dolce	dessert
E	*erbe*	herbs
F	*fagiano*	pheasant
	fagioli	beans
	fagiolini	string beans
	fave	fava (broad) beans

	fegatelli	pork livers
	fegatini	chicken livers
	fegato (alla Veneziana)	calves' liver (with onions and olive oil)
	fettunta	garlic bread with fresh olive oil (Florence)
	fichi	figs
	filetto	filet
	finocchio	fennel
	fior di latte	mozzarella made from cow's milk
	fior di zucca/fiori di zucchino	zucchini flowers stuffed with mozzarella and anchovies, dipped in bread batter and quickly fried
	focaccia	flat bread
	Fontina	delicate, buttery cheese
	formaggio	cheese
	fragole	strawberries
	fragoline	tiny wild strawberries
	freddo	cold
	fritelle	fritters
	frittata	unfolded omelette
	fritto	fried
	fritto misto	assorted deep-fried foods (fish, vegetables)
	frutta	fruit
	frutti di mare	shellfish
	funghi	mushrooms
	funghi porcini	wild boletus mushrooms
G	*gamberetti*	shrimp
	gelato	ice cream
	gianduia	chocolate hazelnut ice cream treat
	gnocchi/gnocchetti	small potato dumplings
	Gorgonzola	blue-veined cheese
	granchio	crab
	grappa	alcoholic spirit distilled from grape mash
	grissini	bread sticks
H	*Hag*	brand name of the most popular decaf coffee; used to mean decaffeinated in general
I	*imbottito*	stuffed
	insalata (di mare)	salad (seafood)
	integrale	whole wheat
	involtini	stuffed meat or fish rolls
L	*lampone*	raspberries
	latte	milk
	legumi	vegetables
	lenticchie	lentils
	lepre	wild hare
	lesso	boiled
	limone (limonata)	lemon (lemonade)
	lingua	tongue
	lombatine	veal chop
	lumache	snails
M	*macedonia di frutta*	dessert of chopped fresh fruit
	maiale, maialino	pork, piglet
	mandarino	tangerine
	mandorla	almond
	manzo	beef
	mela	apple
	melanzane	eggplant
	melone	melon
	merluzzo	cod
	miele	honey

	mille foglie	puff pastry
	mozzarella di bufala	delicate fresh cheese made from the milk of a water buffalo
N	*nazionale*	domestic, meaning made in Italy
	noce	walnut
	nocciola	hazelnut
O	*oca*	goose
	olio di oliva	olive oil
	osso buco	veal knuckle
	ostriche	oysters
P	*pajata*	baby veal intestines
	pancetta	spicy, salted bacon rolled, eaten raw
	pane (tostato)	bread (toast)
	pane e coperto	bread and cover charge
	panettone	light cake with candied fruit peel
	panna cotta	vanilla cream pudding
	panna (montana)	cream (whipped)
	panino	sandwich or roll
	panzanella	Tuscan specialty made with stale bread, olive oil, tomatoes, and onions
	pasta e fagioli	pasta and bean soup
	patata	potato
	pecorino	sheep's cheese
	pepe	black pepper
	peperonata	grilled peppers served in olive oil
	peperoncino	hot red peppers
	peperoni	peppers
	pera	pear
	pesca	peach
	pesce	fish
	piselli	peas
	polenta	cornmeal
	pollo	chicken
	polpette	meatballs
	polpo	octopus
	pomodori (ripieni)	tomatoes (stuffed)
	porchetta	roast piglet
	porri	leeks
	prezzemolo	parsley
	primi piatti	first courses
	produzione artiginale, propria	homemade, usually ice cream
	prosciutto	air-dried, salt-cured ham
	prosciutto cotto	cooked prosciutto
	prosciutto crudo	raw prosciutto
	provolone	smooth, cow's-milk cheese
	prunga	plum
	prunga secca	prune
	puntarelle	wild chicory greens dressed with oil, vinegar, mashed anchovies
	purè di patate	mashed potatoes
R	*radicchio*	red chicory
	rape	turnip greens
	ravanello	radish
	ribollita	bean, bread, cabbage, and vegetable soup (means "reboiled")
	ricotta	soft, mild sheep's cheese
	ripieno	stuffed
	risi e bisi	rice and pea soup, sometimes with ham and Parmesan cheese

	rombo	turbot
	rognoni	kidneys
	rucola, rughetta	arugula
S	*sale*	salt
	salsicca	sausage
	saltimbocca	veal rolls with ham, flavored with sage
	sarde (in saor)	sardines (marinated)
	scampi	prawns
	secondi pratti	main courses
	sedano	celery
	semifreddo	creamy, ice cream
	seppie in nero	squid (cuttlefish) cooked in its own ink
	servizio	service charge
	sogliola	sole
	sorbetto	sherbet
	spezzatino	stew
	spinachi	spinach
	straccetti	stir fried strips of veal or beef
	stracciatella	broth with egg and Parmesan cheese stirred in at the last minute
	straccino	soft cream cheese
T	*tacchino*	turkey
	tartufo	ice cream coated in hard chocolate
	tè, the (con latte, limone)	tea (with milk, lemon)
	tiramisù	rich, creamy dessert made with mascarpone cheese, liqueur, espresso, chocolate, and ladyfingers (means "pick-me-up")
	tisana	herbal tea
	toast	toasted ham and cheese sandwich
	tonno	tuna
	torta	cake
	tostato	toasted
	tramezzino	sandwich (also called *panino*)
	trancia	slice
	trippa (alla romana)	tripe (in tomato sauce)
	trota	trout
U	*un'etto*	100 grams, about 4 ounces
	uova	egg
	uva	grape
V	*verdure (cotta)*	green vegetables (cooked)
	verza	cabbage (also called *cavolo*)
	vitello, vitella, vitellone	veal
	vino (rosso, rosato, bianco)	wine (red, rosé, white)
	vin santo	sweet dessert wine, served with *biscotti*
	vongole	clams
Z	*zabaglione*	custard dessert made in a copper pot to order with beaten egg yolks, sugar, and white or marsala wine, and served warm.
	zucca	pumpkin
	zucchero	sugar
	zuppa de pesce	fish soup
	zuppa inglese	trifle

Index

FLORENCE

($) Indicates a Big Splurge

Big Splurges in Florence

ROME

($) Indicates a Big Splurge

Big Splurges in Rome

VENICE

($) Indicates a Big Splurge

Big Splurges in Venice

Readers' Comments

In *Cheap Eats in Italy,* I recommend places as they were when this book went to press. I hope they will stay that way, but as all travelers know, there are no guarantees. While every effort has been made to ensure the accuracy of the information presented, the reader must understand that prices, menu selections, staff and management, opening and closing times, vacation schedules, and ownership can change overnight. Therefore, the author and publisher cannot accept responsibility for any changes that do occur in the advice or information given that may result in loss or inconvenience to anyone.

Cheap Eats in Italy is updated and revised on a regular basis. If you find that someplace has changed, or make a discovery you want to pass along, please send me a note stating the name and address of the restaurant, the date of your visit, and a description of your findings. Your comments are extremely important to me, and I read and follow through on every letter I receive. Thank you.

Please send your letters to Sandra A. Gustafson, *Cheap Eats in Italy,* c/o Chronicle Books, 85 Second Street, Sixth Floor, San Francisco, CA 94105.